Chūshingura

Act II, scene 2: Enya Hangan (Onoe Baikō VII) preparing to commit *seppuku*. He composes himself mentally and spiritually in the center of the stage. Kabuki production of *Chūshingura* at the National Theater of Japan, Tokyo. *(Photo: Don Kozono.)*

Chūshingura

*Studies in Kabuki and
the Puppet Theater*

Edited by
JAMES R. BRANDON

UNIVERSITY OF HAWAII PRESS • HONOLULU

*Published with the support of The University of Hawaii Japan Studies
Endowment—Funded by a Grant from the Japanese Government*

Library of Congress Cataloging in Publication Data
Main entry under title:

Chūshingura: studies in kabuki and the puppet theater.

　　Includes text of the Forty-seven samurai.
　　Includes index.
　　1.　Kabuki—Addresses, essays, lectures.
2.　Puppets and puppet-plays—Japan—History and
criticism—Addresses, essays, lectures.
3.　Takeda, Izumo, 1691–1756. Kanadehon Chūshingura—
Addresses, essays, lectures.　I.　Brandon, James R.,
1927–　　　.　II.　Takeda, Izumo, 1691–1756. Kanadehon
Chūshingura. English.
PN2924.5.K3C48　　　　　895.6'23　　　　　82–1921
ISBN 0–8248–0793–6　　　　　　　　AACR2

Contents

Preface

KANADEHON CHŪSHINGURA, written in 1748, is perhaps the most highly praised drama of Japanese popular theater. Certainly it has been an enduring audience favorite, year in and year out, in the puppet theater, for which it was written, and in kabuki, where it is performed by live actors. Scarcely a year passes without it being seen in one form or another on the stage, or as a movie or television play. It is also the one classic Japanese play that is widely known in the West. It was first adapted into English by John Masefield, as *The Faithful* in 1915, and the story is variously known in English as *The Forty-Seven Ronin, The Loyal League, The Treasury of Loyal Retainers,* and, in this book, *The Forty-Seven Samurai.* In Japan it is commonly known by its shortened title *Chūshingura* (literally "storehouse of loyalty").

The play is popular in part because it provides a remarkable panorama of Japanese life as numerous fascinating characters act out moments of extreme duress. The two scenes in which Lord Enya Hangan and his retainer Kampei must commit *seppuku* are exemplars of the samurai code that places fulfillment of obligation *(giri)* before human life. The arch villain, Kō no Moronao, is one of the great figures of evil in Japanese drama, and his henchman Bannai is considered the finest comic role in the kabuki repertory. In its eleven acts and eighteen scenes, *Chūshingura* contains pitched battles, love scenes, ceremonial gatherings of lords, a highway murder, delicate dances, and half a dozen intricate plots and intrigues. A second reason for the play's phenomenal hold on Japanese imagination is that it is a dramatization of actual events that took place between 1701 and 1703, involving attempted murder, enforced suicide, debauchery, a vendetta, and eventually the mass suicides of more than forty former samurai, or *rōnin.* This indeed is the stuff of which drama is made. The raw material of history has been fashioned with great success in this play; to take one example, few scenes in all of world theater are as powerfully moving as Hangan's death in Act IV.

Kabuki theater has been a subject of special interest at the University of Hawaii since the 1930s, when yearly productions of Japanese plays, usually kabuki, were first staged in English on the campus. There were in those days still a few professional kabuki actors living in Hawaii (troupes from Japan would tour Hawaii and California, and some actors did not return home). In the decades following World War II, Earle Ernst inaugurated the first academic courses in Japanese theater to be offered in an American university and directed productions of *The House of Sugawara* (1951) and *Benten the Thief* (1953 and 1963). Beginning in 1970, the Department of Drama and Theatre, in cooperation with the Department of Music, began a series of biannual productions of kabuki in English: *Sukeroku the Flower of Edo* (1970), *Narukami the Thunder God* (1972), *The Scarlet Princess of Edo* (1975), *The Road to Kyoto!* (1977), and *The Subscription List* (1981). Guided by the professional kabuki actor Nakamura Matagorō II and by choreographer Onoe Kikunobu, these productions were acted in authentic style, based on training and rehearsal periods extending as long as ten months. Live *nagauta* instrumental music and singing for each play were directed by Ricardo Trimillos and Yamada Chie of the Department of Music. Research in play translation, dramatic theory, theater history, performance style, costuming, and makeup has been conducted in conjunction with the productions. Courses in these topics have become a regular part of the University's Asian Theater Program, established in 1967 to provide a full academic program leading to the M.A., M.F.A., or Ph.D. degree in Asian theater.

It was in the context of this fifty-year history of research, performance, and instruction in kabuki theater that it was decided to organize a special year-long program, Kabuki Hawaii 1978–1979, that would be focused on the play *Chūshingura. Chūshingura* was a logical choice since it is a challenging play for students to perform and an exciting drama for an audience to see. It also offered an opportunity to study how a puppet theater (jōruri) text had been adapted to kabuki performance, thus expanding our work into a new field. *Gidayū,* the music which accompanies the puppet theater, had never before been examined by Western scholars or performed by Western musicians, nor had a kabuki production of a jōruri play ever been performed in English using live music.

Four related activities were carried out during Kabuki Hawaii 1978–1979: permanent faculty members and six professional kabuki artists offered intensive instruction in kabuki performance, history, and literature to American students; a kabuki acting version of the play was translated; this translation was rehearsed and performed; and prominent scholars presented a lecture series about the play to the public. Training and production aspects of the program were directed by Nakamura Matagorō II, chief instructor, Kabuki Training School, National Theater of Japan.

This book brings together a number of the contributions made during the program. Donald Keene, Columbia University, describes how the historical Akō vendetta of the early eighteenth century became the basis of scores of plays in the years following, including *Genroku Chūshingura,* a modern reinterpretation of the event. Government censorship of kabuki and bunraku plays is examined by Donald H. Shively, Harvard University. He uses *Chūshingura* as a telling example of how dramatists, to avoid censorship, placed current events into historical worlds safely past. William P. Malm, University of Michigan, analyzes, for the first time in English, the music of jōruri, the puppet theater, citing examples of musical form in *Chūshingura* performance; jōruri music was taken over into kabuki and hence it can be found in kabuki versions of *Chūshingura* as well. These three papers were first presented in the public lecture series given on the Manoa campus in the spring of 1979, and were revised for publication here. The fourth paper, by the editor, is an account of how kabuki actors and managers adapted the original puppet text, adding wholly new scenes as well, to accommodate the nature of kabuki performance, and was originally intended to be part of the public lecture series. Except for obscure play titles, Japanese terms used in the book have been translated into English equivalents.

The book concludes with the text of *The Forty-Seven Samurai.* Drafts of the translation were written by the editor and two graduate students, Junko Berberich and Michael Feldman, in the fall of 1978. Theater students used these drafts for study and rehearsal of the play in acting classes in the winter and spring of 1979. At the same time, music students adapted the text to the requirements of jōruri and *nagauta* performance. The translation published here is the final version which was performed by the cast of student actors and musicians under Nakamura Matagorō's direction. Forty performances of *The Forty-Seven Samurai* were given between February and May, 1979, first at the John F. Kennedy Theatre on campus, then on the neighbor islands of Hawaii, and finally at colleges and universities in fourteen states during a seven-week national tour. The translation is illustrated by photographs of the production and by photographs of Japanese kabuki and bunraku productions, some of which were shown on campus by James T. Araki in his talk given as part of the public lecture series. A brief introduction to *The Forty-Seven Samurai* describes the translation approach.

From the beginning, Kabuki Hawaii 1978–1979 was conceived as an opportunity to interpret the theatrical achievement of *Chūshingura* from diverse perspectives. Unfortunately, we too often tend to live on our own disciplinary islands, talking only to ourselves and our friends. It seemed especially appropriate to approach in a multidisciplinary fashion the subject of the Akō vendetta, an event which so deeply stirred the Japanese dramatic imagination. It was therefore both intellectually and artistically exciting to find that much new light was shed on this topic during the course of the year. It is hoped that whether the reader has a special interest in history, social science, literature, drama, theater, or music, he will find in one or another of the chapters new ideas and information that will be of value.

Kabuki Hawaii 1978–1979 could not have been carried out successfully without the support of many organizations and interested friends. A generous grant from the University of Hawaii Japan Studies Endowment—funded by a grant from the Japanese Government—provided major funding. A grant from the Endowment also supports the publication of this book. The public lecture series was sponsored by the University of Hawaii Asian Studies Program and was funded by the Program's East Asian Language and Area Center, the Office of the Dean of Arts and Sciences, and the Office of the Chancellor of the Manoa Campus. The entire project was developed and encouraged in tangible and intangible ways by the Department of Drama and Theatre and the Department of Music. The production of *The Forty-Seven Samurai* was funded by the University Theatre. The national tour of *The Forty-Seven Samurai* was underwritten by grants from the Japan–United States Friendship Commission, the President's Fund of the University of Hawaii Foundation, United Airlines, and more than four hundred individual donors. Photographs are by James T. Araki, Donald Kozono, Yoshida Chiaki, Shochiku Co., and the editor.

Honolulu
March 1981

Guest Artist-Teachers
Nakamura Matagorō II, Director of Instruction
Nakamura Matazō, Kabuki Acting
Nakamura Matashirō, Kabuki Acting
Takemoto Ayadayū, Gidayū Music and Chanting
Tanaka Satarō, Narimono Music
Hamatani Hitoshi, Kabuki Production

Public Lecture Series
James T. Araki, Department of East Asian Literature, University of Hawaii
Donald Keene, Department of East Asian Languages and Cultures, Columbia University
William P. Malm, Department of Music, University of Michigan
Donald H. Shively, Department of East Asian Languages and Civilizations, Harvard University

Playscript
Adaptation: Nakamura Matagorō II, James R. Brandon
Translation: James R. Brandon, Junko Berberich, Michael Feldman

University of Hawaii Contributing Faculty
Department of Drama and Theatre
Edward Langhans, Chairman
Mark Boyd, Technical Direction
James R. Brandon, Japanese Theater
Sandra Finney, Costume Design
Richard Mason, Set Design
Takeo Miji, Publicity

Department of Music
Ricardo Trimillos, Chairman
Nishikawa Koshirō, Japanese Dance
Barbara Smith, Ethnomusicology
Yamada Chie, Kabuki Music

Staff
Director: James R. Brandon
Program Coordinators: Douglas Rosentrater and Michael Feldman
Tour Coordinator: Penny Bergman
Liaison: Junko Berberich
Lecture Series Coordinator: Michael Manson
Audio-Visual: Robert Bethune

Chūshingura

Variations on a Theme:
Chūshingura

DONALD KEENE

SO MUCH of Japanese life can be understood in terms of the *nenjū gyōji*, the festivals, memorial services, and even theatrical presentations that reoccur each year on the same days. In every country, of course, there are public holidays—independence days, the birthdays of sovereigns, feasts associated with the prevailing religion, and so on —but in Japan the concern with the orderly repetition of prescribed events goes far beyond that of most other countries. For example, at the first performance of nō offered in January by each company, the festive play *Okina* is invariably presented at the head of the program. The meaning of this play, the oldest of the repertory, has been much discussed by scholars of Japanese theater, and elaborate explanations have been advanced for the seemingly unintelligible sections, but for most members of the audience the words are of much less significance than the event itself; attending a performance of *Okina* at the beginning of the year not only is traditional but helps to make one feel a special, felicitous excitement appropriate to the season. The performance, however imperfectly understood, contributes to the atmosphere of the New Year in much the same way as the traditional New Year's food or the custom of displaying pine boughs at one's gates. Nobody wants to be surprised by a performance of *Okina;* a stunningly original interpretation, far from impressing the spectators, would deprive them of the special pleasure of sensing the ties linking themselves with the past. To hear the familiar words, recited in the familiar way, at the appropriate time of year is an important reason for attending the Japanese theater. It is also a reason for the unfailing popularity of a work like *Chūshingura,* which elicits annual participation as a cherished part of Japanese tradition.

Some plays, like *Okina,* which have the status of semireligious presentations, were unconsciously altered many times over the centuries before they achieved their present, bafflingly obscure form, but it is hard to imagine anyone tampering with the words now in the attempt to restore their original sense. There are other works for the theater, similar to *Okina* in their ritual importance within the repertory—*Chūshingura* is a conspicuous example—which have deliberately been changed in response to the talents of particular performers or the demands of new audiences. The most popular story presented in Japanese drama is the vengeance carried out by the two Soga brothers on their father's enemy. Plays on this theme have been staged by actors associated with every variety of Japanese theater, whether the austere nō, the more lyric puppet theater, the boldly exaggerated kabuki, or the realism of the modern stage. Spectators over the centuries, far from becoming bored by this often-told story traditionally presented in the first month of the new year, have enjoyed it as a particularly characteristic *nenjū gyōji* of that season. The story of the Soga brothers is eternally compelling, but, because it is not sacred, it has been subject to innumerable alterations by both dramatists and performers. The dramatists have always retained the central features of the vendetta story, but they have felt free to embroider, to add fresh details of motivation, to provide contemporary allusions in the hopes of amusing the audience, and even to call attention to the presence in the cast of particular actors. Sometimes, as in the popular play *Sukeroku,* the story of the vendetta carried out by the Soga brothers in the twelfth century is all but obscured by the overpowering atmosphere of the seventeenth-century licensed quarters, and the identification of the swaggering Sukeroku and the sake vendor Shimbei as being in reality the two Soga brothers does not fool anyone. In an even more extreme departure from the original story, in Chikamatsu Monzaemon's play *The Soga Heir (Yotsugi Soga),* first performed in 1683, the main characters of the original story are dead by the time the play opens, and what we see is a vendetta in the second generation carried out by retainers of the Soga brothers against a second generation of villains. Even this "Son of the Sogas" approach was acceptable as a part of larger traditions.

Variation on an original theme is one of the most striking characteristics of Japanese literature. The aim of most classical poets, to give the clearest example, was not to impress readers with their fresh conceptions or their unusual choice of language. On the contrary, a poem which lacked recognizable antecedents was considered to be faulty; a poem which could not be tested against similar poems of the past did not provide an adequate measure of a new poet's abilities, and it lacked the special resonance provided by associations with earlier poetic tradition. In a short poem, moreover, it was essential to expand the stated content by suggestion or by allusions if it was not to seem merely an epigram or a fragment of a full poem. It was hardly possible to write a totally original poem on cherry blossoms in any case. Even the mention of cherry blossoms evokes predictable reactions and remembrances of other poetry. In China peach blossoms had much the same appeal for the poets, but in Japan peach blossoms, for all their loveliness, were rarely celebrated, if only because they summoned up fewer associations with the past. A good poem on cherry blossoms succeeds by coming a tiny bit closer to the absolute center of their beauty than similar poems by earlier writers, or by imparting to the conception in some indefinable way a modernity or individuality that appeals to the connoisseur.

Many Western and some Japanese readers find the use of allusive variation on familiar themes a less exciting kind of poetry than works of more striking individuality. Rather than read one more poem on the cherry blossoms or on reddening maple leaves or on the cries of the cuckoo *(hototogisu),* these readers would prefer a poem describing an unfamiliar flower like the lesser celandine, or a conspicuously unpoetic insect, or a bird whose raucous cries defy beautification—anything in preference to the hackneyed old themes. An eminent critic of Japanese poetry once wrote that to read through all the poems on cherry blossoms and crimson maple leaves in the major collections would be nearly as bad as being condemned to the perpetual torments of hell. The haiku poets were less restricted than *waka* poets in their conception of appropriate material for poetry, and some took special delight in startling their readers. Even the great Bashō was not above mentioning the droppings of the *uguisu,* a bird known in classical poetry for the beauty of its song and its fondness for sporting among plum blossoms. Novelty of this kind, however, tended to develop into a new kind of orthodoxy rather than put an end to orthodoxy, and the haiku poets, for all their experimentations, usually fell back on the familiar, even the ritual.

The theater in Japan today is also largely a theater of the familiar. It is true that there are brilliant innovators: the avant-garde theater of a man like Abe Kōbō bears comparison with that found in any country. But the audiences are relatively small and tend to be restricted to young intellectuals who are consciously rejecting the theater of the past. Yet more and more young people are also attending performances of nō, despite the predictions made twenty or thirty years ago

that the young had lost all interest in a theater that had so little connection with their own lives.

Nō is, of course, a repertory theater. Not a single play composed
for this theater during the past four hundred years has won a place in
the repertory. Among the two hundred and more plays included in
the repertory, many are performed irregularly or on special occasions
only. This means that the staples of the repertory tend to be presented again and again, regardless of the school of nō or the special talents of the available performers. To see the same nō play for the
twentieth or thirtieth time, following every note of the musical delivery and every gesture, is considered to be a far more satisfying experience than attending the revival of a forgotton play. A friend once
asked me, "How do you know an actor is good unless you have seen
other actors in the same role?"

It used to be true that audiences in England and the United
States had the opportunity to attend plays by Shakespeare so often
that they could acquire the same kind of expertise that Japanese theatergoers still possess with respect to nō or kabuki. An unexpected
gesture by Iago in a performance of *Othello* could cause the audience
to gasp; it was precisely such a gesture that established the fame of
James O'Neill, Eugene O'Neill's father, but today only a great ex-
pert would even be aware that anything unusual had occurred. The
closest that we in this country come to this expertise today is with
opera. Someone who has attended *Tosca* twenty or thirty times waits
for the key moments as tests not only of the singers' voices but of
their dramatic ability: what does Tosca do when she first enters the
church where Cavaradossi is painting? How does Scarpia greet Tosca
when she enters his room? How does Cavaradossi express his scorn for
the betrayal by Tosca? At what part of the stage does Tosca deliver
her aria *Vissi d'arte?* When does she first notice the fruit knife? And
so on. These moments obviously mean more to a person seeing *Tosca*
for the twentieth time than for the first.

There is a difference, however, between seeing exactly the same
play or opera again and again—the experience of an audience going
to a nō play or to *Tosca*—and seeing a play which departs frequently
from the original version. This is much less common in the West, but
is typical of Japanese theater. The closest parallel in the West is perhaps that of the Greek theater. Aeschylus, Sophocles, and Euripides
all wrote plays about the unhappy Elektra, and undoubtedly there
were many others by forgotton dramatists. The broad outlines and
even many details of the different versions of her story are similar,

but there are important differences too, and sometimes (especially in the case of Euripides) the dramatist was at pains to make audiences aware of the modernity of his work. Elektra, in Aeschylus' play, recognizes her long-lost brother by seeing a lock of his hair—the same color as her own—which has been offered at their father's tomb, and by the garment he wears, which was of her own weaving. The same situation as described by Euripides has her deny the validity of these proofs. She says, "How should our hair correspond? His is the hair of a gallant youth trained up in manly sports, mine a woman's curled and combed; nay, that is a hopeless clue. Besides, thou couldst find many, whose hair is of the same colour, albeit not sprung from the same blood." As for the robe she wove for Orestes when he was still a child, she rejects it with irrefutable logic: "Even if I had woven him a robe, how should he, a mere child then, be wearing the same now, unless our clothes and bodies grow together?"[1]

Euripides' attitude was very close to the manner of the Japanese dramatists when they made adaptations of familiar stories, whether it was the vengeance carried out by the Soga brothers or the vendetta waged by the forty-seven loyal retainers of Lord Asano. The revisions were not made so as to mock earlier versions, and certainly not in order to destroy the original story by pointing out its contradictions, but to make it seem more plausible, more compelling to later and more sophisticated audiences.

The story of the vendetta carried out by the loyal retainers in the twelfth month of 1702, or on January 30, 1703 by the Western calendar, quickly became known to the public by word of mouth. A severe censorship was exercised over books and the theater, and so controversial a subject, dealing with the punishment meted out by the government to various samurai, could not be discussed openly. But it was impossible to silence all the people who had knowledge of the events: for example, those who lived near Lord Kira's mansion, the scene of the successful break-in; those who had watched the victorious samurai as they marched in procession to the Sengakuji, the temple where Lord Asano was buried, to offer up Kira's head; those belonging to the different households where the retainers were incarcerated pending a decision as to the punishment they were to receive for having disturbed the peace; and those who knew of the ritual suicides subsequently performed by every one of the retainers.

Mayama Seika's modern kabuki play, *Genroku Chūshingura* (written between 1934 and 1942), contains an extended passage in which Ōishi Kuranosuke, the leader of the vendetta, expresses his embarrassment on learning that he and his associates have been raised by popular gossip to the status of great heroes. No longer do people refer to the forty-six (or forty-seven) as the *rōnin* of Akō but as the *gishi* (righteous warriors) of Akō. Kuranosuke protests that he and the others are just ordinary men who have done no more than their duty. Of course, Mayama's play was written almost two hundred and fifty years after the events, and for all his pretentious display of erudition and historical accuracy, there was certainly an admixture of fiction; but the public response to the vendetta was apparently exactly as Kuranosuke described. The retainers of Asano, the lord of Akō, were acclaimed as heroes who had given new life to samurai ideals.

It was not surprising that the theater which, especially during the eighteenth and nineteenth centuries, served as a kind of mirror for Japanese society, should have taken up the theme of the vendetta. The first play we know of which treated the loyal retainers was called *Night Attack at Dawn by the Soga (Akebono Soga no Youchi)*, staged at the Nakamura Theater in Edo not two weeks after Kuranosuke and the others had committed *seppuku* in obedience to the order from above. The authorities closed the play after three performances. Nothing survives of its contents—kabuki plays were in any case rarely printed before the Meiji era—but the title suggests that, under the pretext of describing the celebrated night attack of the Soga brothers during the twelfth century, the playwright had made unmistakeable references to the assault on Kira's mansion by the forty-six retainers. The censorship of the theater at the time prohibited the reenactment of events of political implications, but this rule was often circumvented by changing the setting to the distant world of the past or by disguising the names of the characters. Apparently the 1703 kabuki play was too close to the events for such dodges to fool the censors, and the discouraged actors did not immediately attempt a fresh variant on the theme of the vendetta. The theater may have been a mirror of the time, but it was taken for granted that the mirror must distort sufficiently to confuse unsophisticated persons in the audience about the real intent of the author.

The oldest surviving play dealing with the vendetta is *A Chronicle of Great Peace Reenacted on a Chessboard (Goban Taiheiki)*, written in 1710 by the great dramatist Chikamatsu Monzaemon. Less than a month earlier he had written the puppet play *The Sightseeing Carriage of the Priest Kenkō (Kenkō Hōshi Monomiguruma)*, which described how Kenkō, famed as the author of *Essays in Idleness (Tsu-*

rezuregusa), attempted to save a court lady from the unwanted attentions of the fourteenth-century general Kō no Moronao. Kenkō persuaded Moronao to shift his attentions to Kaoyo, the wife of Enya Hangan, but she rejected his suit. Moronao, greatly annoyed, denounced Kaoyo's husband as a traitor and forced him to commit *seppuku*. The play, in two acts instead of the customary three, ended at this point and probably seemed incomplete. A few weeks later Chikamatsu supplied a third act which had a title of its own, *Goban Taiheiki*. For unknown reasons, the three acts seem never to have been performed together.

Goban Taiheiki, on the surface at least, is a continuation of the play about Kō no Moronao, and it is therefore set in the same period as the two earlier acts, the fourteenth century. The accidental circumstance—a play about the vendetta written as a continuation of one about Moronao—determined the period not only of this work but of most subsequent versions of the story. The names that Chikamatsu invented to hide the true names of the participants in the vendetta would also be used by most dramatists when writing their own versions. The historical Ōishi Kuranosuke became Ōboshi Yuranosuke; his son Chikara became Rikiya (using another pronunciation of the same character for *chikara*). Most of the minor characters had only slightly altered names. Lord Asano, on the other hand, became Enya Hangan, and his enemy became Kō no Moronao, the totally unrelated name of a historical figure of the fourteenth century.

Goban Taiheiki, opens as messengers arrive from various of the loyal retainers. Ōboshi Yuranosuke, Enya Hangan's chief retainer, is not at home to receive them, and his son, Rikiya, is amusing himself by playing *go*. Okahei, an illiterate servant, accepts the messages and delivers all but one to Rikiya. He furtively reads the note, then burns it. Rikiya, detecting the smell of burning paper, demands to know who sent the letter. Annoyed by Okahei's evasive answers, Rikiya slashes and all but kills him. Yuranosuke appears at this point. He says that he has known all the time that Okahei was only pretending to be illiterate, and that he is in fact a spy for their enemy, Moronao. The dying Okahei weeps, then tells his story.

His father was formerly a retainer of Enya Hangan but was dismissed from service. When the father learned that Hangan's castle had been confiscated by the authorities, he begged to be allowed to return to the clan, if only to die in a last show of resistance, but he was refused. The disappointed father committed suicide, leaving Okahei (whose real name is Teraoka Heiemon) a last injunction that he must take Moronao's head and bring it to him in the afterworld. In order to fulfill this injunction Okahei has obtained employment with Moronao. At first he hopes to kill him in an unguarded moment, but no opportunity presents itself. He agrees then to become Moronao's spy and report on activities in Yuranosuke's household. However, his main work as a spy consists in reporting untruthfully that Yuranosuke and Rikiya have become so debauched that there is no danger of their seeking vengeance. Okahei is so convincing that Moronao has relaxed his guard, and now diverts himself by composing *renga* (linked verse), practicing the tea ceremony, and arranging flowers. Okahei declares that now is the time to strike. With a faltering voice he gasps out his last words, that his only regret is that he will be unable to join Yuranosuke in the vendetta. Yuranosuke asks as a last favor that Okahei describe the disposition of the buildings of Moronao's mansion. No longer able to speak, Okahei uses black and white *go* stones to represent the buildings before he breathes his last.

Yuranosuke and Rikiya hide Okahei's corpse under the tatami, to keep Moronao from learning the death of his spy. Soon afterwards Yuranosuke's wife appears. She bitterly complains that her husband appears to have forgotten his resolve to seek vengeance and rebukes him for indulging in *go* and other idle pursuits. She also denounces Rikiya for not having reproved his father. She reminds him that when he was a small boy he was taken on Lord Enya Hangan's knee and had made water on it. Far from angering his lordship, this childish act had only made him smile indulgently.

Yuranosuke sharply answers his wife. He cynically remarks that he enjoys life and its pleasures. If he tries unsuccessfully to kill Moronao, his own head will assuredly fly; and if he is successful, he will have no choice but to commit *seppuku;* either way means certain death. He declares that it is better to live, even in disgrace, than to be praised after one is dead. Yuranosuke threatens his wife for speaking out of turn, but his aged mother rushes in, asserting that she has the right to rebuke her son. As a mark of her contempt for his cowardice, she flings a handful of *go* stones into his face.

Yuranosuke's wife and mother leave. Only then does he explain to Rikiya that he has deliberately refrained from involving his wife and mother in the plot for fear of causing trouble to their families. He examines the letters that have arrived from Kamakura. All urge swift action now that Moronao is off guard. Yuranosuke decides to take a last look at his wife and mother. He goes to their room and finds them lying on the floor with their throats slit. They have killed themselves to strengthen his resolve. He declares that Moronao is now the enemy not only of his master but of his mother and wife. The mother, who has not quite expired, murmurs with her last breath that this was what she had hoped for.

The second scene takes place in Moronao's mansion in Kamakura. He is relaxing with friends, unaware of the plot. Suddenly the loyal retainers of Enya Hangan burst in. They carry all before them, but have difficulty in finding Moronao. Finally he is discovered in the woodshed, and the retainers cut off his head, which they offer before Enya Hangan's grave.

This, in general, is what happens in Chikamatsu's play. It is by no means skillfully written, and even the most tolerant reader is likely to weary of the constant surprises which writers of puppet plays employed to keep the audience's attention. For example, nothing has prepared us for the suicides of the mother and wife, though they do provoke a startling change in our interpretation of the previous scene, where both women are so vehement in their condemnation of Yuranosuke's behavior. The writing on the whole is unworthy of Chikamatsu, although the play contains many elements that would be retained by later dramatists in other versions, especially *Kanadehon Chūshingura,* which was written forty-two years later, in 1748. The carousing of Yuranosuke, intended to make Moronao believe he has given up all thoughts of revenge, and the discovery of Moronao in the woodshed can be found in almost all versions of the play, perhaps because they had a basis in reality. The rebukes the wife directs at Yuranosuke for his failure to avenge his lord, though not repeated in *Kanadehon Chūshingura,* are found in other versions, notably Mayama Seika's play, though here it is the son, rather than the wife, who voices disapproval.

In the years following *Goban Taiheiki* many plays were written about the vendetta, too many to number with accuracy. The public came to expect new plays on the theme almost every year, and each dramatist added something, whether a slightly different interpretation of the motivation or merely an eye-catching scenic trick. Some additions did not survive the play in which they first appeared, but others were imperceptibly incorporated into the body of "truth" about the loyal retainers. Numerous subplots came to be considered integral to the telling of the story of the vendetta. It would be possible to trace precisely when each accretion to the original story was made. But the repetition of plot summaries becomes boring, and anyone who conscientiously attempted to read *all* the variants on the theme of the vendetta would have his life work cut out for him. These accretions by no means came to an end with the triumph of *Kanadehon Chūshingura* in 1748 but have continued to our day in response to the demands of the films and television. Between 1748 and 1900 over fifty full-length plays on the *Chūshingura* theme were written for the jōruri and kabuki theaters. The nineteenth-century dramatist Kawatake Mokuami alone wrote six entirely different plays on the theme, and there was hardly a playwright of significance for almost two hundred years who did not write at least one *Chūshingura* of his own.

Quite apart from the original or semioriginal works inspired by accounts of the vendetta, there were many revivals of *Kanadehon Chūshingura,* both at the puppet theater, for which it was written, and by the kabuki actors, who made revised versions very soon after the appearance of the 1748 play. In general, the puppet theater was more faithful to the text than the actors. Even today a performance of the puppet play begins as the *tayū* (chanter) reverently lifts the text to his forehead as a sign of his respect. Even though he probably knows every word by heart, he carefully turns the pages of the text before him at the appropriate times, as if to indicate his dependence. For the kabuki actors, on the other hand, the text has always tended to become a vehicle for the histrionic talents of particular performers. The audience, in the eighteenth century as now, attended the kabuki theater mainly to see favorite actors in the parts, rather than the play itself, and alterations to the texts were accepted if they enhanced the performance. But the successes enjoyed by later versions of the play never obscured the special importance of *Kanadehon Chūshingura.* It is the only play of its great length which is still regularly produced in entirety or at least in large part, as opposed to the custom of performing a few chosen scenes torn from longer works. The additions made by the kabuki actors to *Kanadehon Chūshingura* have been accepted by the public as authentic, and in some cases the puppet performances depart from their usual observance of fidelity to the original texts and copy the kabuki variations. The *michiyuki* (travel scene) for Okaru and Kampei, first performed by the eighth Danjūrō and the fourth Kikugorō in 1833, is now usually performed by the puppets too, in place of the scene in the original text.

A number of tricks peculiar to kabuki found their way into performance. For example, the actor Ichikawa Danzō discovered a way of making such quick changes that he could appear in the three major roles of the fifth act, Sadakurō, Yoichibei, and Kampei. This display of virtuosity has not been imitated, but another in the same act—Nakamura Nakazō's suppression of all the dialogue for Sadakurō to make the part one of mime only—is almost universally followed today in kabuki, though not in the puppet theater. Again, in the sixth act, "Ichimonjiya," the proprietor of the brothel in Kyoto to which Okaru has been sold, is metamorphosed in the kabuki version into Ichimonjiya's wife Osai, who contributes to the picturesqueness of the scene by using Kyoto dialect.

The number of variants between the currently performed puppet and kabuki versions is so great that to note all of them would be time-consuming, and in the end would not prove much more than what one knows from the start, that kabuki actors have never hesitated to change a play in whatever ways seemed most effective. The puppets, if only because they lack human temperament, are more docile, though it would be rare to see a performance of *Kanadehon Chūshingura* exactly as it was first written. Despite all the changes, however, certain elements remained constant. The character Ōishi Kuranosuke (however called) is an embodiment of samurai ideals. In the Genroku period many people feared that these ideals had been corrupted by the luxury and frivolity of the age, but Kuranosuke and his men demonstrated that any special crisis would still bring them forth into action. The audiences craved novelty in details, but not in this fundamental ethic. For them *Kanadehon Chūshingura* was the grand summation of ideals which even the most unmartial Japanese of the Tokugawa period felt were his own. The annual performances of the play strengthened this conviction; faith in the samurai ideals was renewed by ritual participation in this massive testimony.

Of course, it was not only the grand themes of the work but the variety of the spectacle of a performance that gave *Kanadehon Chūshingura* its special popularity. Each act established a contrasting mood with the previous one, giving the illusion of a complete world. Although Yuranosuke is the central figure in only two of the eleven acts of *Kanadehon Chūshingura,* his presence is felt throughout, and the seventh act requires him to behave like a drunken reveler, a reprobate samurai, a man who is ready to kill even those he loves to preserve the secrecy of his plans, and finally, a man of wisdom and mercy. This one act alone makes for a full experience in the theater, but the cumulative effect of the entire eleven acts, which require at least that many hours to perform, is overpowering.

In many of the later versions of the play key episodes of the vendetta story were sometimes omitted, probably because it was assumed that everyone was familiar with the original work. Parodies were also written, without fear that they might be interpreted as being disrespectful of the heroes of the samurai tradition. One example is Kawatake Mokuami's *A Picture Competition of Figures in Chūshingura (Chūshingura Sugata no Eawase)*, first staged in 1865, in which snatches of the original *Kanadehon Chūshingura* were mixed with frivolous dialogue delivered by anonymous menials. The breathtaking short résumé of the first seven acts manages to omit almost every incident of significance, but every pretext for song and dance is joyously expanded. The second act, for example, opens with jolly recollections by the servants of Moronao, Wakasanosuke, and Hangan about what happened at the Tsurugaoka Shrine the previous day. In the original *Kanadehon Chūshingura* this information is reported by Wakasanosuke's servants in one short paragraph, but here it is stretched out to a full-scale drinking bout with innumerable repetitions of *ha, ha, ha, ha, ha.* This play was a great success and was frequently revived, probably less because of its intrinsic merits than because of the ingenious manner with which the old themes were treated by a master dramatist writing a century later.[2]

The enormous popularity of *Kanadehon Chūshingura* inspired boundless curiosity about episodes in the lives of the characters that were not dealt with in the play. Even accounts that suggested that the heroes were actually far from perfect were accepted without qualms because nothing could shake the conviction that Yuranosuke and his men transcended ordinary human standards. New interpretations or evaluations of the characters were also welcomed, no matter how farfetched. For example, Shikitei Samba, a comic writer of the early nineteenth century, acclaimed Sagisaka Bannai as the supreme hero among all the heroes of *Kanadehon Chūshingura.* Bannai is in fact a lecherous, cowardly underling whose nature is at once revealed in puppet performances as soon as the audience sees the *sammaime chari* head, with its gaping mouth and comically tilted eyebrows, used for the puppet. This head is reserved for foolish villains, but Shikitei Samba, if only because of boredom with more conventional appraisals of the character, insisted that Bannai was a paragon of loyalty. He serves his master Moronao with absolute and unswerving fidelity, cleverly suborns the villainous Kudayū to do Moronao's work, daringly penetrates deep within the enemy stronghold to ferret out Yuranosuke's secret plans, and even after Moronao's death bravely and loyally fights on against hopeless odds to his last breath. "Hooray for the loyal retainer!" is Samba's admiring conclusion.[3] Surely he did not expect anyone to take him seriously, but such farcical commentary indirectly reveals the avid interest readers displayed in each detail of the play.

The most massive attempt ever made to satisfy audiences whose curiosity had been whetted by fictional presentation of the *Chūshingura* themes is Mayama Seika's play *Genroku Chūshingura,* in nine acts that run to over six hundred pages of print. The most puzzling feature of this incredibly long play, which would surely take several days to perform if anyone were enterprising enough to stage the work in its entirety, is that Mayama fails to touch on some of the most important themes of earlier versions. The play opens just after Asano (the characters are known by their historical names) has slashed the villainous Kira (Moronao). We are never told what occasioned this display of anger, though there are a few references to Kira's avarice later on. Mayama devotes pages to an overpowering display of pedantic information; in the stage directions, for example, he describes the costume and crest of every samurai who appears and even states his annual salary, but he neglects to supply the background of the quarrel that has set the tragedy in motion. For that matter, Kira does not appear once in the entire course of the play. Perhaps Mayama assumed that his audiences were thoroughly familiar with the circumstances of the dispute, but one critic has stated that Mayama wished to show that Kuranosuke was indifferent both to the nature of the quarrel and the enemy; his only concern was to do what his loyalty as a retainer commanded.[4]

Be that as it may, the vital question in the first act is not why Asano attacked Kira but whether or not the wound was likely to prove fatal. Asano cheerfully commits suicide after being informed by a compassionate, but untruthful official that although the wound was superficial Kira is an old man and likely to die from loss of blood. Enya Hangan in *Kanadehon Chūshingura* expresses regret that he did not kill Moronao, but is resigned to this failure; the disappointment voiced by Asano in Mayama's play is more affecting. One matter not taken up in *Kanadehon Chūshingura* is why Moronao failed to defend himself when attacked. In Mayama's play some officials praise his forbearance, but one, who is sympathetic to Asano, declares that it was cowardly and unworthy of a samurai not to have drawn his sword when attacked, even in the palace. This seeming contradiction within the samurai code was more likely to have been noticed by a modern writer like Mayama than by dramatists living in the same period in which the incident took place.

Although Mayama occasionally admits that for dramatic purposes he has somewhat altered the facts gleaned from his extensive research, on the whole he is ready to sacrifice even the most affecting
scenes of *Kanadehon Chūshingura* in order to achieve verisimilitude.
For example, the superb scene in *Kanadehon Chūshingura* when Yuranosuke rushes up to his master just after the latter has plunged his
dagger into his abdomen, is completely omitted. Mayama had discovered, after examination of available evidence, that Kuranosuke
did not in fact go to Edo on this occasion; there simply wasn't sufficient time for him to learn the news and rush all the way to distant
Edo. Other research provided Mayama with evidence of the dispute
between the presiding officials as to whether Asano should be permitted to commit *seppuku* indoors or would be required to die outside. Such matters of samurai protocol are unlikely to affect modern
audiences as much as more openly dramatic conflicts, but Mayama
was eager to establish the authenticity of his treatment of the age,
even at the risk of seeming dull. The Tokugawa period dramatists,
both because of censorship and because of their natural instincts as
men of the theater, were more concerned with providing effective
scenes.

The second act of Mayama's play deals chiefly with Kuranosuke's decision with respect to the disposal of the castle of Akō. The
choices before him are to deliver the castle without resistance to the
authorities, to die fighting with his men in its defense, or to commit
mass *seppuku*. Most of the samurai, including Kuranosuke's own
son, a boy of fourteen, favor taking a firm stand; they even give Kuranosuke the nickname of *hiru andon,* or "daytime lantern," to suggest his overly cautious deliberations. But Kuranosuke refuses to be
hurried. He recalls how short-tempered Asano was, even as a youth,
and wonders why none of the retainers in Edo had had the foresight
to appease Kira's greed and thereby spare Asano the necessity of
avenging the insult to his pride. This attitude is in marked contrast to
the one Yuranosuke displays in *Kanadehon Chūshingura,* where he
expresses contempt for Kakogawa Honzō, who saved his master Lord
Wakasanosuke by paying Moronao a bribe.

The most arresting moment in the second act of *Genroku Chūshingura,* at least for contemporary readers, occurs towards the end of
the act. A member of the Asano clan who has been serving in Kyoto
reports the rumor that the emperor himself has been heard to mur-
mur from behind his screen of state that Asano was to be pitied be-

cause he failed to kill Kira. Kuranosuke is stunned by this news, given by Onodera Tonai, and the following dialogue ensues:

KURANOSUKE *(grasping Onodera's hand without realizing it):*
   Tonai-dono!
ONODERA: Kuranosuke-dono!
KURANOSUKE: Tonai-dono!
ONODERA: Kuranosuke-dono!
   (They weep together.)
KURANOSUKE: Aaa, mottainashi, mottainashi. *(He prostrates himself in the direction of Kyoto.)*[5]

Kuranosuke reveals that his chief fear all along had been that Asano's rash action in the palace, where an imperial envoy was being entertained, might have been interpreted as lèse majesté; but when he learns that the emperor has vouchsafed sympathy, and that many court nobles in Kyoto have also expressed regret that Asano did not kill Kira, he feels that his worst fears have been alleviated. Asano is dead, but he has been saved. *(Takumi no kami, sukuwaremashita, sukuwaremashita, sukuware, sukuware, sukuwaremashita.)*[6] It is unfortunate that Asano's estates are to be confiscated and that his family line is to be cut off, but the ultimate disgrace would have been for him to have been considered guilty of disrespect towards the imperial family. The emperor's words have relieved Kuranosuke of this anxiety.

Such sentiments are not to be found in any Tokugawa version of the play to my knowledge. Mayama, who often states his sources, supplied none in this instance, but the sentiments are so familiar, so clearly identifiable as those of the 1930s, that we probably need not look far for older sources. The incident involving Asano and his loyal retainers served as a reminder to Japanese of the eighteenth century, living in an age of peace when the samurai virtues could not easily be displayed, of what they still meant. (Act I of *Kanadehon Chūshingura* contains just after the first words the statement, "The same holds true of a country at peace: the loyalty and courage of its fine soldiers remain hidden, but the stars, though invisible by day, at night reveal themselves, scattered over the firmament").[7] Various dramatizations of the story emphasized this philosophy, and even the parody or debunking that went on never completely concealed this theme.

In the 1930s the samurai virtues were remembered with nostalgia. Allegiance to one's lord was an old-fashioned ideal that had been replaced by allegiance to the emperor. Mayama probably could not resist the impulse to extend this particular kind of loyalty to his samurai heroes. Another ideal of the 1930s is treated in the third act of Mayama's play, in the section concerning the disposal of Asano's assets. The crafty Ōno Kurobei (the Ono Kudayū of *Kanadehon Chūshingura*) urges Kuranosuke to pay off the clan's obligations to the peasantry at the rate of twenty or twenty-five percent of the sums owed. He says that paying more would only invite the derision of other clans. But Kuranosuke is indifferent to the possibility that others may laugh at him; if he had the means, he would pay eighty percent or even one hundred percent to the creditors in the domain, anything to make the lives of the ordinary people more comfortable.[8] Tokugawa scholars often voiced the Confucian principle that the common people, especially the farmers, should be treated with benevolence, but Kuranosuke's remarks at this point in the play seem an echo of the politics of the 1930s, when a love of the soil and sympathy for the farmers were an integral part of the philosophy of the young army officers who rose in rebellion.

Much of the hundred pages of the third act of *Genroku Chūshingura* involves the impatience of Asano's retainers and their bitter complaints over Kuranosuke's delaying tactics. His son, later called Chikara, is eager to have the *gembuku* ceremony performed so that he can do his duty as a full-fledged man and repay his debt to his late master, but Kuranosuke, in a statement that seems strikingly modern and not typical of the Tokugawa period, warns the boy that among the worst pitfalls a samurai must face are praise and worrying about what people will say about him. He assures the boy that even in his youthful garments and forelock he can still display his loyalty to the full. He adds, "I dislike the kind of loyalty that gets praised by everyone who sees it."[9]

Similar voices from the twentieth century are heard from time to time in *Genroku Chūshingura*. They are more attractive than those extolling fanatical loyalty in the eighteenth-century plays, in which men are praised for committing *seppuku* without a second thought. Kuranosuke's prudence is the sign not of cowardice but of a man who is not to be swerved from his ultimate goals. This calm determination in the face of extreme provocation is obviously a quality that Mayama personally admires, and even though he is far more artistic than other twentieth-century adaptors of the *Chūshingura* story, he may fairly be taxed with tailoring the facts to suit his own tastes or those of his age. When, for example, a popular postwar writer of historical fiction like Yoshikawa Eiji makes Taira no Kiyomori express concern over the hardships suffered by the common people or regret that Japan has stagnated for centuries instead of forging ahead and becoming a modern nation, he is obviously pandering to modern tastes.[10]

Perhaps the only scrupulous way to write historical fiction is to emulate Flaubert in *Salammbô,* who deliberately made his characters as remote and unmodern as possible, emphasizing not the similarity of people of the past and those of the present, but their great differences. This method was clearly not the one favored by Mayama or by the many adaptors of *Chūshingura* for the films or television. Kuranosuke was for Mayama the embodiment of samurai ideals which seemed of special importance in the late 1930s. He is determined to avenge his late master, but not if it involves stooping to base deceit. At one point he says, "It is desirable to search out weak spots in one's enemy's defenses and then attack, but I would not wish to satisfy our desire for vengeance if this involved luring our enemy into a trap."[11] Mayama asked more of the samurai ideals than did Kuranosuke's contemporaries, who were impressed by his skill in persuading Kira there was nothing to fear from so debauched a retainer; this act of deception—one might call it a trap—was not considered to be incompatible with the samurai code, but Mayama and his contemporaries were eager to believe that Japan's military actions in China were inspired by righteous ideals and not merely by expedients.

Kuranosuke is of course brave, but he is also a model of prudence and foresight. Aware that not all of Asano's retainers, despite their outrage when they learned of their master's death, can be counted on to persist to the end in the vendetta he plans, he holds repeated meetings of the samurai of the clan, ostensibly to discuss the course of action, but actually to give those who wish to back out the chance to leave without disgrace. Only fifty or so men attend the last meeting, but Kuranosuke knows he can trust them. He tells them that the easiest course would be to die fighting, in the traditional samurai manner, but that this would not bring comfort to their late master. The hardest course is to turn over the castle peacefully, resolved to bide their time until the opportunity to strike arises. This is the course he has chosen, much to the consternation of most of the retainers. He intends to wait, first of all, for a response to his petition that the house of Asano be preserved through the succession of Asano's younger brother Daigaku as *daimyō.* One impassioned hothead cries out, "I don't like it! I don't like it! I don't care if the government bestows the whole of Japan on Daigaku, throwing in China and

India to boot, and he is made a great, great daimyō. I still won't agree if this means leaving our enemy Kira unharmed and our master unavenged. I won't have it!''[12]

Kuranosuke listens patiently to such outbursts, aware of the danger of division, but insists that the men present swear absolute obedience to him and seal their oaths with their blood. Fifty-six men agree.

The fourth act is set in a teahouse in Fushimi, a scene reminiscent of the less historically accurate seventh act of *Kanadehon Chūshingura,* which takes place at the Ichiriki Brothel in Gion. Kuranosuke's son expresses indignation over his father's dissipation, but other samurai suggest that he is probably only pretending to be dissolute, in order to calm Kira's fears of a vendetta. The impetuous Horibe Yasubei, who has already participated in a vendetta and seems to have acquired a taste for them, proposes that they go ahead with the attack on Kira, regardless of whether or not Kuranosuke joins them. Chikara asks Horibe to take him along to Edo.

In the next scene of this act Kuranosuke is shown in full dissipation. He plays the samisen, banters with prostitutes, and, when urged by the samurai to set the vendetta in motion, puts them off by remarking that wherever he goes in Kyoto these days people recognize him and praise him for his self-sacrifice in frequenting the brothels in order to deceive Kira. ''They over-estimate me,'' he comments wryly. The closely guarded secret of *Kanadehon Chūshingura,* that Kuranosuke's dissipation is a pretense, becomes common gossip in Mayama's version. When informed that even the shōgun is now sympathetic to Asano's retainers, and that the ordinary citizens of Edo, hating Kira's avarice, wish that the *rōnin* will kill him soon, Kuranosuke still does not waver. Even the prostitutes at the brothel mock his prudence. One says, ''I've heard people say his name's not Ōishi [Big Stone] but Karuishi [Lightweight Stone], and that he is not a *karō* [chief retainer] but an *ahō* [idiot].''[13] Only when he learns that his son is about to desert him does Kuranosuke intimate that he is following a carefully organized plan. In the most stirring speech of the play, Kuranosuke declares that it is not the result but the manner of the vendetta which is most important:

> If by some unlucky accident Lord Kira should die of old age before we
> have had the chance to exact vengeance, this would indeed mean that
> for the fifty and more of us our luck as samurai had run out. In that
> case, we would have no choice but to go as quickly as possible to the

Sengaku-ji and, taking our places around the stone monument erected to his lordship, follow him manfully by disembowelling ourselves. We would have proven our sincerity and followed the will of heaven. Sincerity is our most important consideration *(Shisei wa daiichi ja).* The vendetta is of secondary importance. As I have always told Hashimoto Sanai and the others, vengeance must not be our final objective. Our first principle must be to perform our duties of utter sincerity to our late master.[14]

The words *shisei,* which may be rendered as "utter sincerity," can be found in the Confucian classics and have been used by Japanese of various periods, but they were peculiarly appropriate to the young army officers of the 1930s whom Mishima so admiringly portrayed in his film *Patriotism (Yūkoku),* which takes place against a backdrop of the two characters starkly written on a vertical plaque. *Shisei* was more clearly an ideal of the 1930s, certainly, than of the Genroku period, although Mayama is at pains to introduce such philosophers as Arai Hakuseki and Kada no Azumamaro in the roles of mentors for the *rōnin;* the latter insists on the differences between Japanese and Chinese—a theme of particular relevance in the 1930s —and declares that people all over Japan are looking to the *rōnin* for proof that the samurai code of Bushidō still exists.[15] Tsunatoyo, who soon afterwards became the shōgun, also demonstrates his sympathy with the *rōnin,* but insists that the vendetta be carried out in a noble manner: "Do you suppose that Lord Asano's chagrin and pent-up wrath will be dissipated merely by your act of placing Kira's freshly severed head before his grave? If you follow the course of duty and possess the truth of those who make justice their only principle, even if you should unfortunately not kill Lord Kira, there will certainly be no blemish on your chivalry and iron resolution."[16]

The fifth act, called "Lord Tsunatoyo at the Ohama Palace" *("Ohama Goten Tsunatoyo-kyō"),* is probably the most frequently performed section of Mayama's play, though it contributes virtually nothing to the main theme of the vendetta. It is more conventionally in the kabuki style and contains such stock figures as evil court ladies who cruelly treat an innocent girl freshly arrived at the court, a wise nobleman (Tsunatoyo) who indirectly expresses admiration for the *rōnin* while maintaining his severe outer demeanor, an impetuous young samurai who wants to kill Kira or die, and so on. There are many implausible developments in the plot that have purely theatrical, as opposed to historical or ideological, appeal. Mayama certainly could write effectively in an old-fashioned style, but he preferred to inject his modern awareness into his works, even if this involved long debates which probably bored many in the audience. The popularity of the fifth act, despite the total absence of Kuranosuke and the other principal figures, is probably in consonance with the similar popularity of scenes in the original *Kanadehon Chūshingura* which appeal to the eye or the ear more than to the intelligence.

The final acts of *Genroku Chūshingura* represent a return to Mayama's more philosophic mood. The successful attack on Kira's mansion is conspicuously understated: everything happens offstage, and the reminiscences of different retainers on their parts in the attack are marred by occasional disputes as to who should be credited with what achievement. This was not Mayama's way of expressing disillusion with the motives of the loyal retainers but a demonstration that these were not supermen untouched by ambition or pride but believable human beings capable of faltering even in their most glorious hour. The concluding act is devoted to the last day of Ōishi Kuranosuke. Alone of the many works treating the story of Chūshingura, Mayama's depicts the final hours of the loyal retainers before they receive the order to commit *seppuku*. Although admirable in execution, these acts have little excitement, and probably only someone as passionately devoted to the story of the gallant forty-seven as Mayama would wish to know all the details presented. But the last act lends a solidity to Mayama's play that has the weight of history. Of all the many dramas written about the retainers of Lord Asano both before and after *Kanadehon Chūshingura,* Mayama's is the only one which can stand up to comparison with that masterpiece of Japanese theater, though its methods are strikingly dissimilar.

The excessive attention to historical detail which is sometimes obtrusive in *Genroku Chūshingura* is certainly not true of the films on the subject, which follow oft-tried patterns of good and bad guys fighting and eliminate the shadings that Mayama was so careful to establish. But a disregard of historical accuracy is not in itself a test of the merits of a play. Its effectiveness on the stage or as a work of literature depends on quite other factors. If, for example, a dramatist were to follow the research of those historians who have determined that Kira was in fact a better ruler than Asano, a man much revered by the people of his domain because of the irrigation works and other beneficial projects that he launched, he might reach conclusions that would destroy the play. The successful vendetta of the forty-seven *rō-nin* is an irresistible theme, but it would be turned topsy-turvy if the audience sympathized with Kira and decided that Asano had been a headstrong, stingy fool. Perhaps Mayama avoided all mention of the original dispute between Kira and Asano because he had reached such conclusions about the two men. Indeed, the point of his play and of all other plays on the *Chūshingura* theme, that loyalty is unconditional, might even have been more forcefully presented if Lord Asano's retainers had died to avenge a thoroughly contemptible master. But that is too much to ask of a dramatist who is aware of the ritual nature of the audience's attendance. Allusive variations on the main themes will no doubt continue to be made, telling us as much about the time of the new work as about the events that occurred in January 1703, but *Chūshingura* will be what it always has been, the ultimate exposition of samurai ideals. And it is to these ideals that Japanese are likely to turn in the future, at least once every year, feeling that this play helps them to understand themselves and their special destiny.

NOTES

1.   Translation by E. P. Coleridge, in Whitney J. Oates and Eugene O'Neill, Jr., eds., *The Complete Greek Drama,* vol. 2 (New York: Random House, 1938), p. 81.

2.   Kawatake Shigetoshi, ed., *Mokuami Zenshū,* vol. 20 (Tokyo: Shunyōdō, 1924–1926), gives the text of the play and a brief introduction.

3.   Shikitei Samba, *Chūshingura Henkichi Ron,* in *Kokkei Meisakushū,* Teikoku Bunko Series (Tokyo: Hakubunkan, 1894), p. 433.

4.   See Tanabe Akio, *Mayama Seika* (Tokyo: Hokuyōsha, 1976), p. 106.

5.   *Mayama Seika Zenshū,* vol. 1 (Tokyo: Dainihon Yūbenkai Kōdansha, 1940), pp. 79–80. The expression *mottainashi* means to be more than one deserves.

6.   Ibid., p. 80.

7.   Translation by Donald Keene, in *Chūshingura: The Treasury of Loyal Retainers* (New York: Columbia University Press, 1971), p. 29. The original Japanese text of this passage was used as an epigraph at the request of Mishima Yukio, to whom the book was dedicated before his death.

8.   *Mayama Seika Zenshū,* p. 98. See also p. 122.

9.   Ibid., p. 124.

10. See, for example, *The Heike Story,* trans. Fuki Wooyenaka Uramatsu (New York: Knopf, 1956), p. 484, where Kiyomori declares, "It's strange that we've made no progress. We've stagnated for five hundred years."

11. *Mayama Seika Zenshū,* p. 373.

12. Ibid., p. 167.

13. Ibid., p. 233.

14. Ibid., p. 245.

15. Ibid., pp. 304, 308.

16. Ibid., p. 350.

Tokugawa Plays on Forbidden Topics

DONALD H. SHIVELY

CHŪSHINGURA is a play on a forbidden topic. Official regulations forbade the depiction of "unusual events of the day," and the raid of vengeance by forty-seven *rōnin* of the Akō domain on the mansion of Lord Kira in 1703 was one of the most sensational incidents in the entire Tokugawa era. Although a special order warned against the dramatization of this raid, year by year stage references to the affair appeared with increasing boldness. Public curiosity about the event itself, and how it might be treated to escape censorship, led playwrights of both the kabuki and puppet theaters to ever more skillful depictions. Over one hundred plays were performed during Tokugawa times about the Akō *rōnin*'s story, but the most popular to this day is *Kanadehon Chūshingura*, staged in 1748. It is, in fact, the most famous play in the repertory of both the puppet and kabuki theaters.

Composition of the original plays about this affair represented an important development in the history of the popular theater. These plays were the first we know of to treat any forbidden topic, and their success quickly inspired portrayals of other sensitive events. They appealed to audiences in part because of the authors' ingenuity in skirmishes with the censors. Disguising "unusual events of the day" as "history" or period pieces, they camouflaged stories sufficiently that officials let them pass.

To appreciate the peculiar form taken by plays about the Akō *rōnin* and other forbidden topics, we must consider both the concerns of the official censors in the Tokugawa period and the character of the period piece *(jidaimono)* which was the staple dramatic form of the day. The two subjects are linked inextricably, for if government regulations placed volatile material beyond the boundaries of the stage, the versatility of the *jidaimono* format helped playwrights to redefine those boundaries in an ever-widening fashion. Little concerned with historical accuracy and imprecise in chronology, the period piece could incorporate proscribed subject matter of recent years into the world of centuries past.

As we shall see, however, the agility of the playwrights in putting the *jidaimono* to new purposes cannot alone explain the successful dramatization of the Akō story. Official tolerance of the exceedingly flimsy disguises used in the period pieces had a variety of motives which raises questions about the changing nature of censorship as well as the objectives of the popular theater in the Tokugawa era. After surveying basic censorship policy and the development of the period piece, we shall turn to the depiction of the Akō affair and the dramatization later of even more sensitive topics.

Censorship

We have two major sources of information regarding principles of censorship in the Tokugawa era: orders to theatrical managers and book publishers that forbade the depiction of certain matters, and the scripts of a few suppressed puppet plays (jōruri) from which we can deduce what officials found objectionable. Neither source is altogether satisfactory, but taken together they outline the guiding concerns of Tokugawa censors.

The earliest laws governing the popular theater attempted to contain licentious behavior on stage and the brawls that often followed. Like prostitution, kabuki was considered both a necessary diversion for the urban populace and an attraction useful to draw commerce to cities under Tokugawa control. Authorities were nonetheless assiduous in their determination to eliminate indecent pantomime and suggestive language from the stage through repeated reforms.

Skits depicting the flirtation of a prostitute and her suitor, known as *keiseikai* ("hiring a prostitute") and *chaya asobi* ("playing in a brothel"), were the common fare of early kabuki. Women were banned from the stage in 1629 to discourage this open advertisement of their charms as well as quarrels over their services among samurai and *rōnin* onlookers. Boys, who had sometimes played women's roles even in earlier times, henceforth monopolized these parts. They were also sought as sexual partners by samurai who occasionally quarreled over them, leading to further attempts to reform the theater in the 1640s and later. "*Shimabara* plays" *(Shimabara kyōgen* or simply

Shimabara) made up much of the kabuki repertory by the 1650s. Named for the licensed pleasure district in Kyoto, these acts were a vicarious guide to the quarter, complete with demonstrations of alternative styles for engaging a prostitute and disporting oneself in a brothel.[1] Such plays were banned in 1655, 1658, and again in 1664 but reemerged in other guises.[2] The vivid portrayal of love scenes and the glamorous treatment of the courtesans' affairs with their lovers continued to engage the attention of the authorities through the eighteenth century.

Although moral concerns inspired some of the restrictions on kabuki, officials were more intent on the maintenance of public decorum, quiet audiences, and peaceable pleasure quarters. The theater and the prostitute quarters were separated and placed at some distance from each other. The authorities continued to regard theater people as riffraff and classified them as semioutcastes beyond the pale of commoner *(chōnin)* society. They continually regulated the behavior and dress of actors, their costumes and wigs, and the theater buildings, to prevent the stage world from appearing too glamorous, too distracting to samurai and commoners alike.

Perhaps their most familiar restrictions involved plays on the theme of double suicide *(shinjū)* by thwarted lovers. Writers of kabuki and jōruri vied in describing young couples in Kyoto and Osaka who were driven in desperation to die together in the belief that they would be reborn on the same lotus calyx in Amida's western paradise. The sympathetic and poetic treatments of their plights, particularly those by Chikamatsu Monzaemon (1653–1725), gave such publicity to double suicides that the officials proscribed both suicides themselves and plays concerning them in 1723.[3] Again, a concern with sensational acts threatening to peace and order was more apparent than moral outrage.

It is the political interests of the censors, however, that most concern us here. Less frequent and less specific than their orders regarding sumptuary matters and public decency, their laws on political subjects go to the heart of the controversy over the forty-seven *rōnin*. One of the earliest orders to theater managers, issued in 1644, states that: "In plays the names of existing people will not be used."[4] Publishers were warned in 1673 not to print matters which would disturb people, or later, "false opinions" and "rumors about people."[5] A prohibition to publishers of 1722 deals with the censors' concerns more specifically: "New books have been written and circulated through society which say various things that are wrong about people's lineage, their ancestors, and the like. This must cease henceforth. If there are books like this and the descendants file suit, the matter will be strictly investigated."[6]

A stricter law forbade mention of the name of Tokugawa Ieyasu, founder of the regime, or any shōgun who followed him. So stern was the proscription that more than a century after Ieyasu's death publishers of scholarly and technical materials still felt constrained about direct references to him. In 1735, therefore, publishers were advised that serious books such as histories and gazetteers might mention the names of shōgun but that lighter pieces (jōruri included) could not allude either to the Tokugawa or stories concerning them.[7] Implicitly, references to distinguished samurai of more recent generations were also forbidden. For the Tokugawa, sensitivity extended back to the latter half of the sixteenth century when they began their rise to power. Playwrights never described events of that troubled time directly.

The determination of the Tokugawa to maintain respect for their own house and the samurai elite reflects the preoccupation of the time with face and family honor. As there were no military campaigns after 1615 in which military men could gain distinction, status was largely determined by the exploits of great forebears and by hereditary privileges. It was critical to put the best possible representation on the service of household ancestors. In a society in which honor was guarded and dignity preserved by strict rules of conduct, moreover, samurai did not wish to see themselves or their progenitors portrayed on stage. Since the performers were semioutcastes or puppets, any depiction of warrior class (buke) histories would be an intolerable indignity.

The prohibition against publishing matters which would "disturb people" seems to have been enforced only with regard to people who counted, that is, samurai and especially the upper buke. The domestic plays (sewamono), which took the lives of common people as their material, dealt quite openly with scandals and love suicides among townsmen, sometimes using real names or transparent substitutes. The authorities overlooked sensational jōruri or kabuki as long as their subjects failed to touch persons of importance who might lodge complaints.

Even the emperor and the court nobility received scant protection. Emperors appear occasionally and princes frequently in period pieces. Often portrayed as very human personalities with the foibles of ordinary people, emperors are gentle, absorbed in love affairs, and sometimes played comically. They differ greatly from the shōgunlike overlords of the plays who appear as powerful and disciplined warriors, autocratic and awesome, betraying little human emotion.

The Buddhist church did win some support from the authorities. Despite the absence of laws proscribing the depiction of priests, the censors closed a number of seventeenth-century puppet plays featuring great religious leaders of the past: Shinran, Hōnen, and Nichiren. The most popular sects of the time had been founded by followers of these spiritual figures of the thirteenth century. We may assume that the sects' leaders took offense at the lack of piety displayed toward the saintly founders. Since the sects had such large numbers of adherents, complaints filed by their head temples persuaded officials to halt performances and the sale of offending jōruri texts. Plays about Shinran were suppressed in Edo in 1655 and in Osaka in 1671. Plays as well as books concerning Shinran and Hōnen were suppressed in Kyoto in 1672.[8] Since censorship did not stem from questions of doctrine or belief, government action against the offending plays was political: the authorities complied with the wishes of influential religious groups.

One last set of prohibitions which touch on political matters must concern us. Beyond protecting the names and histories of living samurai, the censors repeatedly warned against depictions in plays or books of "any kind of extraordinary matter" (1673, 1684), "unusual events of the present time" (1684), "any matters which are questionable" (1684), and "unfounded rumors which are current in society" (1721). The government did not want events of the day, not to mention gossip and scandals pertinent to military men, given sensational treatment or published in the tawdry little booklets or one-page extras which were hawked on street corners.[9]

What do we know about the application of these regulations to the plays themselves and the enforcement of censorship in the kabuki and in the puppet theaters? The history of censorship in the kabuki theater is difficult to trace. Kabuki texts were not printed during the Tokugawa period, and complete, reliable manuscript versions are both few in number and late in date. Only a few survive from the middle of the eighteenth century.[10] Our knowledge of eighteenth-century kabuki comes largely from abridged versions *(kyōgen-bon)* of certain plays, which were printed, and illustrated booklets *(ehon)* of others. Information about the casts and roles of some dramas appears in critical booklets on actors *(yakusha hyōbanki)*, yet all too often we know only the title of a play and the date of its presentation (from the *Gedai Nenkan* or *Play Title Yearbook*).

The main reason for the lack of complete kabuki libretti is the continued dominance of the theater by the actor. The focus of interest was his physical charm, dancing ability, voice and elocution, and his reputation—both on and off stage. Because actors demanded material suited to their talents, the playwright was subordinate. As a consequence, plays lacked structure and literary quality. The author sketched out the plot and some of the script, often the opening lines of important speeches, to prompt the actor, but most of the dialogue was improvised. The rough texts that were prepared, and could have been inspected by censors, were not reliable guides to what would happen in a given performance.[11]

It is likely, therefore, that most censorship of kabuki plays in the eighteenth century continued to be carried out by agents of the city commissioners *(machi bugyō)* who visited actual performances to check on the content of the plays as well as the costumes and deportment of actors. Actors and managers were imprisoned or sent off to exile on occasion, but in most instances it is unclear whether they were punished for a specific infraction, for too venturesome a stage record, or for violation of sumptuary laws. There are notations from time to time that kabuki plays were not permitted to open, probably because of an offensive title or foreknowledge about the theme. Some plays were closed after a few performances or suspended until acceptable changes were made. Because we lack both the scripts of problematic plays and the formal indictments of actors and managers, however, the causes of censorship generally remain elusive.

The situation was different in the puppet theater. Texts were written out in full and set to musical notation for the reciter. Since the puppets' movements were choreographed, narrative improvisation during a performance was not possible. Playwrights constructed plots carefully and composed lyrical parts of the text in a polished literary style. Called jōruri, these texts were recited to the rhythmic, musical accompaniment first of the *biwa* and later, from the beginning of the seventeenth century, of the samisen. Jōruri was long established as a form of narrative literature before puppets were added to mime the action. More gifted authors, such as Chikamatsu, preferred jōruri to kabuki for they retained control over plot and text in the puppet theater.

Jōruri were routinely published from the 1630s, and more than four hundred texts printed between 1625 and 1686 were still extant in the 1930s, evidence that they were considered works of literary interest.[12] The requirement that new manuscripts be approved before publication was extended to all types of works in Kyoto by 1698 and in Edo and Osaka some years later. When a new jōruri play was composed, the theater manager took the manuscript to one of the city commissioners.[13] With his consent, the manuscript was given to a woodblock printer who had the libretto ready for sale soon after performances of the play began. These books included notation for the benefit of the amateur reciter but were also bought to be read as literature.

Rich in language and attentive to plot development, puppet plays became source books for kabuki writers. Most period pieces still in the classical repertory of kabuki today, *Chūshingura* among them, were adaptations of jōruri. Approved by the censors before publication, the puppet texts provided kabuki authors—and modern historians—with a guide to permissible dramatic content.

Period Pieces

Most puppet plays are *jidaimono.* Often referred to as "history plays," suggesting an analogy to that group of Shakespeare's works, the *jidaimono* are better called period pieces.[14] The latter phrase describes them more aptly and is a closer rendering of the Japanese term. Only after 1700, when *sewamono* or "domestic plays" dealing with the common people of the day appeared, was a term of distinction needed at all. Even then, period pieces remained the principal fare of the theater; the domestic plays of both jōruri and kabuki were much shorter dramas added at the end of a day-long program. Chikamatsu himself, though most appreciated today for his *sewamono,* wrote far more *jidaimono.* In his last two decades, while composing all twenty-four of his domestic pieces, he produced twice as many period plays.

In taking historical events for their material, the *jidaimono* followed the tradition of earlier drama—nō and *kōwakamai* (balladdrama)—and the "old jōruri" texts of the sixteenth century. By the middle of the seventeenth century, in any event, laws proscribing the depiction of contemporary incidents seemed to leave the playwright no alternative to period studies. The following discussion of the character of eighteenth-century *jidaimono* relies upon jōruri written initially for puppets, since we lack full kabuki libretti.

Jidaimono usually dealt with historical events familiar to the audience. Many concerned samurai exploits of long ago: the heroic struggles of the Taira and Minamoto clans in the twelfth century, the legends of Yoshitsune, the revenge of the Soga brothers, and the fourteenth-century battles and intrigues recorded in the *Taiheiki.*

The occasional play treated remote figures of the imperial court or well-known religious leaders. Sources for the *jidaimono* included not only early histories and military epics, but later—and highly fictionalized—literature of the Muromachi period as well: nō plays, *kōwakamai, otogi zōshi* (storytellers' tales), and old jōruri. The plays also drew upon Edo period storybooks and previous kabuki. Needless to say, such materials added only legend and fanciful embellishment to the original histories. The dramatic products contained as much folklore as fact.

Playwrights came to think of each "story area" as a *sekai*, that is, a "world" embracing several decades and populated by a stock of historical—and sometimes legendary—characters. Thus *Gikeiki*, for example, a chronicle of Yoshitsune's life in the late twelfth century, became the name, too, of a dramatic world. A play cast in that world could be expected to include Yoshitsune's mistress Shizuka or another of his lovers, his companion Benkei, and such retainers as Izumi Saburō, Gonnotō Kanekura, Kamei Rokurō, Kataoka Hachirō, Date Gorō, Nishikida Tarō, and many others.[15] Already intimately acquainted with these characters, the audience needed no introductions. It simply waited impatiently to see what new feats the heroes would perform and what heinous crimes had been invented for the villains.

The custom developed in popular theaters of staging a new *jidaimono* every second month, unless a performance was such a smash hit that it could be carried over. Because each of the three largest cities had five or six theaters for kabuki and jōruri, the number of plays produced is staggering. Pure revivals were rare, as audiences required some curious twist of plot in every production. Recorded titles of "original" plays consequently run to many thousands. Yet audiences also relished reencounters with the best-loved worlds—that of the Soga brothers, for instance. Edo theaters staged plays involving the Soga *sekai* in the first month of each year, Osaka and Kyoto theaters in the fifth month. Chikamatsu alone wrote eleven jōruri about the Soga brothers, a tribute, at least, to his enterprise.

The production of ever new plays on always familiar themes required a great deal of ingenuity. Playwrights often cannibalized old scripts and exploited scenes which had won popular acclaim. In every case, however, they added something new: fresh love affairs or shocking revelations that certain characters were actually long-lost relatives. Stories wandered farther and farther from historical fact with each innovation. Beleaguered by urgent demands for scripts, authors were hardly disposed to worry about the accuracy of detail. Hasty and improbable invention was the custom. Sometimes the playwright borrowed adventures from characters of one world and ascribed them to another. Fanciful allusions to heroes of a distant *sekai* also enlivened well-worn plots. Spurred on by competition with rival theaters, authors rushed into production new variants on hit themes of a neighboring theater which, if they did not succeed in topping the original, at least rode in the wake of a subject's popularity.

Kabuki and jōruri plays were written for the entertainment of *chōnin*, not samurai. The more refined nō drama was considered proper for the warrior class. Hence performances in the popular theater catered to the commoners' less sophisticated taste and lower level of education. Implausible leaps in plot, flights of fantasy, the jumble of fact and fiction were only the beginning. The plays featured miracle after miracle and piled one agonizing event upon another. The separation of families, the sacrifice of an only child, the identification of the severed head of a son or a brother or a parent, the suicide of a hero that turned out, only after the dagger had been thrust into the belly, to be unnecessary—all such scenes were played in a cathartic style. The theater was a place of escape for townsmen where they could fantasize about superhuman feats of brave men and women, the palaces of shōgun and emperors, quarrels and love affairs in the families of great lords, and high living in the finest houses of assignation.

Playwrights enjoyed enormous freedom, therefore, in their treatment of historical sources. An episode from one of Chikamatsu's best-known period pieces will serve to illustrate their heady departures from established fact. The title alone—*The Taira and the Isle of Women (Heike Nyogo no Shima)*—suggests titillating additions to a classic saga. According to the source, *The Tale of the Heike (Heike Monogatari)*, Taira no Shigehira determined to punish the Nara monks who were defiantly opposed to Taira domination of the imperial government. He marched on Nara, burned the Kōfukuji and Tōdaiji temples (including the Great Buddha Hall), and returned triumphantly to the capital with the heads of his adversaries. But Chikamatsu depicts the Taira carrying home, in addition, the bronze head of the Great Buddha. This object, which is actually some sixteen feet in height and weighs a great many tons, is trundled to Kyoto on a cart and exposed at the execution ground as punishment accorded a defeated enemy leader.[16]

Another act of this play casts Tokiwa Gozen, the former mistress

of Minamoto no Yoshitomo who had been defeated and killed by the
Taira in 1160, in a strange role. Chikamatsu tells us that in 1179,
shortly before the rise of the Minamoto against the Taira, Tokiwa
made it a practice to have her maids entice men passing in the street
to come into her mansion. We learn later that gossip has slandered
Tokiwa, whose purpose is secretly to recruit warriors for the overthrow
of the Taira. A maid named Fuetake, who solicits in the manner of a
brothel tart, is actually Tokiwa's son, Ushiwakamaru. He will emerge
a few years later as the leading general of the Minamoto forces and
one of the greatest heroes of Japanese history.[17] The unorthodox re-
cruitment procedure plays on a popular story concerning Ushiwakamaru. According to the tale, the powerful warrior-monk Benkei
stood on the Gojō bridge night after night and challenged and took
the sword of every man who passed that way. One night Ushiwakamaru confronted him, armed only with a folding fan and a flute—
hence his name Fuetake in Chikamatsu's play—and subdued Benkei,
who at once became his loyal retainer and companion in the campaigns against the Taira. But this was not the end of Chikamatsu's
mischief. This episode also plays on the story of Yoshida Goten, a
highborn lady who reputedly brought men in off the street to sleep
with her. Popular belief had it that the lady was Senhime, Tokugawa
Ieyasu's granddaughter.

As this example indicates, playwrights were storytellers, not historians. Not only did they capriciously mix their stories, they told
them as if they took place within the material and ethical culture of
their own day. Seemingly unconscious of the passage of centuries,
they maintained the world view of an urban commoner, expressing a
chōnin's conception of how great warriors and noble ladies of the
past dressed, spoke, and behaved. The moral principles which moti-
vated their characters were values of the Tokugawa period: loyalty to
one's lord and devotion to parents. All the Neo-Confucian precepts
which permeated the schoolbooks of the day found exemplification
in the plays. The political and social institutions of their time had
always existed. In twelfth-century stories we find Tokugawa-style
samurai, village headmen, merchants, and, above all, prostitutes.
Everything is up to date. There are glaring anachronisms such as mus-
kets and tobacco pipes, although these dubious contributions of
European culture did not reach Japan until the sixteenth century.
Furthermore, the authors or actors liked to insert passing references
to matters of current interest in the city: the latest fashion in kimono,
a new cake and the name of the shop where it could be bought, a

brothel which was involved in gossip, the name of a popular courtesan or of an actor in the troupe.

Because *jidaimono* could accommodate current happenings in a historical setting, a setting which was conceived as differing little from contemporary society, they provided a convenient format within which reference to recent events in the samurai class could be made without seeming out of character. The tendency in these period pieces to introduce episodes from unrelated stories, events which might even involve characters from a different century, also eased the incorporation of forbidden material. Offending material could be naturalized into the semifictional world of the *jidaimono* without violating too blatantly the letter of the censorship regulations.

The Dramatization of the Akō Affair

Audiences clearly had a taste for seeing scandals within the warrior nobility played out. Toward the end of the seventeenth century, kabuki playwrights frequently used the *jidaimono* format to depict inheritance disputes and amorous entanglements of military houses. These episodes were cast as fictional dramas of some earlier or indeterminate period and cannot be identified with specific events in Tokugawa times. The larger and more politically sensitive crises of the warrior elite, however, were seldom portrayed before the middle of the eighteenth century. This was not for want of sensational material. The aborted plot of Yui Shōsetsu against the *bakufu* (government) in 1651 ended in a hundred executions, and throughout the seventeenth century there were raids of revenge *(katakiuchi)* which resulted in armed clashes between scores of samurai. Further, succession quarrels and factional disputes in *daimyō* households *(oie sōdō)* had occasioned the confiscation of certain domains, while intrigue, slander, and dissolute conduct had brought about the loss of others.

The eventual dramatization of a number of these events, as well as the introduction of fairly explicit stage references to proscribed material, followed the depiction of the Akō affair. Plays concerning the raid of the forty-seven *rōnin* were the first to camouflage sensitive subject matter sufficiently to pass the censors. The brilliant refinement of the *jidaimono* format in the Akō plays prepared the way for even bolder treatments of volatile issues on stage.

The bare facts of the Akō story are straightforward. On the fourteenth day of the third month, 1701, Lord Asano, the *daimyō* of Akō, drew his sword against Kira, an official of the shōgun's government. Evidently provoked by Kira, Asano slashed out but inflicted only a slight wound on his adversary's forehead. Asano was in the shōgun's court at the time. It was a capital offense to draw a sword in the court, and Asano was sentenced immediately to perform *seppuku*. Some of his retainers thereupon plotted revenge on Kira. Having waited twenty-two months to the day for the opportune moment, forty-seven of them made a night raid on Kira's mansion.[18] They killed or wounded a number of his retainers, and after a desperate search of the premises, they found Kira hiding in the charcoal storage room. They cut off his head and took it to their lord's tomb.

This bold raid on the mansion of one of the shōgun's officials within the city of Edo was an electrifying event. News of the attack spread at once through Edo. Word also traveled quickly to other cities by private letters. In a country long at peace under the strict security of the Tokugawa, this foray in the shōgun's capital was a stirring reminder of samurai exploits of an earlier age. In the Genroku years of prosperity and pleasure-seeking, when the feudal values of the samurai were thought to have grown soft, the dedication of the *rōnin* —their willingness to sacrifice their lives to uphold their honor and atone for what they regarded as the unjust death of their lord—won the admiration of samurai and *chōnin* alike. It seemed to some that the old virtues of loyalty and sacrifice, which survived only in idealized form in plays and stories about the past, had unexpectedly reemerged. Vengeance for the death of a master or father *(katakiuchi)*, one of the favorite themes in literature since the time of the Soga brothers, had been played out in dramatic style in the streets of Edo. Thus the Akō affair was fascinating to the public and an exceedingly tempting story for playwrights.

The problem of how to deal with the Akō retainers posed a dilemma for the Tokugawa government. These *rōnin* had exemplified feudal virtues, but they had also violated the government's regulations for the preservation of law and order by secretly forming a league and carrying out a revenge without authorization. Almost two months after the attack, following extensive debate in the councils of the *bakufu*, the shōgun sentenced the *rōnin* to *seppuku*. They died in 1703, on the fourth day of the second month.

In the same month (the date is not known), the government issued the following notice:

1. As ordered repeatedly in the past, it is again prohibited to take unusual events that occur in today's society and make them into songs and publish and sell them.

2. In the Sakai-chō and Kobiki-chō theaters also, unusual events of the times must not be used as material and acted out.[19]

There can be little doubt that this order was issued to prevent portrayal of the Akō affair. In the face of the prohibition, how could playwrights deal with the story? It took time and persistence, but after some years they succeeded in dramatizing most of the details.

Note that there are three parts to the Akō affair: (1) the sword wound—Asano's attack upon Kira in the shōgun's court; (2) the *rōnin* suffering—the privations and long wait of the samurai who lost their positions and lived in humiliation until they could avenge their lord; and (3) the raid—the night assault on Kira's mansion and the taking of his head. Episodes such as these were not uncommon in *jidaimono,* especially in the subgenre of revenge pieces. Playwrights lost little time in introducing into plays on quite irrelevant subjects some action which had a slight resemblance to one or another of the Akō incidents.

An Edo theater, the Yamamura-za, is said to have staged one of the first kabuki plays to depict the inflicting of a sword wound in the shōgun's court, *Higashiyama Eiga no Butai.* Although there is no reliable evidence concerning either the play or the performance, it was reputedly set in the fifteenth-century world of Oguri Hangan and mounted in the third month of 1702, the first anniversary of the wounding of Kira in Edo castle and long before the raid on his mansion. According to another and more commonly cited story, the Nakamura Theater in Edo opened the kabuki *Night Attack at Dawn by the Soga (Akebono Soga no Youchi)* in the second month of 1703, only twelve days after the *seppuku* of the *rōnin.* This play was ostensibly about the revenge of the Soga brothers, but the raid scene was modeled on the attack of the Akō retainers. The performance was banned after three days. Again, the documentation is flawed and contradictory, and some scholars no longer credit the account.[20] Given the sensitivity of the government to the Akō affair, there is reason to doubt that theaters in Edo—the shōgun's capital and the site of the events—would make even passing references to it. Not until a decade later is there good documentation of an Edo performance of a play depicting the vengeance.

In Kyoto, however, early treatment of the Akō story seems to have been possible, for we know of no objection to pointed allusions to the affair when Chikamatsu's kabuki *Keisei Mitsu no Kuruma* was performed at the Hayagumo Chōdayū Theater in the first month of 1703. A printed booklet *(kyōgen-bon)* containing a synopsis of the play survives. In Act II, the samurai hero seeks to avenge the death of his mistress, a prostitute, in a raid which mimics the Akō episode. The costumes and weapons of the attackers, their decision to scale the walls surrounding the mansion of their enemy and unbar the gate from inside, their swordfights within the mansion compound, and their seizure of the enemy's head which they bear off in a procession —all such details unmistakably record the descent upon Kira's residence. The play also gives expression to the popular admiration of the Akō *rōnin:* "How admirable! They are models of warriors."[21]

Other plays in Osaka and Kyoto with references to the event soon followed. At the end of 1703 and into the next year, two puppet dramas—similar in title and content—hinted at the Akō incident. Takemoto Chikugonojō's *Keisei Yatsuhanagata* and Uji Kaganojō's *Naniwa-zome Yatsuhanagata* both depicted scenes of sword wounds at court in their first acts and raids upon the enemy mansion in their fourth acts. Elements of the Akō story were also worked into storybooks: Nishizawa Ippū's (1665–1731) *Keisei Budō Zakura* printed in 1704 and a variant, *Keisei Harima Ishi,* in 1706. They appeared to be stories about the licensed quarter but in fact contained material about the Akō affair. Aoki Rosui's *Kōmyō Taiheiki,* published about this time, was set in the fourteenth-century world of the *Taiheiki,* and it too referred to the Akō *rōnin.* Although the plots of these storybooks are farfetched, the reader can find in them some of the details concerning the Akō heroes.[22]

On the seventh anniversary of Asano's death in 1708, a time when it was customary to perform special Buddhist services in memory of the deceased, the Kameya Theater in Kyoto opened a kabuki play called *Fukubiki Urū Shōgatsu.* Set in the *Taiheiki* world, it introduced Enya Hangan to represent Asano. The play included a raid scene, but little else is known of it.

In the second half of 1710, there were remarkable developments in dramatizations of the Akō story. At least eight kabuki and puppet plays on the affair were staged in Osaka and Kyoto.[23] Two of these plays, which have survived in their jōruri texts, present the essential facts of the story but disguise them as events of an earlier world. The most celebrated, which was to have great influence on later productions, was a one-act play by Chikamatsu entitled *Goban Taiheiki.*[24] It purports to be the sequel to his two-act play *The Sightseeing Carriage of the Priest Kenkō (Kenkō Hōshi Monomi Guruma).*

Kenkō Hōshi drew much of its material from a story in chapter 21 of the *Taiheiki*, "The Slander and Death of Enya Hangan." That story recounts how Kō no Moronao (d. 1351), one of the most powerful lords of the time, learned of the unparalleled beauty of the wife of Enya Hangan Takasada (d. 1341), lord of Hōki. In the *Taiheiki* account, Moronao attempts to woo her with a poem, but she rejects this advance with a poetic allusion to another lady who refused to be untrue to her husband. One later evening Moronao spies on Hangan's wife as she arises from her bath and, with this fuller revelation of her extraordinary beauty, becomes obsessed with desire. To remove Hangan from the scene, Moronao reports to the shōgun, Ashikaga Takauji, that Hangan is plotting insurrection. Hangan hears of this slander and he and his family flee. They are subsequently overtaken by the shōgun's forces, Hangan's wife and older son are killed, and he commits *seppuku*. His faithful retainer Yawata Rokurō entrusts Hangan's second son to a priest before he, too, commits *seppuku*.[25]

In Chikamatsu's play, Moronao hears of the lady's beauty and has the poet and essayist Yoshida Kenkō (1283–1350) compose a love letter for him to send her. She scorns it with a reference to the poem mentioned earlier. Moronao then learns that she will visit the Kiyomizu temple to perform ablutions in the waters of the Otowa Falls, to pray for her husband's success in a military campaign. Moronao waits for her at the temple and is smitten by passion as she appears in her bathing robe. When he attempts to engage her, Hangan rushes upon the scene and, with a display of martial prowess, frightens off Moronao. In the second act Hangan is dead. His retainer, Yawata Rokurō, vows revenge: "Since our master, Lord Hangan, has been killed we cannot live long in this world, but we will not rest until we have killed the enemy, Kō no Moronao. . . ."[26]

Chikamatsu's one-act play, *Goban Taiheiki*, has a subtitle which indicates that it is a sequel to his play about Moronao and the beauty.[27] In the opening lines we are told that a *rōnin* and former retainer of Lord Hangan's called Yawata Rokurō is now known as Ōboshi Yuranosuke.[28] This speech alerts the audience that the play concerns the Akō story, since the name thinly disguises the leader of the Akō *rōnin*, Ōishi Kuranosuke. The retainer's son is given the name Rikiya; the character for *riki* is also read Chikara, a homonym of the name of Kuranosuke's son. Their lord, Hangan, who was forced to commit *seppuku*, represents Asano, and the villain Moronao, who causes his death, represents Kira. This short play includes the essen-

tial details of the second and third parts of the Akō story: the suffering of the *rōnin;* the seclusion of their leader in Yamashina; his exchange of secret letters with loyal confederates in eastern Japan; his
parting from his wife; the rallying of the other *rōnin;* and the night
attack on the enemy's mansion which ends with the discovery of
Moronao in the charcoal room; the taking of his head; and the delivery of it to the lord's tomb. Most of the devices employed by Chikamatsu—the use of the fourteenth-century Moronao–Enya story as a
cover, the substitute names, the representation of the Tokugawa as
the Ashikaga, the setting of the raid in Kamakura rather than in Edo
—were retained by the authors of *Chūshingura* thirty-eight years
later.[29]

Chikamatsu's *Goban Taiheiki* was not the first of the many
plays about the Akō affair performed in 1710. The earliest is believed
to be the kabuki, *Onikage Musashi Abumi,* written by Azuma Sam-
pachi, which opened in the sixth month. We know of it from a critical booklet of the time, the *Yakusha Daifukuchō,* which notes under
its entry for the actor Shinozuki Jirōzaemon: "Last summer from the
sixth month, tenth day until the ninth month, eleventh day, there
was a great hit which ran 120 days called *Musashi Abumi* on the revenge of the forty-seven men. After that the kabuki theaters of Kyoto
and Osaka without exception put on revenge pieces and turned a
profit. [Jirōzaemon] played the part of Ōkishi Kunai."[30] The *kyōgen-bon* of the kabuki is not extant, but we do know the cast and the
parts they played. The names of the characters are almost identical to
those of a puppet play of the same title, written by Ki no Kaion
(1663–1742), which was probably performed at the end of the year.
The latter play, which survives, contains references to the kabuki version and is thought to have followed its plot.[31] The characters are
from the world of Oguri Hangan of the early fifteenth century.
Oguri's faithful retainer bears the name Ōkishi Kunai to resemble
Ōishi Kuranosuke, and his son is called Rikinosuke, using the same
wordplay as Chikamatsu's Rikiya.

The Oguri Hangan world evolved from one of the early texts of
"old jōruri," *Oguri no Hangan,* published in 1666, as well as a
number of widely differing accounts of Oguri's story in prose literature and early dramatic works. In eighteenth-century jōruri and
kabuki, this world encompassed the adventures of a semilegendary
warrior and skilled horseman and his devoted wife, Terute-hime. In
most versions Hangan is poisoned by his wife's father, Yokoyama,
and her older brother, Saburō. In one version he dies, in another he

lingers deathly ill; in both traditions, Terute-hime places his body upon a cart which she herself pulls to Kumano, where the healing waters miraculously restore him. He returns to punish the Yokoyama.[32]

In Kaion's five-act jōruri *Onikage Musashi Abumi*, Ashikaga Yoshimasa's younger brother, Masatomo, pays a visit to Kamakura. Oguri Hangan Kaneuji is appointed to supervise the reception. But after having been insulted by his greedy father-in-law, Yokoyama Saemon Nobuhisa, and provoked into drawing his sword and wounding Yokoyama, Hangan is forced to commit *seppuku*. Before his death, he expresses his resentment to an attendant who later relays the message to Oguri's senior retainer, Ōkishi Kunai, at his lord's provincial mansion. In Act II, Oguri's wife, Terute-hime, places his body on a cart which she draws to the family temple, Yūgyōji at Fujisawa. Kunai and the other retainers, forty-seven in all, gather at the temple and vow to kill Yokoyama and his son.

Act III is set in the humble house of Katagiri Genzaemon. His son, Gengo, who had been Oguri's retainer, comes to say farewell. Although the father and mother criticize their son for failing to avenge Oguri's death, Gengo does not reply in order to keep secret his plan to give his life in the attempt to avenge his lord.

Act IV is a scene in the Fushimi brothel quarter where the prostitute Agemaki is in love with Rikinosuke, Kunai's son. Kunai buys up her contract in order that she and his son may live together, or so Agemaki believes. In fact, Kunai redeems Agemaki because her life must be sacrificed for his cause. Kunai knows that Agemaki has learned of the secret plan to avenge Oguri's death and he fears also that Rikinosuke, because of his love for Agemaki, will not be singleminded in his pursuit of their mission. Act V is the attack on the mansion. Yokoyama and his son are found in the charcoal room; they are dragged out, and their heads cut off.[33]

Scholars now believe that Kaion's play and Chikamatsu's *Goban Taiheiki* were produced about the same time, late in 1710 or soon thereafter.[34] Kaion and Chikamatsu wrote for competing puppet theaters in Osaka, the Toyotake-za and the Takemoto-za respectively, which sought publicity by billing the playwrights as rivals and staging plays by them in the same year on the same newsworthy event. There are several instances of such competition. In 1711 both authors wrote plays on the double suicide of Okisa and Jirōbei: Chikamatsu's *Imamiya no Shinjū* and Kaion's *Imamiya Shinjū Marugoshi Renri no Matsu*. Both also wrote plays in 1718 concerning the punishment that year of an ostentatious brothel operator: *Keisei Shuten Dōji* and *Sanshō Dayū Yoshiwara Suzume.* In 1722, after the double suicide of Ochiyo and Hambei, Chikamatsu wrote *Shinjū Yoigōshin,* and Kaion wrote *Shinjū Futatsu Haraobi.* With the vogue for kabuki plays on the Akō story in the second half of 1710, it is plausible that the two puppet theaters rushed rival portrayals of that affair into production.[35]

Why the rash of bold plays in 1710? The death of Shōgun Tsunayoshi the previous year was certainly instrumental.[36] Far-reaching changes in government occurred and many of Tsunayoshi's policies were reversed—including some of his controversial decisions concerning the Asano house. A capricious and often harsh ruler, Tsunayoshi had been infuriated by Asano's attack on Kira, especially as it came only minutes before Kira and Asano were to perform as principals in presenting the shōgun's gifts for the emperor to the imperial emissaries. The ambassadors had come to Edo to confer the first court rank upon the shōgun's mother. Tsunayoshi was a stickler for ritual and etiquette and a student of court ceremonial. Thus it was a matter of great concern to him that auspicious observances be performed properly. Instead, he was confronted by an assassination attempt in the corridor near the great hall and the defilement of the court by bloodshed. (The imperial envoys saved the shōgun from further embarrassment by tactfully agreeing that the ceremony should be held as planned, and another audience hall was hastily prepared.)[37]

Superstitious by nature, Tsunayoshi was deeply shaken by the inauspicious omen. The incident recalled a traumatic event of 1684 when his chief minister, Hotta Masatoshi, was assassinated, also in the corridors of Edo castle. The only previous sword attack occurred in 1628 when the shōgun's senior councilor, Inoue Masanari, was slain. In both cases the assassin paid with his life, his property was confiscated, and his house brought to an end.

It is not surprising that Asano was sentenced to *seppuku,* but the way in which the sentence was carried out was unnecessarily severe. Acting against the advice of his ministers, who requested time to investigate Asano's sanity and consider the matter, Tsunayoshi autocratically condemned Asano to die the same day as the attack, before he could speak to his family or retainers. They probably never learned—as historians to this date do not know—what provoked Asano to attack Kira. Asano's domain and property were confiscated, resulting in the dismissal of all 270 of his samurai and the effective end of his house. Asano's younger brother, Nagahiro, one of the shōgun's bannermen *(hatamoto)* with a fief of three thousand *koku* of rice, was also deprived of his position and placed under house arrest. Most controversial, however, was Tsunayoshi's violation of a basic feudal law. Since the fifteenth century feudal lords had followed the principle that, in case of a fight between two retainers, both would be punished without attempting to weigh the blame *(kenka ryōsei-bai)*. Not only was Kira spared, he was complimented by the shōgun for not resisting the attack.[38]

It is often said that had Kira received some kind of punishment, there would never have been a revenge. If Asano's brother had not lost his fief, moreover, he could have carried on the Asano house—even if as a bannerman rather than a *daimyō*—and so averted the attack.[39] But because of the stern circumstances, and because Kira was apparently not well liked, there was considerable sympathy for the Asano family and retainers within the shōgun's administration and, of course, among other samurai and the public.

Following Tsunayoshi's death in the first month of 1709, a general amnesty was proclaimed in the seventh month. The government recalled Asano's brother to Edo and released eighteen sons of Akō *rōnin* who had been sent into exile or placed in custody. In the sixth month of the next year, Asano Nagahiro received an audience with the shōgun and, three months later, was reappointed a *hatamoto* and awarded a fief of five hundred *koku* in Awa. The Asano house was reestablished.[40]

The repudiation of Tsunayoshi's policies by the new regime emboldened playwrights to tell the Akō story in greater detail, which they did in a flurry of dramas that year. Fear of complaints from the descendants of Kira for portraying him as corrupt and villainous did not constrain them. Kira's adopted son and heir had lost his fief for cowardice on the night of the raid and had already died in disgrace; the house of Kira had come to an end.

The reinstatement of Asano Nagahiro in 1710 concluded the Akō affair. In a spirit of celebration, therefore, plays appeared toward the end of the year incorporating the latest news items. In the ninth month, in the kabuki *Sazare Ishi Go-Taiheiki,* the sequel to *Taiheiki Sazare Ishi,* which was staged in the seventh month, the shōgun pardons the children of the *rōnin,* grants a fief to Hangan's son Rokurō (a younger brother according to another account of the play) who succeeds as head of the house of Hangan.[41] At the close of Chikamatsu's *Goban Taiheiki* an official arrives at the tomb of Lord Hangan and reads the government order, sentencing the *rōnin* to death for their armed attack in violation of the law, but commending their loyalty. The order observes that because of Hangan's virtue, his son, Takeōmaru, will succeed to his father's position as lord of the two provinces of Izumo and Hōki. The *rōnin* rejoice and then calmly perform *seppuku*.[42]

The crucial events which enabled playwrights to present details of the Akō affair were the death of Tsunayoshi and the subsequent adoption by the new regime of a settlement of the Akō affair which disassociated it from the controversial judgments of Tsunayoshi. Still and all, the plays obviously violated the ban on presenting sensational events of the time and also identified the samurai involved in the affair. What were the mitigating factors which persuaded the authorities not to interfere in the performances?

It is important to remember that *bakufu* policy was not consistent and unchanging. With the succession of a new shōgun, or even with the advent of a new chief minister, there was often a distinct change in political attitude. The reestablishment of the Asano house is a case in point, and by celebrating this event playwrights were in line with the policy of the new administration. The fact that seven years had passed since the death of Kira also placed the Akō affair, the details of which had become rather well known, at some distance. Further, the samurai identifiable behind their disguises in the play were not from houses which were still of importance, if they survived at all. Only Kira was cast in a bad light.

Perhaps of equal significance to the successful staging of the Akō plays was the playwrights' refinement of the period-piece format to disguise contemporary topics. Indeed, the public's interest in the Akō dramatizations may well have centered on the author's artfulness in devising means to satisfy the censors. The transparency of their disguises, though, suggests that the censorship was really rather light, at least as it affected the Akō story by 1710. We must assume that the plays got safely to the stage because the censors found in them no criticism of the Tokugawa government, nor any action which would impugn the dignity of samurai.

To some extent, the ascendancy of the *jidaimono* illustrates the importance ascribed to form or appearance in Tokugawa society which made it easier to overlook substance. Officials winked, for example, at the samurai practice of borrowing large woven sedge hats at the entrance to the Yoshiwara pleasure quarter to conceal their faces. Another instance of the attention to formal camouflage concerns the young kabuki actors who played female roles. Required to shave their forelocks in the style of adult males, they were nonetheless permitted to wear a small patch of purple cloth over the shaven pate to give the appearance of a forelock. Later in the period, they were even permitted to wear a wig over the shaven area.

The camouflaging of contemporary material in *jidaimono* was facilitated, of course, by the peculiar characteristics of that genre noted earlier. Its jumble of fact and fiction, its vague sense of historical chronology, its mixing of worlds, its tendency to "*chōnin*-ize" earlier cultures, made it possible to accommodate contemporary happenings without seeming anomalies. Neither realism nor a tight logic was expected in the loose structure of the rambling plays. The references to current events were diffused in a mass of historical and fictional material. In the Akō plays written after 1710, the fictional elements were expanded and elaborated in the tradition of *jidaimono*.

Between 1710 and the writing of *Chūshingura* in 1748, there were more than twenty other plays, and many books, which recounted the Akō story.[43] The most important was *Chūshin Kogane no Tanzaku* in 1732, which borrowed heavily from Chikamatsu's and Kaion's plays, even making a hybrid—Ōkishi Yuranosuke—of the fictional names of the hero used by the two authors: Ōboshi Yuranosuke and Ōkishi Kunai. The author, Namiki Sōsuke (Senryū), was one of the three writers in the team which produced *Chūshingura* sixteen years later. Most of the historical details found in the plays written after 1710, however, were already revealed in the works of Chikamatsu and Kaion. While their successors developed and embellished various episodes, most additions were fiction. The aim of later playwrights was not to reveal new facts about the affair, but to write more successful plays.

Some of the fictional elements in *Chūshingura* were already present in the 1710 plays, especially in Chikamatsu's two-part work. By using the *Taiheiki*'s Moronao to represent Kira, Chikamatsu characterized his villain as a lecher who sought an affair with Asano's wife in a most indiscreet manner. This colorful fabrication fixed in the popular mind the belief that Kira needled Asano in anger over his rejection in love. Chikamatsu's unjust depiction of Kira's retainer Yakushiji Jirōzaemon and his introduction of a spy (or apparent spy) who is killed for reading secret correspondence between the *rōnin* are further pieces of fiction.

By the time *Chūshingura* was completed, the story was replete with additional artistic falsehoods. The jōruri *Onikage Musashi Abumi* (evidently borrowing from the kabuki of the same name mentioned before) included a brothel scene which was the source of the famous Ichiriki act (Act VII) in *Chūshingura*. Although the historical Ōishi Kuranosuke did frequent such licensed quarters as Fushimi and Gion during his long wait in Yamashina for an opportune moment to avenge Asano's death, there was, in fact, no prostitute resembling *Musashi Abumi*'s Agemaki or *Chūshingura*'s Okaru.

Other fictional aspects of *Chūshingura* are numerous: the love affairs between Okaru and Kampei and between Konami and Rikiya; the provision of a map of the enemy's mansion by Kakogawa Honzō; and the unsubstantiated (though possibly accurate) allegation that Kira provoked Asano by his greed for more generous gifts (or bribes). One of the more dramatic scenes in *Chūshingura* is the arrival of Yuranosuke, moments before Lord Hangan breathes his last, to hear Hangan's whispered plea that he be avenged. Yuranosuke then receives from his lord's hand the death dagger that will be used to decapitate Moronao. Never mind that the real Kuranosuke was four hundred miles distant from his *daimyō* on the fateful day. These and similar embellishments inspire the assertion, probably a fair estimate, that two-thirds of *Chūshingura* is fiction.[44] The basic facts of the Akō story are nonetheless present, and history was not as abused as was usually the case in period pieces.

By the time *Chūshingura* was performed, there was little concern about censorship since the writers followed the conventions, now well established, of how names and identities should be camouflaged. *Chūshingura* contains no criticism of the regime, and could not be considered subversive in any way. In fact, with its glorification of loyalty and samurai honor, it supports the ethical code in an age when the samurai spirit was considered to be in decline. To take no chances, the play opens with a few lines of flattery of the government, to be interpreted, of course, as the Tokugawa shogunate.[45] (Amusingly enough, these lines were found objectionable by imperial loyalists of the Meiji period.) The authors of *Chūshingura* were nevertheless careful to avoid censure of Tsunayoshi's decisions. Asano's *seppuku* seems to occur days after the sword attack. He is at home with family and retainers. Asano's brother is never mentioned. Tsunayoshi's failure to follow the law of equal punishment for quarreling retainers is ignored.

Plays about the Tokugawa and Other Forbidden Topics

The devices developed by playwrights around 1710 which made it possible to treat the Akō story by transporting it into an earlier world were employed in the following years in plays inspired by other prohibited subjects. Some jōruri of the next decade were even more daring than the Akō plays, for they included stories about the Tokugawa shōgun themselves and historical events which were especially sensitive for the shogunal house.

In 1714 Chikamatsu wrote a remarkably irreverent play. In form, *The Sagami Lay Monk and the Thousand Dogs (Sagami Nyūdō Sembiki Inu)* was about Hōjō Takatoki (1303–1333), the bad last regent of the Kamakura regime. In fact, it wove in a clever satire on Shōgun Tsunayoshi, who had died five years earlier. Both Takatoki and Tsunayoshi were military overlords who ruled from shogunates in the east and were notorious for their capricious rule and self-indulgent lives. Chikamatsu fused these two faulted rulers, separated by more than three centuries, into a single character, achieving a high concentration of reprehensible traits. He played particularly on the obsession of both rulers with dogs: Takatoki collected fighting dogs; Tsunayoshi issued countless laws for the protection of dogs. Toward the end of the play, the hero is rescued by a large white hound called Shiraishi. This name, if given the Sino-Japanese reading, is Hakuseki, and immediately connotes Arai Hakuseki, the Confucian scholar and tutor of Tsunayoshi's successor who was largely responsible for correcting the abuses of Tsunayoshi's regime. The audience was certainly delighted to see this leading minister of government, a sober reformer and pedantic Confucian, represented on the stage as a dog —a puppet dog at that—but a heroic one. Although there is serious satire in this play along with the playfulness, Chikamatsu's main objective was to excite the audience by his daring and wit. As Chikamatsu expected, the authorities chose to ignore the disrespect toward the previous shōgun, whose legacy was still an embarrassment.[46]

The prohibition against writing about recent events theoretically denied authors some of the most dramatic material of Japanese history: the military campaigns of Oda Nobunaga in the 1570s, the brilliant victories of Toyotomi Hideyoshi in the 1580s, and his invasion of Korea in the 1590s. The Tokugawa did not wish to see the accomplishments of these predecessors glorified. To celebrate the achievements of these great men only directed attention to the devious maneuvers by which the Tokugawa had usurped their position and seized control of the country.

Chikamatsu did use such material, however, and may have been the first to dramatize the career of Hideyoshi. In *Japan's Chronicle of the Three Kingdoms (Honchō Sangokushi)* in 1719, he portrayed the assassination of Nobunaga by Akechi Mitsuhide, Hideyoshi's victory over Mitsuhide, and, as he tells it, Hideyoshi's glorious conquest of Korea. The names of the great samurai are changed slightly. Toyotomi (or Hashiba) Hideyoshi becomes Mashiba Hisayoshi. Oda Nobunaga becomes Taira no Harunaga; Katō Kiyomasa is Katō Masakiyo; Shibata Katsuie is Shimada Katsusue; and so forth. Tokugawa, who should play a prominent role in any play about Hideyoshi, is not mentioned. Mitsuhide, the treacherous assassin of his lord, Nobunaga, is called by his real personal name. Real names are also used for nonsamurai such as the tea master Sen no Rikyū, Hideyoshi's storyteller Sorori, and the musician Sawazumi Kengyō. Female characters are added, of course, to provide romantic interest. The prostitute Koiso, for example, procures for Hideyoshi a map of Korea vital to his campaign.[47]

Following Chikamatsu's effort, some twenty puppet plays were written on Nobunaga and Hideyoshi. Most authors employed the name changes that Chikamatsu devised, as did later woodblock print artists who produced series of prints illustrating the Korean campaigns. The plays about Hideyoshi were called *Taikōki mono,* after the title of his biographies.

One of these jōruri about Nobunaga, *Gion Sairei Shinchōki,* was denied permission to open in Osaka in 1757. Since a substantial investment had been made in the production, an attempt was made to perform the play in Edo instead. The Edo city commissioner, to whom application was made, gave his consent. He pointed out that permission had understandably been denied in Osaka, a city built by Hideyoshi and the site of his castle, where some sentiment concerning Hideyoshi's military successes remained. As the situation was different in Edo, the Tokugawa headquarters, and as the Tokugawa did not appear in the play, he said there would be no objection to its production in the shogunal capital. He did require, nevertheless, that the title be changed to avoid the reference to Nobunaga's name. *Shinchōki,* meaning "chronicle of Nobunaga," was changed to *shinkōki,* "chronicle of faith," and the names of some of the characters were altered. Thereupon the text was printed and performances began. Two *daimyō* descendants of the Oda and Toyotomi houses objected. Their complaint went to the city commissioners and to the shōgun's highest ministers for conference, with the result that the theater people were summoned and told gently that performances must stop.[48]

By far the most sensitive topic playwrights attempted was

Ieyasu's assault on Osaka castle in 1615, as a result of which the Tokugawa completed their subjugation of the realm. The Tokugawa had reason to be sensitive about how Ieyasu came to power. He had been Hideyoshi's vassal; he had taken oaths repeatedly, together with the other great lords, to remain loyal to Hideyoshi's heir. Yet after Hideyoshi's death and the succession of his five-year-old son, Hideyori, Ieyasu was able to divide the Toyotomi vassals by devious political maneuvers and establish his own hegemony. He isolated the Toyotomi family in Osaka and, breaking more promises, stormed the castle and destroyed the Toyotomi.

The government made it clear that it did not want this history discussed. Its harsh response to a book published in 1660, forty-four years after Ieyasu's death, demonstrated this determination. The book, *Kojō Zoroi*, contained a selection of famous letters from Japanese history and included what purported to be messages exchanged shortly before the attack on Osaka castle between Ieyasu and the Toyotomi heir, Hideyori, then twenty-one years old and married to Ieyasu's granddaughter. Ieyasu complained that Hideyori was strengthening the castle and recruiting troops. Hideyori replied: "My father said I should become ruler when I was fifteen, and he received oaths from all the samurai of Japan. . . . I have never heard of such a deceitful samurai as you, Ieyasu. You have forgotten your debt of gratitude to Hideyoshi, and you have not let me have even one province, but have isolated me and now intend to exterminate my family." These words were true, and everyone knew it, but that did not save the publisher of the book from being beheaded.[49]

In order to relate the story of the quarrel between Ieyasu and Hideyori, it was necessary for writers to develop a more elaborate disguise than they had for the Akō story. They had to find an episode in earlier Japanese history, already well known to the audience, with enough parallels to the forbidden tale, no matter how tortured, to serve as a cover from beginning to end. The first successful attempt was Ki no Kaion's jōruri, *Yoshitsune and the New Takadachi (Yoshitsune Shin Takadachi)*, in 1719.[50]

The historical episode he chose was the quarrel in the twelfth century between Yoritomo, the head of the Minamoto family who later became the first shōgun, and his younger brother, Yoshitsune, whose military exploits brought victory to the family. Yoritomo's suspicions about the ambitions of his younger brother were fanned by slanderers, and finally Yoshitsune fled Kyoto and took refuge in the Takadachi fortress in northern Japan. Yoritomo sent a large army against him and destroyed him in this stronghold. The story, in kabuki terms, occurred in the world called the Ōshū campaign *(Ōshū zeme)*, the last part of the world of the Yoshitsune cycle and one of the most familiar in the theater. In an elaborate fashion Kaion matched the people of Yoshitsune's world—his mistress, his lieutenants, his envoys—with Hideyori's associates and generals in the defense of Osaka castle. Minamoto no Yoritomo represented Tokugawa Ieyasu; Yoshitsune was Hideyori; Gonnotō Kanefusa was Katagiri Katsumoto; Izumi no Saburō was Sanada Yukimura; Kamei no Rokurō represented Kimura Shigenari; and Kataoka no Hachirō was Gotō Matabei (Motosugu). Yoshitsune's mistress, called Kyō no Kimi by Kaion, but in later versions called by her usual name of Shizuka, had no exact equivalent but replaced Hideyori's mother, Yododono. Takadachi fortress represented Osaka castle. To help the audience identify the defenders of Osaka castle with the familiar twelfth-century figures, or just to entertain those who already understood, there were numerous wordplays and allusions to the names or characteristics of the Osaka generals.

Kaion was remarkably ingenious in forging the details of the two stories. We know that after Yoshitsune reached his northern fortress, for instance, he sent three envoys to attempt a reconciliation with his older brother, just as Osaka sent three envoys to Ieyasu in 1614. This convenient parallel in history was, of course, utilized by Kaion. According to the play, Yoshitsune sent the envoys because he and his followers stood accused of three crimes. The first was that in fleeing Kyoto they disguised themselves as *yamabushi* (ascetic priests) raising funds for the rebuilding of Tōdaiji temple and, thanks to this ruse, passed illegally through the barrier at Ataka. Although there is no actual parallel to this episode in Hideyori's history, it was used to provide the setting for the second crime. At the barrier, the next offense occurred when Yoshitsune's retainer Benkei recited a fictitious subscription list *(kanjinchō)* in an attempt to convince the guard that they were genuine priests. In Kaion's play it included the following sentence: "We request the help of many people to bring virtue to our country's court."[51] This was not only a disguised appeal to rise against Yoritomo's government; it was also intended to put a hex on Yoritomo by separating in one sentence the two characters of his name. (The character *yori* means "request"; the character *tomo*, also read *chō*, means "court.") Although Yoritomo never made such an accusation against Yoshitsune, this is a clever reference to the charge Ieyasu made against Hideyori of having a bell cast for the Hōkōji temple in Kyoto with an inscription which separated the characters *ie* and *yasu*. Whatever we may think of the gravity of that offense, Ieyasu did in fact exploit it fully as a treasonous act by Hideyori—an attempt to kill Ieyasu by magic. The third charge made by Yoritomo in the play was that Yoshitsune attempted to recruit samurai from various parts of Japan for his military force, exactly what Hideyori was indeed doing at Osaka castle.

In Kaion's play, Yoritomo offered the possibility of a reconciliation if Yoshitsune would do one of three things as an act of good faith. These three proposals are similar to those actually made by Ieyasu to the Osaka camp. One of Yoritomo's proposals, that Yoshitsune leave his fortress and move to the western provinces, represented Ieyasu's request that Hideyori leave Osaka castle and become the lord of provinces in western Japan. The second proposal made by Yoritomo required Yoshitsune to come to his court at Kamakura to render homage and service as did other commanders. Ieyasu ordered Hideyori to attend him at Nijō castle like other *daimyō*. Yoritomo's third proposal was that Yoshitsune send his mistress Shizuka to Kamakura as a hostage. Ieyasu wanted Hideyori to send his mother, Yododono, to Edo.

Parallels of this kind were sustained throughout the play. In the campaign against the northern Takadachi fortress, for example, the Koromo River was diverted by the attacking forces, as was the case with the Yodo River at Osaka, causing the water in the outer moat of the castle to drop. The play also describes a temporary truce in the Takadachi siege similar to the pause between the winter and summer campaigns at Osaka castle. Kaion shows the Takadachi forces divided by dissension, as were the Osaka generals, while the attacking forces show no such disunity.

The author was careful, however, not to make reference to Ieyasu's usurpation of Hideyori's rights. Ieyasu is not represented as perfidious, or even crafty; he is a strong, disciplined general of great political and military competence, while Hideyori is played by a Yoshitsune who is indecisive, changeable, and more interested in his mistress and himself than in the welfare of his men. It stands to reason that he should lose in the end. At the price of considerable distortion of history—of both the twelfth-century story and the seventeenth-century events—this play was performed without incident in 1719.

Successive revisions of Ki no Kaion's play did not fare as well. Sixteen years later, in 1735, a new version, the jōruri *Nambantetsu*

Gotō Menuki, was not permitted to open, and the text did not appear in print. Several manuscripts of the play, however, survive. By comparing them to later revisions of the play which were performed, we can surmise why the original was found objectionable. The first problem was that it was set not in the Yoshitsune world but in the *Taiheiki* world of the fourteenth century. Portraying the Tokugawa as Ashikaga, from whom the Tokugawa were more immediately descended than they were from the Minamoto, was a difficulty. Much worse was using the Nitta, revered ancestors of the Tokugawa, to represent the Toyotomi. Acts IV and V posed the gravest problem. In Act IV a samurai's wife, hoping to win back her husband by assassinating the shōgun Ashikaga Takauji (representing Ieyasu), fires a musket at him from close range but misses. Act V has Nitta Yoshioki (representing Hideyoriz rallying his men, all resolved to die in a valiant defense of the castle. The attempt to shoot Ieyasu and the sight of Toyotomi forces bravely preparing to fight the Tokugawa were images which the authorities did not wish to see celebrated on the stage.

The writers set the play aside for nine years, until 1744, then rewrote the first three acts in the Yoshitsune world and changed the title to *Yoshitsune's New Veiled Letter (Yoshitsune Shin Fukumi Jō).* They adapted the final scenes of a different play for the last two acts, depicting a reconciliation of the brothers Yoritomo and Yoshitsune. The play opened in Edo instead of Osaka. But the last two acts did not fit satisfactorily and the attack on the castle, the climax, was omitted. The theaters tried again ten years later, in 1754, using a different title, *Yoshitsune's Letter from Koshigoe (Yoshitsune Koshigoe Jō),* and this time restored the original fourth act which portrayed the attempt to shoot Ieyasu. The theater was ordered to drop Act IV. After another sixteen years, in 1770, a theater finally succeeded in performing the fourth act. Soon after, the text of the complete play appeared in print, which means, probably, that the entire work reached the stage at last, complete to the spirited defense of the castle. The process of performing it without interference required at least five attempts over a period of more than thirty-five years.[52]

A few years before this play was staged in full, Chikamatsu Hanji (1725–1783) wrote a drama on the same theme, *Ōmi Genji Senjin Yakata* (1769). He transposed the play from the Yoshitsune world to the conflict between Hōjō Tokimasa and Minamoto no Yoriie. When the first shōgun, Yoritomo, died in 1199, the title passed to his seventeen-year-old son, Yoriie, but Hōjō Tokimasa, his maternal grandfather, ousted him and replaced him with his younger brother Sanetomo. Hōjō Tokimasa represents Ieyasu, Yoriie represents Hideyori, and Sakamoto castle represents Osaka castle. Wishing to take advantage of the notoriety of the scene in which Ieyasu is shot at, the dramatist shows Tokimasa (Ieyasu) shot and killed by a musket, only to reveal that the dead man is Tokimasa's double *(kagemusha)*, a decoy dressed like him to foil assassins. The play ends with Yoriie and his brother reconciled, and the assault on the castle averted.[53]

As this play was performed without difficulty, the playwright wrote a sequel, *(Ōmi Genji) Taihei Kabuto no Kazari*, the following year in order to resume the battle for the castle. In this piece, the real Tokimasa is shot with a musket and killed, but the Goddess Benten of Izu miraculously brings him back to life. Yoriie realizes that since the Hōjō have divine protection, they cannot be defeated. Hence he abandons the castle and sets off for Okinawa to restore his fortunes. This sequel was closed after twenty-four days. Eleven years later, in 1781, it was given the title of an old play by Kaion, *Chronicle of Three Kamakura Rulers (Kamakura Sandaiki)*, written in 1716, to which it bore no relationship. The author's name was concealed, and it was successfully performed—in Edo instead of Osaka.[54] Scenes of both of these plays are still in the kabuki and puppet repertory.

The depiction of Ieyasu as Tokimasa in these two plays was less flattering than earlier representations. While still shown as more capable than Hideyori, he wins out by sly plotting and is described in Act III as "an old badger who deceives people with his skillful tongue" *(benzetsu takumi ni hito o bakasu Hōjō no tanuki oyaji me)*.[55] The name "old badger" *(tanuki oyaji)* came to be a popular epithet for Ieyasu among Osaka people.

Conclusion

The history of the plays about Osaka castle and the Akō *rōnin* indicates that the Tokugawa regime was sensitive to certain subjects and did intervene on occasion to prevent representations on the stage which it considered undesirable. Not only were there censorship laws; they were enforced to a certain extent. Stories about samurai, if presented at all, had to be cast in an earlier century. Writers could not name the Tokugawa or other high members of the military elite who had lived in Tokugawa times; these persons could be represented only if given the identity of a figure of the remote past. Ordinary samurai of recent times, however, like important warriors of the late sixteenth century, could be given names which were doctored or scrambled.

The ban on portraying unusual events of the day was generally observed—if samurai were involved. The Akō story came to the stage just seven years after the fact, but even so represented something of an exception. No comparable example of the dramatization of a recent episode stands out in later years. There was never any discussion of government policy in the theater, and politically sensitive issues were not treated until considerable time had passed. The Yui Shōsetsu plot of 1651, for instance, received dramatic treatment only in 1729. Not until 1789 did the Battle of Sekigahara (1600) appear on stage. Plays concerning succession quarrels in the great *daimyō* houses *(oie sōdō)* of the early Tokugawa period did not appear until after the first Akō plays. In bringing forbidden topics to the theater, the passing decades and changes in *bakufu* administration were significant factors. It also made a difference where plays were staged.

Nonetheless, the plays described earlier demonstrate that the authorities were often satisfied with thin disguises and cosmetic changes, and that some topics which were specifically proscribed finally reached the theater. In view of the rather draconian language of Tokugawa laws it may seem inconsistent that the officials often displayed a patient, even permissive, attitude. The most persuasive explanation of this inconsistency may be found in the fact that the popular theaters did not pose a challenge to the regime. What happened there was, in the end, not of great concern to the government. The playwrights did not call into question Tokugawa moral values and world views. Indeed, they did not conceive of themselves as social or political critics. Their purpose was to entertain, to tell stories. They treated contemporary, forbidden topics only to titillate audiences curious to hear more about recent occurrences and fascinated by the daring and ingenuity of the theater people who dramatized them.

Also important was the increasing maturation of the Tokugawa regime, which led to a gradual relaxation of controls. The *bakufu's* use of arbitrary power and severe punishments softened from the mid-seventeenth to the mid-eighteenth centuries. Particularly the attitude of the government toward the urban populace, which posed no political challenge, became more and more lenient. Because of the great difference between the governing class and plebeian society, the authorities were more interested in how commoners behaved than in what they thought; they issued far more sumptuary regulations to the theaters than laws concerning the content of plays. The maintenance of social and status distinctions was considered essential to the political order. Thus in dealing with the theater, officials seem to have found it sufficient to follow a policy of containment. They tried to prevent the spirited townspeople from making their theater too irreverent or too outrageous, just as they were constrained from making it too immoral or too luxurious.

This discussion of a special group of topical *jidaimono* has examined the concerns of the playwright on one side and those of the watchful authorities on the other. The significance of the plays for the audience is also of interest, but we lack sufficient understanding of the urban commoners' level of education in the early eighteenth century, or of their knowledge of their world and its history, to hazard very many observations. Did the plays provide them with anything more than escapist entertainment? Although it was not the objective of playwrights to instruct, the *chōnin* of this time—especially those less well educated—did learn from the performances and the printed jōruri texts and kabuki booklets. They were exposed to an abundance of historical names and facts as well as details which were not quite straight. There were certainly many theatergoers who thought Hideyoshi's real name was Hisayoshi and Kiyomasa's name was Masakiyo. Even today some Japanese are not quite sure whether the leader of the Akō *rōnin* was Yuranosuke or Kuranosuke. What the people gained may be better described as consciousness, rather than knowledge, of the past.

The plays taught ethics more effectively than they taught history. Loyalty to one's superior and reverence to one's parents stood above all else. The heroes were models of self-discipline, uprightness, honesty, and compassion; the heroines exemplified fidelity and self-sacrifice. Evil was always punished, and good was rewarded—although that reward was often found in an honorable death. The dramatists did not consciously teach this idealized ethical code which was fostered by the regime. They did not include it just to appease the authorities. Their commoner audiences stood in awe of this idealized vision of samurai who lived by moral principle. They admired it and even aspired to it in the way that social inferiors emulate their betters. They sympathized with heroes and heroines who strove to meet the demands of absolute discipline and ultimate sacrifice. The ethical code was essential to the playwrights, for the plays derived their dramatic quality from the conflicts which arose from the characters' determination to follow the code. The crises in the play involved conflicts between duty and personal desires, or between loyalty and filial responsibilities. To sacrifice one's life was beautiful because it demonstrated purity of motive. No play illustrates this better than

Chūshingura—the title means "treasury of loyal retainers"—in which the forty-seven heroes, in their single-minded dedication to loyalty, make countless sacrifices until, in the end, without a moment's regret, they give their lives to maintain this principle.

NOTES

I should like to express my gratitude to scholars and friends who suggested materials which contributed to this study: Professors Gunji Masakatsu, Hattori Yukio, Hiramatsu Yoshirō, Moriya Takeshi, Munemasa Isoo, and Torigoe Bunzō. I am particularly indebted to Professor Uchiyama Mikiko for her two articles cited in notes 52 and 54, and to Ms. Fujita Yukari and Kawai Masumi for bibliographic assistance. My thanks also to Professor Mary Elizabeth Berry for many invaluable suggestions.

1. For the history of early kabuki, see Hattori Yukio's chapter in Geinōshi Kenkyūkai, comp., *Kabuki: Shibai no Sekai (Nihon no Koten Geinō)*, vol. 8 (Tokyo: Heibonsha, 1976), pp. 34–38; Donald H. Shively, "Bakufu Versus Kabuki," *Harvard Journal of Asiatic Studies* 18 (1955):326–356; Benito Ortolani, *Das Kabukitheater: Kulturgeschichte der Anfänge*, Monumenta Nipponica Monographs, No. 19 (Tokyo: Sophia University Press, 1964).

2. Ihara Toshirō, comp., *Kabuki Nempyō*, 8 vols. (Tokyo: Iwanami Shoten, 1956–1963), 1:69a, 75a, 93a.

3. Takayanagi Shinzō and Ishii Ryōsuke, eds., *Ofuregaki Kampō Shūsei* (Tokyo: Iwanami Shoten, 1934), Nos. 2022 and 2582.

4. Ihara, *Kabuki Nempyō*, 1:57.

5. Takayanagi and Ishii, *Ofuregaki Kampō Shūsei*, Nos. 2220 (1673), 2013 (1684), 2092 (1721).

6. Ibid., No. 2020 (1722).

7. Ibid., No. 2026.

8. Ihara, *Kabuki Nempyō*, 1:69a, 112b, 114b.

9. Takayanagi and Ishii, *Ofuregaki Kampō Shūsei*, Nos. 2220 (1673), 2013 (1684), 2014 (1684), 2015 (1698), 2675 (1713), and 2668 (1703).

10. Rather full kabuki stage texts *(daichō)* began to be written out from about 1700. The oldest known to exist is Nakada Kaemon's *Shinjū Kimon no Kado*, performed in Osaka in 1710; Suwa Haruo, *Shuppan Kotohajime: Edo no Hon* (Tokyo: Mainichi Shimbunsha, 1978), p. 135.

11. There is a record from 1842 of a kabuki text being submitted in advance by a theater to an Edo city commissioner, but we do not know whether this had long been the practice, or whether it was a special measure during the Tempō Reforms. Professor Moriya Takeshi referred me to this notation in Geinōshi Kenkyūkai, comp., *Nihon Shomin Bunka Shiryō Shūsei* (Tokyo: San'ichi Shobō, 1977), 12:639.

12. The earliest printed text extant is *Takadachi* of 1625. Charles J. Dunn, *The Early Japanese Puppet Drama* (London: Luzac, 1966), pp. 42, 70–72.

13. Suwa, *Shuppan Kotohajime*, pp. 90, 105.

14. The English term was suggested by Donald Keene in *World Within Walls:*

Japanese Literature of the Pre-Modern Era, 1600-1867 (New York: Holt, Rinehart and Winston, 1976), p. 239.

15. Since Yoshitsune was a leading general in the struggle between the Taira and Minamoto, he also belongs to other worlds of the late twelfth century such as *Heike Monogatari* and *Gempei Gun.* See Hattori Yukio, ed., *Sekai Kōmoku: Shibai Nenjū Gyōji (Kabuki no Bunken 6)* Tokyo: Kokuritsu Gekijo, 1974), pp. 30–40.

16. Shuzui Kenji and Ōkubo Tadakuni, eds., *Chikamatsu Jōrurishū,* II (*Nihon Koten Bungaku Taikei,* vol. 50) (Tokyo: Iwanami Shoten, 1958–1959), pp. 294–297.

17. Ibid., pp. 324–337.

18. From Asano's death on the fourteenth day of the third month of 1701 until the raid on the night of the fourteenth day of the twelfth month of 1702 (30 January 1703 in the Gregorian calendar) was actually twenty-two months because 1702 had an intercalary eighth month.

19. Takayanagi and Ishii, *Ofuregaki Kampō Shūsei,* No. 2668.

20. For an excellent discussion of these problems, see Yūda Yoshio's "*Kanadehon Chūshingura* Seiritsushi," first published in *Kokubungaku Kaishaku to Kanshō* (December 1967), and reprinted in his *Jōrurishi Ronkō* (Tokyo: Chūō Kōronsha, 1975), pp. 359–370. See also Hattori Yukio's analysis, in Kawatake Toshio, ed., *(Dentō no Bi: Kanadehon) Chūshingura* (Tokyo: Kabushiki Kaisha Rippū Shobō, 1978), pp. 56–61; and Matsushima Eiichi, *Chūshingura* (Iwanami Shinsho 541) (Tokyo: Iwanami Shoten, 1964), pp. 128–142.

21. See Yūda, "*Kanadehon Chūshingura* Seiritsushi," p. 362; Hattori, in Kawatake, *Chūshingura,* p. 57; Matsushima, *Chūshingura,* p. 132; and the text in Takano Tatsuyuki, ed., *Chikamatsu Kabuki Kyōgenshū,* (Tokyo: Rikugōkan, 1927), 2:226.

22. Yūda, "*Kanadehon Chūshingura* Seiritsushi," pp. 361–362.

23. Ibid., pp. 361–367; Hattori, in Kawatake, *Chūshingura,* pp. 57–61; and Kikuchi Akira's chronology in the latter book, pp. 134–141.

24. *Goban Taiheiki* has until recently been dated the first day of the third month, 1706. The date derived from the Meiwa edition (1768) of the *Gedai Nenkan.* Many of the dates for early plays given in this edition which do not appear in the earlier Hōreki edition (1757) have been shown to be incorrect. Yūda (pp. 364–367) has argued persuasively that the play dates from the latter part of 1710, and his opinion is now followed by Japanese specialists. See *Gidayū Nempyō: Kinsei Hen* (Tokyo: Yagi Shoten, 1979), 1:42a.

25. Gotō Tanji and Kamada Kisaburō, eds., *Taiheiki,* II (*Nihon Koten Bungaku Taikei,* vol. 35) pp. 349–364. To avoid confusion in the later discussion, I have used Chikamatsu's latter-day readings of the names rather than the *Taiheiki's*: Hangan for Hōgwan, and Yawata for Hachiman.

26. The play thus ends inconclusively after two acts, instead of the usual three or five acts. For the text, see Fujii Otoo, *Chikamatsu Zenshū,* 12 vols. (Osaka: Asahi Shimbunsha, 1925–1928), 7:703–754; also Kitani Hōgin (Masanosuke), *Dai Chikamatsu Zenshū,* 16 vols. (1922–1925), 7:201–234.

27. The subtitle mentions Moronao, the poem alluded to by the lady, and "the great victory of the forty-seven stone pieces [on the *go* board]"; Fujii, *Chikamatsu Zenshū,* 7:759.

28. Ibid., 7:755–798, especially p. 759.

29. See Kitani's discussion in *Dai Chikamatsu Zenshū*, 7:287–294.

30. Quoted by Hattori in Kawatake, *Chūshingura*, p. 57.

31. Yūda, "*Kanadehon Chūshingura* Seiritsushi," pp. 364–367.

32. For a discussion of various versions of the Oguri Hangan story, see Wakatsuki Yasuji, *Ko-jōruri no Shinkenkyū: Keichō-Kambun Hen* (Tokyo: Shingetsusha, 1938), 1:1080–1094, and Kitani's notes to Chikamatsu's play on the theme, *Tōryū Oguri Hangan* (1698), in *Dai Chikamatsu Zenshū*, 4:337–355.

33. For the text, see *Ki no Kaion Zenshū* (Osaka: Seibundō, 1977–), 1:106–152.

34. The date in the Meiwa edition of *Gedai Nenkan*, first day of the twelfth month, 1713, is rejected by Yūda, pp. 364–367; *Ki no Kaion Zenshū*, 1:109; *Gidayū Nempyō*, 1:109.

35. Yūda, "*Kanadehon Chūshingura* Seiritsushi," p. 366.

36. Matsushima, *Chūshingura*, p. 136; Hattori, in Kawatake, *Chūshingura*, p. 57.

37. Matsushima, *Chūshingura*, pp. 14–17.

38. Ibid., pp. 10–14, 17–24.

39. Ibid., pp. 59, 68–72, 90, 95; Sakae Shioya, *Chūshingura: An Exposition*, 2nd rev. ed. (Tokyo: Hokuseidō Press, 1956), p. 255.

40. Matsushima, *Chūshingura*, p. 125.

41. Yūda, "*Kanadehon Chūshingura* Seiritsushi," p. 364.

42. Ibid.; Fujii, *Chikamatsu Zenshū*, 7:796–797.

43. See Kikuchi's chronology in Kawatake, *Chūshingura*, pp. 135–136.

44. Shioya, *Chūshingura: An Exposition*, p. 225.

45. "His virtuous rule extends in all four directions, and the people, like grass before the wind, bend in obedience. His authority spreads its triumphant wings over the land, . . ." Donald Keene, trans., *Chūshingura: The Treasury of Loyal Retainers* (New York: Columbia University Press, 1971), p. 29; Otoba Hiromu, ed., *Jōrurishū*, I (*Nihon Koten Bungaku Taikei*, vol. 51), p. 293.

46. For a detailed discussion of this play, *Sagami Nyūdō Sembiki Inu*, see Donald H. Shively, "Chikamatsu's Satire on the Dog Shogun," *Harvard Journal of Asiatic Studies* 18 (1955), pp. 159–180.

47. Fujii, *Chikamatsu Zenshū*, 11:675–756. See also Kitani's discussion in *Dai Chikamatsu Zenshū*, 15:169–175.

48. Ihara, *Kabuki Nempyō*, 3:306–307, quotes the story from *Yamato Kaidan Keijitsu Zensho* (1758, in manuscript). The story seems to be incorrect in indicating that the play was not performed in Osaka; it opened at the Toyotake-za in Osaka on the fifth day of the twelfth month, 1757, under the revised title and ran for over a year (*Gidayū Nempyō*, 1:279–281). A kabuki version with the original title was performed the next month in Kyoto, and a kabuki with the revised title opened later in 1758 in Edo, and in 1759 in Osaka (Ihara, *Kabuki Nempyō*, 3:335, 341, 383–384).

49. Miyatake Gaikotsu, *Hikkashi* (Osaka: Gazoku Bunko, 1911), pp. 5–6.

50. *Ki no Kaion Zenshū*, 4:285–338. The title refers to the old jōruri, *Takadachi*, of 1625.

51. Ibid., p. 290.

52. For a fuller account of the various *Nambantetsu Gotō Menuki* manuscripts and later revisions of the play and their fate, see Uchiyama Mikiko, "*Nambantetsu Gotō Menuki* Kō," Engeki Kenkyū, no. 2 (April 1967), pp. 1–57.

53. *Jōruri Meisakushū,* II (*Nihon Meicho Zenshū,* vol. 7) (Tokyo: Nihon Meicho Zenshū Kankōkai, 1929), pp. 514–570.

54. Uchiyama Mikiko, " '*Taihei Kabuto no Kazari*' no Shohon," *Engeki Gaku,* no. 6 (1966), pp. 47–59; Yokoyama Tadashi, " '*Kamakura Sandaiki*' no Seiritsu ni tsuite," *Kinsei Engeki Ronsō* (Osaka: Seibundō, 1976), pp. 280–297; Tsurumi Makoto, ed., *Jōrurishū,* II (*Nihon Koten Bungaku Taikei,* vol. 52), pp. 16–26 (notes); pp. 183–281.

55. Tsurumi, *Jōrurishū,* p. 210.

A Musical Approach to the Study of Japanese Jōruri

WILLIAM P. MALM

FOR MOST ORIENTALISTS, the term jōruri refers to a series of Japanese narrative texts beginning with the sixteenth-century *Tales of the Princess Lapis Lazulae (Jōrurihime Monogatari Jūnidan Zōshi)* and reaching their zenith in late seventeenth- and eighteenth-century dramas for the puppet theater (bunraku) and kabuki. To view jōruri exclusively from a literary standpoint, however, is scholastically and artistically inaccurate, for all these texts were written to be declaimed and sung. The jōruri audiences, like Western opera fans, came (and continue to come) to a performance as much to hear a special singer as to hear a story written by a specific author. The names of all the early forms of puppet-theater jōruri (Bunya, Harima, Doguya, and so on) were, in fact, those of leading singers. These men were free to alter the text as they saw fit. Historical sources seldom mention the names of the original authors whose works these singers were interpreting.[1] With the appearance of Chikamatsu Monzaemon (1653–1725), the author became equal in importance to the performer, but even Chikamatsu's plays can be classified as *gidayū bushi,* after the name of the famous singer, Takemoto Gidayū (1651–1714), for whom he wrote many of them.[2]

Since the time of Chikamatsu and Takemoto, the terms *gidayū bushi, gidayū,* and jōruri have become synonymous, though other genres of samisen narrative music continued to develop both in and out of the puppet theater. Today these also tend to be classified under the general title of jōruri or narratives *(katarimono).*[3] Nevertheless, *gidayū* has remained the standard against which most past and present samisen-accompanied narratives tend to be discussed. In this context it seems evident that a true artistic appreciation and historical understanding of jōruri must at some time take into consideration the characteristics of *gidayū* musical performance.

In the living theater one finds fans who already "understand" *gidayū* music, though they seldom are scholastically inclined. For example, when a man in a modern puppet theater performance shouts, "We've waited for this" *(matte imashita),* he places his call at just the right moment because he knows the text and also because he knows that this is a musical highpoint in the setting of the text. He also is shouting an encouragement to the singer and the puppeteer rather than an appreciation to the author. He has grasped the excitement and the art of contemporary jōruri by experiencing it as a musical-theatrical-literary entity. By the same token, the old lady sitting next to him with her feet tucked under her in defiance of her Western-style theater chair cries not only because the words are sad but also because they are sung with such beautiful pathos.

Clues concerning the musical styles of jōruri in the late seventeenth century are found in instruction books by professional musicians such as the *Takenokoshū* (1678) by Uji Kaganojō (1635–1711) and the *Danmonoshū* by Takemoto Gidayū himself. Both of these important sources have been translated in part by Andrew Gerstle,[4] thus providing English readers with much significant information about the theory and practice of the period. However, it is difficult to assess the degree to which twentieth-century performers maintain the style and spirit of the earlier tradition. Nevertheless, contemporary sources are legion in the forms of books, notations, theater and concert performances, radio or television broadcasts, and recordings of *gidayū* "stars."

Since music is fundamentally a sonic event, this study will concentrate on such contemporary sources in addition to personal experiences in private lessons.[5] The last section presents examples of *gidayū* musical styles transcribed into the Western notation system. The purpose of the study is to enhance our understanding of the musical nature of jōruri as performed today. Perhaps, at a later time, such preliminary attempts will make it possible for us to trace our way back to the actual sonic style of earlier jōruri. This essay makes no pretense of such interpretations, nor can it cover all the musical aspects of modern practice. It may provide information that will assist musical and literary readers in the placing of jōruri studies and performances in their proper musical framework. It may even help us hear the tradition with the same intensity and appreciation of the *gidayū* connoisseurs who can still shout or weep in the theaters today.

Performance Practice

Gidayū can be heard under four circumstances today: (1) as accompaniment to the puppet theater; (2) in the kabuki theater; (3) in dance performances; and (4) in concerts. The basic musical unit in all cases is one singer, the *tayū*,[6] and one player of the three-stringed, plucked samisen or shamisen.[7] In the puppet theater these men appear on a dais set just beyond the stage-left proscenium as shown in figure 1. This dais is set on a revolving disk so that new performers can be spun on stage at the same time that the old ones are removed. At this point in a traditional performance, a masked announcer on stage calls out the names of the performers before the music begins. This procedure is not always followed in modern productions. In kabuki or in a dance performance the musicians are placed either on a dais or in an alcove (the *yuka*) above the entrance of the stage-left flat. In the latter case, a bamboo curtain hides the performers from view. Concert performances of *gidayū* use the normal Western stage arrangement with the performers placed in center stage facing the audience. In all cases, the samisen player is to the left of the singer.

The singer has before him a sturdy, elaborately decorated stand *(mirudai* or *kendai)*, upon which is placed a copy of the text *(maru-*

Figure 1

hon or *shōhon).*[8] The singer sits on a very low stool *(chōshidai),* apparently to aid his breathing posture as well as relieve the pressure on his legs. A covered tea cup is placed by his stand. Frequently it is placed there by one of the singer's disciples who will then sit in the corner of the stage below the dais and attend to the contents of the cup as well as listen to the master's performance.

The samisen player has only a few accessories about him. He never uses notation on stage.[9] Sometimes a small pad is placed under his right knee to raise the instrument slightly. A bag of talcum powder is frequently seen at his side. The powder is used to dust the back of the neck of the instrument as well as the player's hand in order to make it easier for him to slide his hand up and down. Professional players sometimes wear between the left hand thumb and index finger the knitted *yubikake* (finger coverings), borrowed from players of other genres. Talcum powder is also used on the right hand, which can become quite slippery with sweat while holding the thick and heavy ivory plectrum *(bachi)* of the *gidayū* samisen. Some modern players place adhesive tape along the gripping edge for safety.

The *gidayū* samisen itself is known as a *futozao* or "thick-necked" samisen. It is the largest of the traditional samisen and therefore uses the thickest skins and strings and the heaviest body. The bridges are specially weighted with lead, and professional players own a set of these bridges in different weights which they change for the sake of resonance according to the pitch at which the instrument is tuned. The tuning of the samisen is not set. It varies according to the singer's range and to certain formal considerations with which we shall deal later. The basic tuning is called *hon chōshi* and consists of a fourth and a fifth starting from the lowest string. The other two common tunings are *ni-agari,* a fifth and a fourth, and *san-sagari,* two fourths. Finally, we should note the strong buzzing or *sawari* which is so characteristic of the sound of the lowest string. The term *sawari* will be used in a totally different context later in this paper, but *sawari* as a samisen sound gives *gidayū* music one of its most notable flavors.[10]

In a performance there are seldom more than one singer and one samisen player on stage at one time, though we have already indicated that there is usually a change in personnel within each performance. If a dance comes at the end of a long narrative piece, an extra samisen player will often join the basic two performers. His function is to reinforce the sound or add an obligato part. Typical examples of such performances are found at the end of the "Hori River Scene"

("Horikawa no Dan") from *A Recent Rivalry in the River Bed (Chikagoro Kawara no Tatehiki)* and the "Nozaki Village Scene" ("Nozakimura no Dan") from *A Buddhist Hymnal Newly Published (Shinpan Utazaemon)*.

Pieces used as dance numbers often have five or six singers and an equal number of samisen. The final number in a bunraku program is often staged this way. Many traveling scenes *(michiyuki)* such as "The Journey at the First Song of New Year" ("Hatsune no Tabi") from *Yoshitsune and the Thousand Cherry Trees (Yoshitsune Sembon Zakura)* use these large ensembles. The music in such cases is not essentially different from that performed by the basic two men and could be performed by them alone. The difference is primarily theatrical rather than musical.

Men are the sole performers in the puppet and kabuki theaters as well as for most dance programs. There is, however, a strong tradition of female performers in both the music and manipulation of the puppet theater on Awaji Island.[11] In addition, concert forms of female samisen narrative music *(onna jōruri)* became very popular in the late nineteenth century and can still be heard today.[12] The female *tayū* imitate the massive tones of their male mentors with frightening accuracy.[13]

Musical Components of Jōruri Style

The most obvious divisions of any musical-narrative style are the spoken and the sung sections. I have chosen the terms declamatory and lyrical as the best descriptions of their use in jōruri. There is in jōruri yet another important division. It is a half-sung, half-spoken middle ground which will be categorized in this study by the Western term parlando. Finally, there are in *gidayū* purely instrumental sections. Thus, from an analytical point of view one can say that there are four basic components in jōruri style: the instrumental, the declamatory, the lyrical, and the parlando.

If we turn to the traditional view of *gidayū,* equivalent terms in Japanese are not always found. Let us start with the clearer cases. The longer instrumental interludes are called *ai* or *ai no te.* As we shall see later, particular interludes acquire specific titles according to their function or their historical origins. The purely declamatory sections themselves (without accompaniment) are called *kotoba.* Occasionally the kabuki term *serifu* (dialogue) is used to describe such sections, though this term is more commonly used to designate the actual speech of actors.

When we move to the lyrical and parlando components of *gidayū* the native nomenclature becomes less useful in a generic sense. The most common term for lyrical sections is *jiai* or *ji*. The term *fushi* sometimes appears in this general context though it seems more properly applied to specific tunes. The parlando sections vary greatly in name. The most common term for them in writings about *gidayū* is *ji iro* or *iro*. Musically, it seems more proper to reserve the term *iro* for parlando sections which connect lyrical to declamatory sections in contrast with parlandos called *kakari* which make the transition in the opposite direction, that is, from spoken to sung sections. The term *ji iro* would then be left to cover all parlando sections which are more or less complete in themselves or are interjections within a declamatory section.

The basic words *kotoba* and *ji* did not originate in jōruri. Their meanings as they were used in earlier forms vary greatly. For example, in the ancient *kōwakamai* dramas as they survive today, the term *kotoba* means man's dialogue or recollections while *ji* is man's conduct and sentiments.[14] Of the many uses of the term *ji* throughout Japanese music, Utsumi Shigetarō claims that the most important to jōruri history is that of earlier narrative forms such as *heikyoku*, the reciting of *The Tale of the Heike (Heike Monogatari)*. In these forms it meant a manner of intoning the recitations. It entered early jōruri *(kojōruri)* with this meaning. For Utsumi, the term *fushi* came into use when "a special type of voice was used or when it was held together by a special samisen rhythm."[15] This idea would seem to reinforce our earlier definition of *fushi* as a lyrical section relying on a specific stereotyped melody.

Figure 2 schematizes some of the relations *between* the jōruri components listed above. The term *ai* has not been included because instrumental sections may appear between or within any of the other components. The vagueness of the middle ground between speech and song and the circular nature of the connectives in figure 2 are a deliberate attempt to visualize the fluid changes in style and the smooth transitions which contribute so much to the art of *gidayū*. Thus, as we look at each component individually, it must be remembered that they will not always cooperate with our scholarly penchant for categories but will hop about from label to label in a most discouraging albeit musical manner.

Instrumental Sections

The term *ai* is found in all the instrumental-vocal forms of the Edo period. In *gidayū* the word is seen in *maruhon* texts whenever

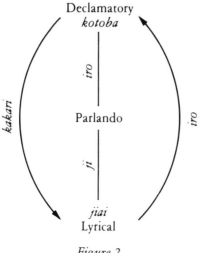

Figure 2

there is a short instrumental passage such as measure 19 of example 1. Technically, the term *ai no te* refers to more extensive interludes. In *gidayū*, however, most instrumental interludes of any length have special names, so the words *ai no te* seldom appear in *gidayū* texts. Most of these named interludes are used in rather specific ways. For example, the pattern called *ōnori* (example 12) is used before rhythmical parlando sections usually of a masculine nature, while the pattern *iri* (measures 24–25 of example 2) often precedes a high vocal cadenza known as a calling out *(oyobidasu)*.[16] The *iri* pattern varies according to the number of syllables in the word that follows. Similar adjustments are made in many melodic patterns, for the raison d'être of *gidayū* music is its support of and reaction to the text.

The instrumental preludes *okuri, sanjū,* and *sonae* used at the start of each section of a play will be discussed later in this chapter. We need note here only that they are among the more extensive instrumental solos in *gidayū*. Even in dance numbers, the more virtuosic instrumental solos tend to be broken up by vocal entrances. When the samisen does play alone there is usually a good dramatic reason for it; for example, when Akoya plays on the *koto*, samisen, and *kokyū* (bowed lute) in the scene "Akoya Forced to Play the Koto" ("Akoya Kotozeme no Dan") from the play *War Tale of the Battle Helmet at Dannoura (Dannoura Kabuto Gunki)*. The longer, more abstract *ai no te* of the *nagauta* and *jiuta* traditions have little place in this narrative art.

The most interesting instrumental pieces are those called *meri-*

yasu.[17] For the most part these tunes are used as background for extended speeches or dialogues. However, the term *meriyasu* can also be applied to some descriptive tunes such as the *nami no meriyasu* for the sound of the waves. Some of the accompaniments for energetic dances or fights *(tachimawari)* are also called *meriyasu.* All three types of *meriyasu* tend to have particular mood or situational connotations. These extramusical implications are an important part of the meaning of *meriyasu,* for the term can be applied to such melodies even when they occasionally occur not with declamation but with a lyrical or parlando vocal part set over them. The greatest part of the time, however, *meriyasu* provide settings for declamatory speech.

Declamation

Purely narrative sections *(kotoba)* might seem to lie outside the topic of this paper. However, anyone who has ever heard the melo-dramatic declamations of the *gidayū* narrators must be aware that their art involves such musical-theatrical problems as breathing, timing, intonation, and pacing. The *Compilation of Gidayū (Gidayū Taikan)* implies as much:

> *Kotoba* differs from *jiai* in that it is not recited to samisen accompaniment. Because of this, *kotoba* must have their own kind of pitch *(chō-shi)* in order that the good and bad points of the words do not become too obvious to the audience. They must also have a sense of tonal variation as well as pauses *(yokuyō tonza).*[18] Moreover, *kotoba* require even greater ingenuity since there is no samisen present to provide the rhythm. Many amateurs who can perform *jiai* fall down when it comes to *kotoba* because they haven't taken the trouble to learn about *chōshi,* *yokuyō,* and breath control *(kassatsu no kyū).*[19]

The concepts found in the quotation above are reinforced by my experience in private lessons. *Gidayū* teachers are as concerned with the correct contour and timing of spoken lines as they are with the proper rendition of more lyrical passages. The opening *kotoba* section of example 1 illustrates both principles. The contour, crudely represented in the transcriptions by pitchless notes on a five-line staff, must rise and fall in the same manner at each lesson, though other teachers will uphold a different standard in keeping with their interpretation. The proper execution of the ritard in measure 4 and the pauses at measures 4 and 5 in particular involve an important *gidayū* principle known as *ma* or pause. This term implies not only a pause but also a manner of breathing. The *Gidayū Taikan* puts it this way:

Whether in *kotoba* or in *jiai*, when it comes to reciting *jōruri*, *ma* is of the utmost importance. This is breathing while reciting *jōruri;* it is catching the breath. The life or death of *jōruri* depends entirely on *ma.* It may be taken in the meaning of taking a breath and making a pause in the *jiai* or *kotoba* and then reciting on. It may appear that way to the audience but if it is looked at from the standpoint of the narrator, it is a breath taken at the instant when the meaning of the preceding phrase has not yet finished and that of the following phrase is about to begin.[20]

The problems of *ma* and its ancillary concepts of rhythm *(hyōshi)* and speed *(nori)* are even more evident in the musical sections. However, it is important to note from the first example that, in such an integrated art as *gidayū,* the problems of performing musical and nonmusical sections are often quite similar.

It has been my experience that the greatest amount of time in lessons is spent in learning declamatory rather than lyrical sections. This may simply reflect on my inadequacies as an actor. However, it is also in keeping with the attitudes of Japanese writers on the relative importance of speaking and singing to the art of jōruri. The *Gidayū Taikan* contains the following opinion:

> *Kotoba* is seventy percent of the importance [of jōruri]. While the main object of *jiai* is to depict surrounding scenery and the actions of characters, the forte of *kotoba* is that it makes a direct communication between the audience and the characters as though the audience were hearing confessions of agony, pain, sorrow, or regret from people standing before them. . . . Although in reciting *jiai* one can't arouse complete sympathy and identification with characters, in *kotoba* one can.[21]

Though I would argue with the last sentence, I readily admit the power of the purely narrative art. Some of its grandeur is caught in the following passage from the book *Bunraku:*

> The *kotoba* section is the place where the special qualities of *gidayū* are displayed. The *kotoba* attempts not only to express completely the position, class, occupation, age, sex, character, virtue or vice, and degree of intelligence and ability of the character on stage, but also to show the person's emotion of joy, anger, wrath, or happiness.[22]

Since one *tayū* portrays all the characters, he must rely heavily on stereotyped vocal mannerisms to help him differentiate the parts in the detail mentioned above. Of course, the text, like the dialogue of any good play, reveals the character of the speakers as well.

However, *gidayū* texts do not always make it clear who is speaking, and often the *tayū*'s voice placement is the best guide to the division of parts in a given dialogue. Like the heads of the puppets, the voices of the various character types are carefully regulated. When a *tayū* has mastered all these types he has become an accomplished actor, but he is not yet a complete *gidayū* artist, for he must be able to balance this narrative prowess with an ability to sing as well as a skill at connecting the declamatory and lyrical styles into a smooth single dramatic unit.

Lyrical

As intimated earlier, the terms *ji*, *jiai*, and *fushi* are often used interchangeably without any attempt to define them or with definitions which are confusing or contradictory. The following quotation from the *Gidayū Taikan* is a good case in point. "*Ji*—to recite a *fushi* in accompaniment to a samisen from one pause to the next with good *ma* is called *jiai*. . . . *Jiai* is a passage in which *kotoba* is recited with expression to the accompaniment of the samisen. It is almost like *ji* and so is often confused with it."[23]

What can such a jumble of terms mean? My tentative opinion is that the writer of this passage is using the terms *ji*, *jiai*, and *fushi* in the following manner. *Fushi* here means the more specific melodic patterns such as will be discussed in other sections of this chapter. Part of the confusion is that *fushi* is both a general word for tune as well as a specific but poorly defined technical term in *gidayū*. As for the use of the term *jiai* in the first sentence, it should be noted that the term *jiai* does not appear in actual *maruhon* texts and therefore seems the closest to a true generic term such as our Western choice, lyrical. Its use here may have that generic sense. On the basis of the second sentence of the quotation it would seem that *ji* sections make greater use of the more specific *fushi* patterns, while *jiai* sections set the text, the meaning of *kotoba* in this sentence, with less dependence on such patterns, particularly those derived from other genres or indicative of a particular *tayū*'s style.

Some of the most developed and lovely *jiai* are found in *sawari* sections, particularly the class of *sawari* known as *kudoki*. A *sawari* is the musical highlight of a scene, in which the central emotional situation is given its fullest musical treatment. This may occur in a rather bright and quick section such as the end of the "Nozaki Village Scene" mentioned earlier. More often, however, *sawari* are sad laments. Such *sawari* are more commonly called *kudoki*. This term is found in nō drama and in other samisen genre with a similar implication. *Kudoki* in *gidayū* are rather like soliloquies, for their texts consist of the words and thoughts of one character. *Kudoki,* along with other kinds of *sawari,* are complete in themselves and can be performed separately in concerts. One of the few detailed notations of *gidayū* is in a collection of such *sawari* from many plays.[24] Students usually begin by learning a *sawari,* and new *sawari* recordings by famous artists appear each year in Japan with the inevitability of new releases of Beethoven's Fifth in the West.

The musical reader may wonder why the Western term aria has not been applied to *sawari.* It is true that *sawari* serve the same general functions in *gidayū* that arias serve in opera, just as many *gidayū* parlandos function like opera recitatives. However, such analogies have not been used because, once one leaves the functional level, the stylistic implications of the Western terms are quite at variance with the *gidayū* idiom. Space and the present topic do not allow a full explanation of these differences nor a discussion of the very interesting formal structures of *sawari.* Within the context of the components of *gidayū,* however, it should be noted that any given *sawari,* while emphasizing the lyrical, contains sections in the other three styles (narrative, parlando, and instrumental) at some point in its structure. A case in point is example 1 which is the start of a *kudoki*-style *sawari.* Its constant shift of styles and tempos is one indication of why the term aria does not readily apply to this music.

A typical lyrical section can be seen in example 1 beginning in measure 24. In addition to the steady flow of melody in rhythm (measures 24–32) there is a cadenza (measure 33) and a short instrumental interlude before the next vocal entrance (measure 35). A comparison of this long section with measures 5–9 gives a clear idea of the difference between lyrical and parlando styles. By contrast, measures 10–18 are more difficult to classify. This passage lies somewhere closer to the parlando than to the lyrical on the hypothetical line in figure 1. Part of its parlando quality arises from its restricted melodic development, while its sense of rhythm pulls it towards the lyrical. The presence or lack of rhythm does not in itself imply either style, but the problem of rhythm warrants special attention if we are to understand the subtleties of the components of *gidayū* style.

We have already discussed the problem of *ma.* Two concepts remain to be explained, *nori* and *hyōshi.* The term *nori* (speed) is derived from concepts of tempo which go back to Buddhist chanting but are best known in the theory of rhythm in the nō drama.[25] Its use in *gidayū* is generally simpler than that in nō since it is primarily an indication of a steady beat, as found, for example, in measures 19–21 of example 2. The term *nori* is frequently applied to lyrical sections with moderate-to-fast tempos. In *sawari, nori* sections appear with greater frequency as the piece progresses. *Nori* can be found in declamatory and parlando sections as well.

The term *hyōshi* (rhythm) as used in *gidayū* is concerned primarily with the more characteristic sections of flexible, changing tempo. The *Gidayū Recitation: A New Book (Gidayū Dokusho Shin-sho)* gives the following example of a problem in *hyōshi.*

> To the side of the texts notated in this book there are places where there is one samisen note for one character of the text. There are also places where there are three samisen notes beside one character and places where one samisen note hangs between two characters of the text. These all depend on *hyōshi* to form any kind of connection.[26]

Hyōshi and the concept of *ma* are more intense versions of the kind of coordination required of a Western vocal-piano team performing in the French impressionist tradition. These concepts involve the give and take of any good artistic team as they listen to and react to each other and to the necessities of the music. Teamwork is certainly necessary to perform such passages as measures 5–9 of example 1. Because of the constant shifting of tempos and styles, such coordination remains equally critical in *nori* sections as well. Example 2 is an excellent illustration of the rhythmic variety of *gidayū,* for it goes from the very free style of measures 9–16 to the fast *nori* of measures 19–20 and 26–30. To render all these changes in notation is extremely difficult. To perform them correctly is not easy either.

We have discussed the *gidayū* lyrical style in terms of its nomenclature, the places where it is best found, and its rhythmic implications. These are only the first steps towards a true understanding of *gidayū* lyricism, but they should be sufficient to show the relation of lyricism to the other aspects of *gidayū* style as they appear in this study.

Parlando

We have found that the term *ji iro* is the closest Japanese equivalent for parlando style. The word parlando itself literally means "in the style of speaking." As it is used in Western music, it implies that the rhythm and accent of speech have a greater than usual influence on the musical line. The melodic contour of such sections, therefore, is less lyrical and the rhythm is often, though not always, rather free. This flexible rhythm has given rise in the West to the term parlando-rubato. The parlando-rubato style is common to many narrative traditions. It is found, for example, all over eastern Europe and has its place within the Anglo-American balladic tradition as well. It is also an extremely important part of *gidayū* style.

Since *gidayū* is characterized by a strong tendency towards changes in rhythm, it is not always easy to separate the lyrical from the parlando. Measures 5–8 of example 1 are clearly in the parlando style. The *maruhon* text for this section, however, is not marked *ji iro*, for this term, like the word *jiai*, is seldom seen in *gidayū* songbooks. Both words are used as general descriptive terms rather than as practical reminders for the performers. The particular passage in question is marked in the text as a *kakari*,[27] since it links a declamatory and a lyrical section. By contrast, the pattern seen in example 3 is called an *iro* or *iro todome*. The word *iro,* as indicated earlier, is often used as a synonym for *ji iro.* In addition, *iro,* as it appears in practical music guides, has two more specific meanings beyond the general one. All three are implied in the following:

> *Iro* is a mode of expression halfway between *jiai* and *kotoba.* It may be said to be kotoba which has been put to a simple melody [heightened speech] and sometimes it is used in the middle of *jiai* to break up the monotony of the *jiai.* Sometimes it is considered to be *kotoba* having *iro* or *kotoba no iro.* Most often, however, *iro* is used as *iro todome* to make a shift from *jiai* to *kotoba* inconspicuously.[28]

The first sentence above implies a general parlando style. The second refers to the interjection of one or two spoken words in the midst of a lyrical section. The fourth sentence refers to the kind of transitional passage shown in example 3. It is the most frequently used type of *iro.* Note in the example how it lapses into words before the music has stopped. The samisen part is characterized by a concentration on the note of the top open string (b in our transcriptions), usually in the pattern shown in example 3. This form of *iro* is a standard way of setting short connective texts between speeches such as "Then he turned to her with heavy heart and said . . ." or "As he spoke he thought of their long separation."

Example 4 shows a typical accompaniment for a long parlando section starting at measure 5. Note how the sparse samisen accompaniment concentrates on the open strings (B, E, and b) plus the notes *harikiri*[29] (e), *gin* (f sharp), and occasionally *ya* (a), or *kan* (b'). The placement of such notes against a vocal line has yet to be studied in detail. Preliminary analysis implies that there may be an influence of the eight-beat framework *(yatsubyōshi)* of nō[30] on the settings of *gidayū* parlando sections. In this context the samisen part is analogous to the sounds of the drums in nō which are known to mark off poetic units within the text.[31]

There is one more set of terms to be dealt with before we leave the discussion of basic components: *haru, u,* and *chū* and with their many semilegitimate offspring such as *ji u, ji haru, haru bushi, fushi haru,* and so on. *Haru* originally seemed to have meant a kind of music expressiveness and had the meaning "to cover,"[32] that is, the voice should cover the silent moments of the samisen part. Since we have already implied that emotion-laden words tend to exploit higher pitches, it is not surprising to find that the term *haru* became associated with the concept of a higher range emphasizing the notes between the open top string and its octave. The open top string itself has sometimes been called *haru*. The term *u* was used for the next range and the next string down, while the term *chū* implied the lowest string.[33] Passages marked with these terms in *maruhon* are generally though not consistently interpreted in this manner in modern performances. For example, compare the term *chū* at the top of the fifth line from the right in figure 3 and the term *haru* slightly below it with their interpretations in example 2 on the words *"uchi"* in measure 17 and *"okamu"* in measure 20. The symbol for *u* is found in the second, third, fourth, and sixth lines (from the right) of figure 3. Its rendition varies as can be seen in example 2 on the words *"nui"* in measure 4, *"kubi"* in measure 8, *"me"* in measure 16, and *"tama"* in measure 22. The term *chū* is used for measures 39–40 of example 1.

With the prefix *ji* these terms still tend to maintain their range distinctions, that is, *ji haru* sections tend to start higher, *ji u* sections are in a moderate range, and *ji chū* are low. Measure 9 of example 1, for instance, is marked in the *maruhon* as a *ji u,* as is measure 24. The symbol *ji haru* is seen in the middle of line one in figure 3, which is measure 1 of example 2.

From the standpoint of general components of *gidayū* style these terms are sufficient. It should be noted, however, that some of the permutations of these words have become attached to melodic patterns of a totally different type. *Haru ji,* for example, is a specific stereotyped melodic pattern derived from the *itchūbushi* tradition, while *haru chū* is yet a different melody. *Haru u,* by contrast, means

Figure 3

the note one-half step above *haru,* c above b in our notation. In this case *u* means *uku,* to float. Using the same meaning, the term *chū u* is the note above the second string, F above E. *Chū bushi* is a stereotyped tune which ends heavily on the middle string but does not go below it, while *haru bushi* (example 7) is a well-known opening pattern which seldom rises above the fourth position on the top string (e) and tends to use notes down to the bottom string. *Fushi haru* is yet another totally different melody.

If some of these examples have seemed less than helpful in clarifying the nomenclature of *gidayū* they have at least implied one important point: *gidayū,* basically a performer's art, has been less concerned with consistent terms than with good performances.[34] It is doubtful that one could ever construct a detailed music theory for *gidayū* like that developed for nō drama music. The concept of four basic, constantly interlocking components, however, provides a matrix into which other aspects of *gidayū* music can be set in meaningful patterns. One of the most important of such patterns is that created by musical devices which give a sense of form.

Music as an Indicator of Form

Although jōruri began as a twelve-part form it soon was reduced in size as various sections were absorbed into larger units.[35] It was traditional to divide period pieces *(jidaimono)* into five *dan* (scenes) and the so-called genre plays *(sewamono)* into three *maku* or acts. When one turns to the modern repertory, however, these distinctions are not terribly useful for two reasons. First, complete plays, particularly period plays, are seldom performed, *Kanadehon Chūshingura* being a major exception. Hence, any sense of overall form in the play is lost, as, for example, symphonic form would be if one played only one movement of a given composition. Second, since each of these large sections was historically a composite of previously separate units, there are within most *dan* or *maku* several semi-independent units which can be performed by themselves. The question, then, is at which level does form become musically meaningful? In order to answer that question we will have to discuss briefly the traditional placements of units within units in jōruri plays, concentrating on period pieces since the nomenclature is similar in genre plays.

The most general terminology used by writers on jōruri form is the three-part concept of *jo-ha-kyū;* the introduction, breaking apart, and rushing to the end. This concept is deeply rooted in Japanese traditional music and is best known for its use in nō drama.[36] Its application to the three *maku* of genre plays is obvious. The most common method of applying it to period pieces is as follows:[37]

1st *dan*	2nd *dan*	3rd *dan*	4th *dan*	5th *dan*
JO		HA		KYŪ
		jo ha kyū		

The placement of the *ha* of the *ha* in the third *dan* is the aestheticians' explanation for the great importance and frequent performance of the third *dan*.

The *jo-ha-kyū* principle is applied in other Japanese musics to units of every size from single melodic phrases to entire pieces. To some extent this is done in *gidayū* also, though two other sets of terms are more closely associated with the jōruri tradition. These are *sei-san-kyū* and *kuchi-naka-kiri*. *Sei-san-kyū*—peaceful, mountainous, and rushing—can be applied in ways similar to those indicated for *jo-ha-kyū*. Its most common use, however, is in relation to performance technique. The *Gidayū Taikan* describes one such use in this way:

> In the beginning of a piece one recites calmly and deliberately. This is *sei*. Around the middle of the piece one recites more and more firmly, majestically, and grandly with full force like a mountain. This is *san*. At the end one recites at full speed and finishes the piece at a swift pace. This is called *kyū*. These are the three principles of reciting, the mastery of which is necessary whether a play is a period piece or a genre play.[38]

While *jo-ha-kyū* and *sei-san-kyū* are rather general aesthetic terms, *kuchi-naka-kiri* refers to the specific subdivisions of each *dan* that are like scenes within an act. This is the set of terms which the practitioners of *gidayū* as well as the theorists use when discussing a play and its music. *Kuchi, naka,* and *kiri* mean the opening, the middle, and the cutting off. Traditionally, the *kuchi* of the first *dan* is called the *daijo* (the big introduction) while the fifth *dan* is without subdivisions.[39] All three subdivisions do not always appear in every *dan*, and other subdivisions may also be found such as *kakeai, tsugi, ato,* or *mae*. Nevertheless, the *kuchi-naka-kiri* divisions mark off the basic dramaturgical-musical units from which the fundamentals of *gidayū* style will be eventually discovered.

In modern productions, one seldom hears all the subdivisions of one *dan*, and it is difficult sometimes to know what one is hearing without previous knowledge of the play. This difficulty is caused in part by the word *dan*, which, in addition to its meaning of one of the five acts of the play, is also used as a generic term for a formal division of any sort.[40] For example, one sees in the program of the June 1964 production of *Chronicles of Prosperity and Decline (Hiragana Seisuiki)* by the Bunraku Kyōkai troupe at the Mitsukoshi Theater in Tokyo what appears to be a five-*dan* play listed as follows:

1. "The Inn at Ōtsu" ("Ōtsu Yadoya no Dan")
2. "Pulling the Corpse on Bamboo Grass" ("Sasabiki no Dan")

3. "Matsuemon Beaten" ("Matsuemon Uchi no Dan")
4. "Rowing Backwards" ("Sakaro no Dan")
5. "The Kanzaki Brothel" ("Kanzaki Ageya no Dan")

A look at the original play[41] shows that these *"dan"* are all parts
of the third and fourth *dan* as shown below (the numbers correspond
to those of the list given above):

Third *dan*   Fourth *dan*

kuchi   -   *naka*   -   *kiri*   *naka*   -   *kiri*

kuchi ─── *kiri*

1.   2.   3. - & - 4.   5.

sei - *san* - *kyū*

The *kiri* of the third *dan* has been split in two. Such sub-subsections
are sometimes called the *kuchi* and *kiri* of the *kiri*. Thus, we see that
these terms can be applied, like the other sets of three terms discussed earlier, to still smaller units.[42] Perhaps the ultimate in the system is seen in number 4 above with the added *sei-san-kyū* division.
This allows one to say that the climax of the entire work is the *kyū* of
the *kiri* of the *kiri* of the *ha* (third *dan*) of the *ha* of the play! The
kuchi of the fourth *dan* has been omitted and the *naka* and opening
of the *kiri* combined. The rest of the *kiri* was deleted from this production. Even to perform this chopped-up version of the play, however, requires over two hours. In such a time span the violence done
to the theoretical form of the entire play has little effect on the concepts of form which can be recognized and retained in the musical
ear. A study of one *kiri,* traditionally the musical climax of each act,[43]
will tell us more about jōruri as music than any struggle with the
five-*dan*-form leviathan can hope to do. There are, however, a few
points of musical interest in the overall form of jōruri which should
not be ignored in theory, though they may not always appear in
practice.

We have already indicated a relation between the *sei-san-kyū*
concept and performance practice. According to both the theorists
and the practitioners of *gidayū,* the five-part form itself and the
kuchi-naka-kiri subdivisions have their musical implications as well.
Most of these deal with the pitch level which should be used for each

section. These pitch levels involve not only the concept of range, such as the terms *haru*, *u*, and *chū* sometimes imply, but more particularly the note to which the samisen is tuned. Pitches in samisen music are indicated by the term *hon*, the numerator for things like poles and strings. Thus, the first *dan* is said to be tuned normally to the fourth or fifth *hon* (C or C sharp) while the *kiri* sections[44] of the second *dan* use the fifth to seventh *hon* (D–E); the *kiri* of the third *dan*, the fourth and fifth; the *kiri* of the fourth *dan*, the fifth through seventh; and *michiyuki* (travel scenes), the eighth *hon* (F). Under this arrangement one can see a general pitch relation between the first and third and second and fourth *dan* in a manner reminiscent of, though not necessarily analogous to, the tonality concepts of the Western symphony in which each movement starts in a key which relates to the overall tonal structure. The fifth *dan* is not given a special pitch preference.

Other factors besides form influence the pitch of *gidayū*, such as the range preference of a particular singer or the predominance of male or female parts in the musical section that follows. However, it is the formal implications of pitch which concern us now. Many times the samisen will be changed from its normal *hon chōshi* tuning or have the pitch of all three strings in the same tuning raised in order to mark off a certain section of a piece. New tunings are most common when a piece from another genre, such as *hauta*, *kouta*, or *koto* music, is performed in the midst of a *gidayū* play. Asagao's song in the "Inn Scene" ("Yadoya no Dan") of *A Tale of Close Resemblance and the Morning Glory (Shōutsushi Asagao Banashi)*, for example, is performed in *ni agari*. Sometimes an actual *koto* part is played in order to further underline the origin of the piece as well as to accompany the pseudo-performance on the *koto* by the puppet. The opening song of *The Tale of the Miracle of Kannon at Tsubosaka (Tsubosaka Kannon Reigenki)* is in *ni agari* as the blind samisen teacher, Sawaichi, sings his sad *jiuta*. The finale of the "Nozaki Village Scene" in *A Buddhist Hymnal Newly Published* is in the standard *hon chōshi* tuning, but all the pitches have been raised to give a fresh forceful sound to this famous boat scene.

From the discussion above we can conclude that pitch level and tuning relate to form in two ways. First, the preference for certain general tuning pitches in each *dan* or section of a *dan* is believed to have a subliminal effect on the listener because a given *dan* set in a given pitch "feels right." By the interrelation of pitches from *dan* to *dan* the principle of a larger architectonic concept of tonality and form also is implied,[45] though, as we have seen, present practice seldom allows such a relationship to be tested. The second use of pitch is to set off special songs, particularly those borrowed from other traditions. Special songs provide a welcome change in pitch, though they do not really represent modulations in the Japanese sense of the term. Modulation in Japanese music means a change in the kind of scale used or the move to a mode within such a scale. Such movements do occur in *gidayū,* but their use is related more to the subtleties of melodic structure and to mood devices than to the subject at hand. Of more importance to form are the melodic formulae to which we turn next.

Melodic patterns are of formal significance when they mark off specific divisions of a piece. The four most obvious ways in which they do this in *gidayū* are by acting as preludes, sectional cadences, intermediate cadences, or trailing cadences. The term prelude is self-explanatory. These preludes appear before major sections of the play such as a *dan,* a subdivision of a *dan* such as *kuchi* or *kiri,* or the point at which there is a change of performers within such a subdivision. Sectional cadences clearly mark off the end of these same major sections of the play. An intermediate cadence is any firm (in Western musical terms, complete) cadence which indicates the end of a specific dialogue or thought. In literary terms, one might say that intermediate cadences mark off paragraphs while sectional cadences end chapters.

A trailing cadence is more specialized than the other two, but its frequency of use gives it a place in our general list. A trailing cadence is often used to connect a lyrical or parlando section to a declamatory section. It does not come to a firm stop but fades out under the dialogue to make a smooth transition (see measure 19 of example 1).

A study of the use of these four formal devices in the living tradition is complicated by the fact that the modern repertory contains only a few plays which survive with all their *dan,* and few of these surviving *dan* are performed with all their subdivisions. This makes it particularly difficult to give a clear picture of the true pattern, if any, in which the preludes and sectional cadences are used in jōruri form. In addition, both concert and theater performances may be cut or arranged in such a way that preludes or cadences will be used which differ from those marked in the *maruhon.* Data are still being collected on this problem and at present only a few general observations and tendencies can be noted.

The most common terms attached to preludes or sectional cadences are *sonae, sanjū,* and *okuri.* Theoretically, the melody *sonae* is used to indicate the beginning of the first *dan* or sometimes, in a slightly extended form, the fourth *dan.* A typical *sonae* is shown in example 5A. It is called typical because it must be remembered that the examples given in this study are only single versions of patterns which can vary greatly from piece to piece and player to player. Example 5 is taken from the very start, the *daijo,* of the first *dan* of *Kanadehon Chūshingura.*[46] The fourth-*dan* version of *sonae* can be found before the *kuchi,* the so-called *terairi* section, of "The Village School Scene" ("Terakoya no Dan") from *The House of Sugawara (Sugawara Denju Tenarai Kagami).* An example of *sonae* in a different *dan* can be heard before the *kuchi* of the third *dan* of *Kanadehon Chūshingura.*

The terms *sanjū* and *okuri* have four characteristics familiar to us from our study of the components of jōruri style. First, the terms do not originate in *gidayū* but reach back into ancient Buddhist music. Their meanings changed as they passed through other traditions on their way to *gidayū.* Second, the same terms are not always applied within *gidayū* in the same way. Third, there are a host of compound words which use *sanjū* or *okuri* as bases but which do not necessarily perform related functions. Finally, there are patterns which serve the same functions as *sanjū* or *okuri* but have different names.

The standard way to move from one *dan* or large section to another is to use the last five-syllable line of the previous section as the first line of the next section, even though the line is meaningless in the context of the section to which it is added. Many times this last line is marked in the *maruhon* with the word *sanjū.* Thus, it would appear that the same melody is used to both close one section and open another. However, the sectional-cadencing *sanjū* is a melody totally different from the preluding *sanjū.* Example 5B shows a typical preluding *sanjū* from the start of the second *dan* of *Kanadehon Chūshingura.* The previous first *dan* ends with the pattern *osanjū* shown in example 5C. In addition to being an example of a cadencing *sanjū, osanjū* illustrates a variation of pattern which has dramaturgical significance. *Osanjū* is only used if the scene involves the emperor or some other high-placed person. In this case the first *dan* has involved the brother of the shōgun, several feudal lords, and a lady from the court of the emperor Godaigo.

Theoretically, the use of a *sanjū* pattern indicates that the section which follows takes place in a location different from the previous one. By contrast, *okuri* is said to be used when the same set appears for both scenes. When either pattern is used at the moment of a change of performers within a scene, the spot chosen for the transfer is usually one in which a main character has just left or is about to come on stage. The standard preluding form of *okuri* is shown in example 6. It is known variously as *okuri, yodanme no okuri*,[47] or *hiki dashi*. Its main variant, *komadayū okuri*, is also shown in example 6B. It represents originally a difference in style between various schools of players.

Though only the samisen part is seen in example 6A, there is a standard manner in which the vocal part follows this introduction. It is also part of the *okuri* pattern. There are many other standard ways in which important vocal sections are begun. Example 7 shows the most common such patterns, called *haru bushi*, which, one may note, has little to do with the terms *haru* or *fushi* as they were discussed earlier. There are many other preluding patterns for the voice and/or samisen which, like *haru bushi*, do not use the term *sanjū* or *okuri* in their titles. Their use generally relates to the specific dramaturgical situation of the scene that follows.

The most common *okuri* class of sectional cadences is *iro okuri*, shown in example 8A. The extended syllable at the end is sung as the *tayū* removes his small support seat, raises his *maruhon* to his forehead, and bows as the dais rotates him off stage. Formally, the very end of a major section of the music can be called a *dangire*.[48] There is also another common melodic pattern called *dangire* which, like the *iro okuri* pattern, may appear in the *dangire* section of the scene. It is shown in example 9.

As one becomes more familiar with the *gidayū* idiom, these various preluding and cadencing patterns enable the listener to identify the major divisions of a play and anticipate to some degree the situation that is to follow. From such anticipations come part of the pleasure of the *gidayū* connoisseur. Within individual scenes the intermediate cadences are of even greater importance, for they mark off the less obvious divisions.

The most common intermediate cadences are those whose names involve the root words *okuri* or *yuri*. All these patterns settle firmly on one of the open strings of the samisen (B, e, or b in our transcriptions). All these patterns are subject to extensive variations which may be caused by the particular text they set, the dramatic situation, or the interpretation of their meaning by individual performers. Of the many *okuri* patterns the two most intriguing are *ko okuri* and *u okuri*.[49] They are shown in example 8. *Ko okuri* is said to be used when a word three syllables long is being set, and *u okuri* is used for four-syllable words. Other *okuri* patterns relate to the general pitch levels *(chū okuri)* or note preferences *(gin okuri)*. In such cases there is seldom a consistent use of the terms, even as they relate to a specific passage as discussed by various performers.

The *yuri* patterns are numbered from one to nine. Originally there seemed to have been only seven. Machida Kashō is of the opinion that the number originally meant the number of times the pattern *yuri* was repeated.[50] As time went on, these terms came to stand for separate melodies, though they all served the same intermediate cadencing function. In some *maruhon* only the term *yuri*[51] appears, leaving us to wonder which pattern might have been intended.

Example 10 gives typical versions of the nine *yuri* used today. The vocal part has been left out of these examples since it usually follows the samisen line in a one-syllable vocalise. Each of these *yuri* has versions which differ greatly from those shown,[52] but the material in example 10 should give the reader some idea of the manner in which these intermediate cadences are handled. Two examples of the most common pattern, *mitsu yuri,* have been included to give some indication of how one pattern varies from piece to piece. The longer *yuri* patterns tend to show up in more rhythmical sections of *gidayū* such as the *michiyuki,* a *dangire,* a *sawari,* or during a dance. *Itsutsu yuri* and *nanatsu yuri* are said to be best used in *michiyuki* sections, the latter being particularly useful for very picturesque traveling scenes. *Kokonotsu yuri* is used when a heavy effect is wanted after some major masculine event has occurred.

In the versions shown in example 10 it should be noted that most of them end on E after extensive emphasis on melodically unresolved tones such as F and A. The only exceptions to this are *nanatsu yuri,* a *michiyuki* pattern, and *yatsu yuri,* a pattern seldom heard today. When these cadences are compared with those of our other examples it would appear that the orientation of *gidayū* is towards the open middle string (E) as a general pitch center. The work of plotting out pitch centers in entire *dan* remains to be done, but after hundreds of hours of hearing *gidayū,* my general impression is that the music circles around E and B with only occasional excursions to A,[53] F sharp, C sharp, or D as pitch centers.

Before we concentrate on the dramatic aspects of *gidayū,* there remains the subject of trailing cadences. In measure 19 of example 1 one finds a cadence which ends on d after a long passage which has emphasized e and b. The d either sounds like an unresolved note requiring another e which never appears, or it sounds like a sudden change of pitch center which leads nowhere. With either interpretation, the result is a feeling of incompleteness, a desire to go on. The musical line has taken a sudden turn, and, while our ears are distracted by this, the style of the text has switched to declamation. This is the essence of the trailing cadence. The same thing occurs at the very end of example 1, which also leads into declamation. Example 2 shows another of the most common uses of such a cadence as it appears after the crying motive, *naki*. Note that the music seems to modulate suddenly to an exotic pitch center (C sharp). Most of these trailing cadences are played with a decrescendo in order to make the transition even smoother. They help to overcome that very difficult moment of aesthetic change when one must stop regarding the *tayū* as a singer and start to hear him as an actor.

The trailing cadences along with the *iro* pattern discussed earlier add greatly to the flow of *gidayū* music, while the other cadencing and preluding patterns help us distinguish the formal division of the play. In the next section we turn to some of the musical elements which contribute to the dramatic significance of this unusual narrative art.

Music to Indicate Mood and Action

The subject of music for mood and action in jōruri is especially interesting because, in such a theatrical tradition, music is seldom isolated from the dramatic situation. We have already seen, in example 2, measure 35, and example 4, measure 2, a pattern known as *naki*, which is the standard way to denote crying. This melody belongs to a class of *fushi* which in Japanese academic terms are called *senritsukei;* in English, we would say stereotyped melodic patterns. Functionally, these *gidayū* patterns resemble the European baroque technique known as the doctrine of affections. Both traditions developed standard musical procedures for depicting emotions. These were repertory-wide, that is, they could be used by all composers in any piece in which similar situations arose. In both East and West, these melodic patterns tended to portray emotions or actions rather than specific persons or objects as do the leitmotives of Wagner. And in both traditions, the individual melodies were subject to great variation as they were applied to specific passages. Indeed, it might be better to call them standard procedures rather than actual melodies, though one can learn to recognize many of them quickly in any of the permutations.

A further study of the *naki* pattern shows the manner in which such melodies are varied in *gidayū*. The tears in example 2 are male and those in example 4 are female; therefore, there is an octave difference in their placement. The tears in example 4 are in the midst of a declamation, are not a complete breakdown, and are therefore rather brief. The tears in example 2 are at the end of a lyrical section leading into a declamation and are a complete breakdown. Hence, they are more extensive and end in a trailing cadence as noted before. A tear-filled eye can be felt in many passages of *gidayū* by the brief use of a and b′ in alternation, while a lamenting wail can appear with all its sobbing in the midst of a lyrical section of a *sawari* with a melody like the one shown in example 5. This does not mean that all emotional outbursts must be accompanied by the *naki* pattern. For example, a general welling up of emotions with or without tears can be felt by a repetition of one or more notes somewhat in the manner of measures 18–20 in example 2.

Example 11 shows a totally different mood device. This is a *meriyasu* used whenever farmers or gauche townspeople appear on the scene. It is used when the farmers come to call their children out of school in "The Village School Scene" and also is heard when the innkeeper appears to announce bedtime in "The Inn at Ōtsu" from *Chronicles of Prosperity and Decline*. The use of a very exotic pitch center (F sharp) and scale add to the humorous quality of this tune.

Meriyasu and preludes contain many such action indicators. For example, the Edo-period popular song called "Shika Odori" is used to open "Sabu's Home Scene" ("Sabu Uchi no Dan") in *Summer Festival (Natsu Matsuri Naniwa Kagami)* since the text begins by mentioning the summer festival that is taking place at the time of the scene. The same popular tune is used to begin the "Castle Tree Store Scene" ("Shirokiya no Dan") from *A Beloved Maid and an Heirloom Kimono (Koi Musume Mukashi Hachijō)*, which opens with a mention of a crowded district well known to Edo dandies. The seventh *dan* of *Kanadehon Chūshingura* begins with a brothel tune as the scene opens on Yuranosuke's revels in the Ichiriki house of assignation in Kyoto.[54] A *kiyari* woodmen's song is used while a log is being hauled in the "Willow Tree Scene" ("Yanagi no Dan") from *The Sanjūsan Gendō Temple (Sanjūsan Gendō),* and the rough actions of the boatmen are well depicted in the finale of the "Nozaki Village Scene" mentioned earlier.

Less specific but more important delineations in character are often heard in music used for entrances. The *ōnori* pattern shown in example 12A is especially suited for warriors, while the pattern in example 12B is used for the entrance of children. Both these patterns exploit very strong tones—*ya, kan,* and *gin* (a, b′ and f sharp). These same tones are important to the *naki* pattern and also tend to precede cadenzas set on emotion-laden words, as seen in measure 16 of example 4. To explain what is meant by a strong tone, we must move to the subject of music as an indicator of mood.

For any foreigner to speak about mood in another culture's music is rather dangerous, not only because of the prejudices of his own cultural background, but also because of the great scorn that modern ethnomusicologists have heaped on their predecessors for similar judgments about happy Western and sad oriental music. Nevertheless, a careful study of the settings of jōruri plays, when linked with the comments of performers, provides much evidence that the musical tones of *gidayū* frequently convey intense mood and feeling. Let us first look at them in their most neutral form, as parts of a tone system.

Gidayū uses two basic scale systems—the *yō* and *in/miyako* shown in example 13. These scales can be built on other notes and have modal forms.[55] In addition to the alternate tones (marked in black in example 13), there are frequent borrowings between the scales to make different ascending and descending patterns, as is seen in measures 2–3 of example 2. While all samisen musics exploit such techniques, it seems that *gidayū* uses a much richer tonal vocabulary and is more daring in its modulations. The close connection of *gidayū* to its very dramatic texts may be one reason for this variety. The text is certainly helpful in explaining sudden tonal changes such as measures 34–39 of example 1. The use of the *in* scale on A with its exotic note, b flat, seems a very appropriate setting of the moment in Asagao's story when, after having been accidentally reunited with her lover in Akashi, they are again cruelly separated as if by a storm.

When we begin to interpret *gidayū* music in this manner we have reached the most controversial, and aesthetically interesting, part of our study. The interpretation of "meaning" in *gidayū* melodies has only just begun, but it will eventually add much to the scholar's appreciation of the art of *gidayū*. The interpretations will deal not only with changes in scales but also with the significance of individual notes in relation to the mood of a given passage.

The most obvious examples of individual pitches used as mood devices are the notes *gin* (f sharp) and *kowari* (c sharp), which are considered to be brighter than *urei* (f) and *sankami* (c). This does not mean that every time one of these notes is used an equivalent mood is produced. Even from what little we have seen of the uses of scales and modes, such a theory would be untenable. In the proper situation, however, the mood effect of these notes seems definite and deliberate. The best examples appear at the start of parlando sections in which a single f or f sharp is struck, as shown in example 14. If the moment is particularly pathetic, the note f is preferred. This does not mean that striking an f sharp instead will make the mood happy. It will make it more lyrical. In the first passage of example 14, Kumagai has just seen Atsumori in the midst of the Heike army, dressed in his gorgeous armor. In the second passage, Kumagai has thrown Atsumori to the ground and now sees his blackened teeth and young noble face, so much like that of his own son whom he must later sacrifice to save Atsumori. Both moments are intense, but their moods require different treatments, a part of which is the selection of the first samisen note. In measures 5–6 of example 4, the use of the e as a starting note shows the more neutral manner in which parlandos are begun when they are leading to intense or lyrical passages.

From what has been said one might be tempted to conclude that the *yō* scale is bright and the *in* scale is sad. The problem, however, is not that simple. For example, in the Japanese theater there is a general rule that when a scene becomes too intense in any direction there must be a counterbalance. Thus, many kabuki fight scenes are done in a kind of slow-motion pantomime while many *michiyuki* in which lovers are traveling towards a suicide spot are accompanied by rather forceful, gay tunes. The intense crying at the climax of a *kudoki* will often use a version of the pattern *naki* which makes great use of c and f sharps, as seen in example 15. There is yet another factor which controls the use of specific notes. This is the difference between styles known as *nishi fū* and *higashi fū*.

Originally, western style *(nishi fū)* referred to the music of the Takemoto Theater and the eastern style *(higashi fū)* to that of the Toyotake Theater.[56] As the terms are used today they refer to a change in style within one scene performed by one singer. The *higashi fū* style is said to prefer the notes f and c sharp, while *nishi fū* uses more of f and c natural. Thus, a player may describe one passage as *higashi fū* and another within the same piece as *nishi fū*. It may turn out that this is merely the performer's way of referring to the *yō* and *in* scales, though further research may show that each style has its characteristic melodic patterns as well which help the performer in identifying it. The same passage may be treated in either style according to the interpretation of individual artists. For example, the rather eastern style of measures 26–28 of example 1 could be made very western by replacing all the c sharps and f sharps with naturals. This, however, would spoil the effect of the f naturals in measure 29. These f naturals are not a matter of changing to western style, for they form the opening of a stereotyped pattern called *tataki* which is found frequently in *kudoki* sections and traditionally exploits the half-step movement between f and e. One can see from such an example that the defining of these two styles in actual compositions is one of the more nebulous aspects of an already difficult subject.

A deeper understanding of the uses of mood in *gidayū* music would require much detailed discussion of specific passages in various plays and would only be meaningful if the reader were acquainted with the repertory in equal detail. Nevertheless, for an introductory study the basic points concerning mood have already been made. Through cultural conditioning the *gidayū* fan has learned to accept specific musical passages as abstractions of action while other melodies and melodic styles are felt to permeate an entire scene with a certain mood.

Perhaps the most striking example of such mood music in *gidayū* is a series of very widely spaced pluckings on the open string of the samisen which are played as the various accessories of a formal suicide are being placed before Enya Hangan in the fourth *dan* of *Kanadehon Chūshingura*. The great waves of silence that occur between each lonely note engulf the audience and Hangan's sorrowing but silent retainers in a mood of sadness as intense as anything the throbbing laments of Puccini ever produced. The fact that these notes are missing in the recorded version of this piece[57] only reinforces one of the general theses of this study, that *gidayū* is a musical-theatrical art and can best be appreciated when it is studied synchronically.

Jōruri as a Performer's Art

One great disadvantage of academic studies in music is that they must isolate moments in an art whose beauty can best be appreciated in a time continuum. In the preceding sections of this study we have displayed some of the facts and sounds of *gidayū* music as if they were a collection of exotic butterflies, carefully arranged and classified by species and place of origin. However, both butterflies and musical facts take on a totally different meaning when they are free to float and mingle. In *gidayū* it is the performer who gives the music wings.

From all that has been said it should be obvious that, while the aesthetic laws of *gidayū* are demanding, their applications in performance are subject to individual interpretation. A *gidayū* piece has certain set musical moments, but it is never as rigid in structure as a Beethoven sonata, for example, or a Verdi opera aria. In both the *gidayū* and the Western examples, variations in tempo and nuance are important to what is called style in performance. In *gidayū*, however, the notes may change as well. Variations in melodic interpretation can be easily noted by listening to the same composition as recorded by different artists.[58] They are even more evident when two *tayū* in a kabuki try to sing together. Disconcerting discrepancies appear and there is a general lack of that sense of ensemble found in other kinds of samisen music which have a tradition of unison singing, such as *nagauta* or *kiyomoto*.[59] This is not a matter of carelessness but a reflection of the basically soloistic nature of the storyteller's tradition.

The performing art of *gidayū* involves the individual interpretation of the *tayū* as it is governed by tradition, by his concept of the play and its characters, and, in the theater, by the choreographic requirements of the stage action.[60] The sense of ensemble, less evident in vocal duets, is constantly evident in the relation of the *tayū*'s performance to its samisen accompaniment. To foster this coordination, *tayū* and samisen players tend to work in teams which over the years develop their own sense of style. This does not mean that the distinctiveness of one team becomes so great that another samisen player could not be used. All *gidayū* teams operate under certain general rules of style within which they are free to vary the music according to individual taste. One often hears the word *ashirai* (ornamentation) in discussions of *gidayū* style, meaning that an extra flourish here or a different turn in the melody there is considered an enhancement rather than a distortion of the original melodic intent. Although once again one is reminded of the European baroque tradition, the freedom in *gidayū* is much greater than in baroque vocal music, and this freedom is reflected in the traditional notation (see fig. 3) which indicates musical phrases by rather indefinite marks *(shu)* alongside the text. These marks either name a pattern *(naki, tataki,* and so on) or a general range *(haru, chū,* and so on) or indicate a vocal turn with various shaped lines. None of these symbols can be read as we do the Western five-line graphic notation or the figured bass of baroque music. *Gidayū* remains basically a guild art, and the secrets of its notation must be learned at the feet of one of its master interpreters. A more accurate traditional notation does exist which uses the Japanese syllabary *(i, ro, ha,* and so on) to represent finger positions on the samisen.[61] The rhythmic indications in this notation are rather general, however, as might be expected in such a rhythmically flexible music. The interpretations of old manuscripts using this notation vary greatly.[62]

These vague notations and variations in style do not denote a cavalier attitude towards the music. Rather, they are in keeping with the freedom necessary to storytellers all over the world. When one hears *gidayū* with all its theatrical panoply of puppets, stagings, famous plays, and singing stars, one tends to forget that at its base it is a narrative tradition. One of the greatest fascinations of *gidayū* is the fact that it has managed to retain the direct power of the narrator while becoming a totally theatrical form. Few narrative arts have been able to achieve this synthesis. The great epic poets of eastern Europe and the storytellers of Africa, the Moslem world, and central Asia have remained basically folk artists. They rely on their skill as weavers of tales and generally limit their music to repetitive tunes on a stringed instrument. The professional storytellers of ancient Greece and premodern Europe were not far removed from these folk artists. In Europe, the narrative tradition became theatrical with the rise of opera, at which point the story was taken out of the control of a narrator and put into the mouths of individual singers. Except for the oratorio, the narrator disappeared from European art music.

In *gidayū* there is a unique synthesis of the folk art of storytelling with the fine arts of operatic theater and professional playwriting. As the secrets of its tradition are gradually brought to light, *gidayū* will find its rightful place among the higher art forms of theatrical music in the world. In the meantime, these preliminary remarks may prove useful to those who might wish to listen to *gidayū* without concern for any Olympian contest of the muses. The pleasures of the knowledgeable *gidayū* listener are many and can be discovered by anyone with a feeling for theater and a willingness to learn a new musical idiom. Fortunately, modern Japan still contains a group of skilled artists who can turn the scrawling words and vague symbols of *gidayū maruhon* into musical-theatrical portrayals of affecting emotions from the human comedy.

TRANSCRIPTIONS

The *gidayū* musical style does not lend itself readily to notation of any kind. The examples in this study can become musically meaningful only after one has listened to the actual style of the music they attempt to represent. Western notation has been used in the interest of communication with Western readers, but one should be aware of the meaning of the special markings and the limits of the standard markings.

Measure lines have been placed in all examples in order to facilitate the location of given passages. They do not always mark off accent groups. Since the rhythm and tempo constantly shift, many of the examples are given without time signatures. Where practical, metronome marks are given, though the beat seldom lasts for long in one speed. Since Western keys have no relevance to Japanese music, there are no key signatures. Note that all examples are notated one octave above their actual range. The selection of actual pitches (centering around B and E) are traditional. The pieces may start on any pitch. In speaking about pitches in the text, capital letters are used for all pitches from the lowest string (B) through the fourth position on the middle string (A, on the second space of the staff); the next octave is written in small letters; and above that a prime sign is used (such as b′) for the note two spaces above the staff.

Notes with x's for heads represent declamation and are written to show the general contour rather than the actual pitches. An arrow pointing down above a note indicates that it is lower than the tempered pitch and an arrow pointing up means that the note is higher than tempered pitch. A straight line connecting two notes represents a sliding between them. A curved line leading in or out of the head of a note indicates a slide to or from that note in the direction of the curve.

The sources for the examples are as follows:

Example 1: "Yadoya no Dan" from a lesson version of *Shōutsushi Asagao Banashi* recorded by Toyozawa Wakō.

Example 2: "Nozakimura no Dan" from *Shimpan Utazaemon.* Side two of King record LKD 19.

Example 3: "Kumagai Jinya no Dan" from *Ichinotani Futaba Gunki.* Lesson version.

Example 4: Same source as example 3.

Example 5: From the first and second *dan* of *Kanadehon Chūshingura* as heard on King record KC 1019.

Example 6: From a lesson version of "Kumagai Jinya no Dan" from *Ichinotani Futaba Gunki.*

Example 7(A): The opening of "Sakaya no Dan" from *Hade Sugata Onna Maiginu* on King record KC 1018.

Example 7(B): The opening of the *sawari* from a lesson version of "Sakaya no Dan" from *Hade Sugata Onna Maiginu.*

Example 8(A, B, and C): From Machida Kashō, *Samisen Seikyoku Senritsukei no Kenkyū,* vol. 5.

Example 9: From the ending of the same source as example 7B.

Example 10: 1. Machida, vol. 4, no. 3.
2. Machida, vol. 4, no. 9.
3. (A) Lesson version.
(B) "Kumagai Jinya no Dan."
4. "Terakoya no Dan." Lesson version.
5. Lesson version.
6. Lesson version.
7. Lesson version.
8. Machida, vol. 4, p. 21.
9. Lesson version.

Example 11: Lesson version.

Example 12(A): "Kumagai Jinya no Dan."

Example 12(B): From taped discussion of Tsuruzawa Wakō.

Example 13: Malm, *Nagauta,* p. 61.

Example 14(A and B): "Kumagai Jinya no Dan." Lesson version.

Example 15: "Yadoya no Dan." Lesson version.

EXAMPLE 1

EXAMPLE 1 (Cont.)

EXAMPLE 1 (Cont.)

EXAMPLE 2

EXAMPLE 2 (Cont.)

EXAMPLE 2 (Cont.)

EXAMPLE 3

IRO TODOME

su - su - me sa-shan-shi - ta - ka   so - na - ra

EXAMPLE 4

EXAMPLE 4 (Cont.)

EXAMPLE 5

EXAMPLE 6

OKURI

EXAMPLE 7

HARU BUSHI

EXAMPLE 7 (Cont.)

EXAMPLE 8

EXAMPLE 9
DANGIRE

EXAMPLE 10
YURI

EXAMPLE 10 (Cont.)

EXAMPLE 11
A MERIYASU

EXAMPLE 12

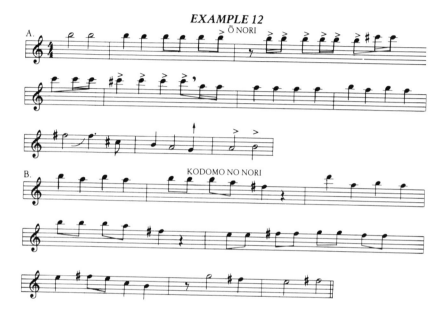

EXAMPLE 13

EXAMPLE 14

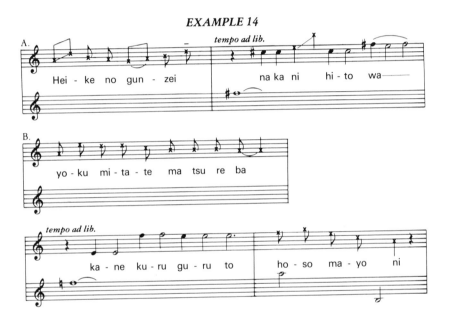

A.

Hei - ke no gun - zei   na ka ni hi - to wa

B.

yo - ku mi - ta - te   ma tsu re ba

ka - ne ku - ru gu - ru to   ho - so ma - yo   ni

EXAMPLE 15
NAKI

Music copyist: Carol Jenkins

NOTES

1.   For details, see Charles J. Dunn, *The Early Japanese Puppet Drama* (London: Luzac and Co., 1966); Tsunoda Ichirō, *Ningyōgeki Seiritsu ni Kansuru Kenkyū* (Osaka: Asahiya Shoten, 1963); or Utsumi Shigetarō, *Ningyō Jōruri to Bunraku* (Tokyo: Hakusuisha, 1958).

2.   The names of the puppeteers, the *ningyō tsukai*, are found in old jōruri documents, but their social position in the bunraku world has generally been lower than that of the musicians. This reflects their supposed origin from the lowest class *(eta)*. The tension caused by such attitudes is still found in the theater today. See further Yūda Yoshio, *Jōrurishi Ronkō* (Tokyo: Chūō Kōronsha, 1975).

3.   See further Dunn, *Early Japanese Puppet Drama.* A chronological list of better-known genres is found in *Encyclopaedia Britannica* (15th ed.), 12:688. Narrative forms that existed before *gidayū* are called *kojōruri* ("old jōruri"). See also Tanabe Hisao, *Samisen Ongakushi* (Tokyo: Chuyoda, 1963).

4.   See Andrew Gerstle, "Circle of Fantasy" (Ph.D. diss., Harvard University, 1980).

5.   I am particularly grateful to Tsuruzawa Jūzō in 1961 and Toyozawa Wakō in 1963–1964 for their lessons and their patience.

6.   The term *tayū* was originally a fifth-rank position in the Chinese court and became the same in the Nara period court of Japan. However, it also became an honorific suffix on the names of actors and musicians in shrine ceremonies and theatricals. Later the term was adopted by singers of samisen music and even high-ranking prostitutes. Its best-known use since the Edo period, however, is as a suffix in the stage names of jōruri singers, and so the term *tayū* itself came to mean the singer of jōruri. See further Kawaguchi Yoshitarō, ed., *Geinō Jiten* (Tokyo: Kōhōkai, 1953), pp. 420–421.

7.   Variations in the pronunciation of the name of the instrument are regional or by genre. In the Osaka area and in *gidayū* the standard term is samisen.

8.   When plays were originally printed complete with all *dan* (scenes) in one volume, they were called *maruhon* to distinguish them from *nukihon* which contained excerpts. The term *shōhon* was also used to mean that these books contained correct texts. The printing of *maruhon* ended around 1832 with the creation of new five-sectioned jōruri pieces, though some two thousand original *maruhon* have survived. These are used as the basis of many modern editions, and thus the old terms are still applied though the actual book used is seldom if ever a complete play. See Shimonaka Yasaburō *Ongaku Jiten* (Tokyo: Heibonsha, 1957), 10:122–123.

9.   In the early days of a month's performance, one can occasionally see players peeking at notation discreetly placed on the floor before them. Even such an aid is seldom seen except in newly arranged dance numbers. The major repertory is all memorized.

10. For a technical study of this feature of the samisen see Lorraine Sakata, "The Comparative Analysis of Sawari on the Shamisen," *Ethnomusicology* 10, no. 2 (May 1966):141–152.

11. See further Watatani Kiyoshi, *Bunraku to Awaji Ningyōza* (Tokyo: Nara Shobō, 1956).

12. See further Okada Dōichi, *Meiji Taisho Onna Gidayū Seikan Monogatari.* (Tokyo: Meitoku Shuppansha, 1953). The Honmokutei Theater in Tokyo traditionally performs *onna jōruri* the first four days of every month.

13. Listen, for example, to records such as *Shimpan Utazaemon* (King LKD 19) sung by Takemoto Tokitayū.

14. Utsumi, *Ningyō Jōruri,* p. 630.

15. Ibid.

16. The term *iri* is used for the samisen part in measure 5 of example 2. The lowest part of the second line from the right in figure 3 shows the symbol. Its meaning is different as can be seen in the transcription. The symbol for the *iri* of measure 24 is seen in the lower left corner area of figure 3.

17. For other uses of the term *meriyasu* in other genre, see William P. Malm, *Nagauta: The Heart of Kabuki Music* (Tokyo: Tuttle, 1964), pp. 52 and 108; and James R. Brandon, William P. Malm, and Donald H. Shively, *Studies in Kabuki* (Honolulu: University Press of Hawaii, 1978), p. 156.

18. The precise meaning of *yokuyō tonza* is problematic. The text does not elucidate them further. In all their possible meanings, however, they indicate a musical approach to a narrative passage and are thus germane to the point of the quotation.

19. Akiyama Sei, *Gidayū Taikan* (Dairen, Manchuria: Nichi Nichi Shimbunsha, 1918), 2:52.

20. Ibid., p. 68.

21. Ibid., p. 55.

22. *Bunraku* (Osaka: Kōdansha, 1959), p. 187.

23. Akiyama, *Gidayū Taikan,* pp. 194–195.

24. See *Gidayū Sawarishū,* nos. 741 and 742, in *Samisen Bunkafu* (Tokyo: Hōgakusha, 1952). The notation is discussed briefly in William P. Malm, *Japanese Music and Musical Instruments* (Tokyo: Tuttle, 1959), pp. 273–274.

25. See Minagawa Tatsuo, "Japanese Noh Music," *Journal of the American Musicological Society* 10, no. 3 (Fall 1957): 181–200.

26. *Gidayū Dokushō Shinsho* (Osaka: Bunrakusha, 1920), 1:8.

27. The term *kakari* has several other unrelated uses. In general these refer to tunes borrowed from other musics.

28. *Bunraku,* p. 186.

29. The name *harikiri* came from the fact that the pole of the samisen is made in sections and one of the joints was at the spot that produced this note.

30. See Miyake Kōichi, *Jibyōshi Seikai* (Tokyo: Hinoki Shoten, 1954), p. 223.

31. See William P. Malm, "The Rhythmic Orientation of Two Drums in the Japanese Noh Drama," *Ethnomusicology* 2, no. 3 (1958):89–95.

32. Machida Kashō, *Samisen Seikyoku Senritsukei no Kenkyū,* mimeographed (*Tōyō Ongaku Gakkai,* 1956) 7:3 ff.

33. One might wonder why the term *chū*—middle—was used for the lowest string. The answer seems to be that *haru* indicated a range from b upward, *u* floated between b and the middle string, while *chū* proceeded from around the middle string (the old *chū*) downward towards the bottom string. See ibid., p. 1.

34. The Nippon Victor Album *Gidayūbushi no Kyokubushi* (SJ 3016–3017) is an important source of examples concerning the variety of sounds that fall within any one category we have discussed.

35. For a detailed discussion of this change see Utsumi, *Ningyō Jōruri,* p. 223 ff.

36. For further discussion of *jo-ha-kyū* see Shimonaka, *Ongaku Jiten,* 5:159. See also Malm, *Nagauta,* pp. 27–28.
37. Utsumi, *Ningyō Jōruri,* pp. 231–233.
38. Akiyama, *Gidayū Taikan,* p. 50.
39. Several plays can be seen broken down according to these subdivisions in Utsumi, *Ningyō Jōruri,* pp. 233–238.
40. The use of the term *dan* in this sense is common to most Japanese traditional music.
41. See Utsumi, *Ningyō Jōruri,* p. 234.
42. They have occasionally been applied to larger divisions as well. Utsumi uses them to show the arrangement of plays for a day's production. See ibid., p. 239.
43. Because of their musical importance, *kiri* sections are heard most often both in the puppet theater and on the *gidayū* concert stage. The term *kiri* is also important in nō music. See Minigawa, "Japanese Noh Music."
44. It should be remembered that the *kiri* sections are scenes within a *dan* and are, therefore, complete in themselves. Thus, all these tunings do not represent a great deal of changing in a given performance. A standard length for a *kiri* is around thirty minutes or more.
45. In the West, similar claims have been made for the acts of operas, particularly those of Wagner. However, such claims in the West have seldom been made by the composers and performers of the art as they have in *gidayū*.
46. Many of the *dan* of *Chūshingura* have been recorded by King records of Japan, on records KC 1006–8, 1003, 1010, 1012, and 1019.
47. Though this name means the fourth *dan okuri,* the pattern may appear in any *dan*. It is, of course, found frequently in the fourth *dan* as well, particularly at the start of the *kiri*.
48. Formally, this section is generally smaller in scope than, for example, a *kiri* of a *kiri*. The term *dangire* has similar meaning in other genre. See Malm, *Nagauta,* pp. 36, 161.
49. See Machida, *Samisen Seikyoku,* vol. 5.
50. Ibid., vol. 4. This study has many examples of each type of *yuri*.
51. The term *yuri,* like *sanjū* and *okuri,* has its roots in Buddhist chant nomenclature, where it stood for a kind of vocal ornamentation.
52. See Machida, *Samisen Seikyoku,* vol. 4.
53. See measures 34–38 of example 1 for an A pitch center.
54. In the kabuki, this scene is *kakeai,* that is, it uses other genre of samisen music along with *gidayū* on stage. This prelude is usually played by *kiyomoto* musicians. The Ichiriki Brothel and Gion geisha to which the song refers still exist in Kyoto, but one needs to be as rich as Yuranosuke to visit them.
55. For a chart of Japanese modes and scales see Malm, *Nagauta,* p. 61.
56. The former is named after Takemoto Gidayū and the latter is derived from Toyotake Wakadayū, a pupil of Takemoto.
57. Listen to King record KC 1012.
58. For example listen to King record 1020 and Victor J1 12 for two interpretations of "Kumagai Jinya no Dan" from *Ichinotani Futaba Gunki*.
59. Groups of *tayū* are used in the puppet theater for many dance numbers. In such cases they train together and the blend is excellent.
60. At present the *tayū* has the dominant artistic and financial position in the bun-

raku puppet theater and tends to look down on the puppeteers. Nevertheless, he must cooperate with them when the demands of stage action occur.

61. For one chart of these symbols see *Bunraku,* p. 180.
62. One of the most famous manuscripts is the *Fukuzukushi* which lists over one hundred and fifty melodic patterns in *i-ro-ha* notation. Three different interpretations exist in Japanese tape archives.

The Theft of *Chūshingura:* or The Great Kabuki Caper

JAMES R. BRANDON

IT DID NOT TAKE kabuki producers and actors long to recognize that the jōruri play *Kanadehon Chūshingura* was a valuable stage property well worth the effort to appropriate for the kabuki stage. Even before the puppet play opened on the fourteenth day of the eighth lunar month in 1748 at the Takemoto Puppet Theater, it was the talk of Osaka. Audiences clamoring to see the exciting events of the well-known Akō vendetta made the play an instant success, and its run of two months would surely have extended through the year and into 1749 had it not been for an artistic dispute that arose between the company's chief puppeteer, Yoshida Bunzaburō, and its chief chanter, Takemoto Konotayū. At issue was the tempo at which a passage from Act IX should be chanted. Bunzaburō was manipulating the puppet of Yuranosuke while Konotayū chanted, " 'I will show you.' In the garden just then weighted under heavy snow was a great bamboo. . . ." Bunzaburō wanted to have Yuranosuke rise on "I will show you," step into his wooden clogs on "in the garden," and cross to the bamboo grove on "just then." To do this he needed the chanter to pause longer between phrases. Konotayū was troupe artistic director *(zagashira)*. He felt deeply insulted that a mere puppet manipulator would question his performance. When Takeda Izumo, the Takemoto Theater owner and main author of the play being performed, did not intervene on Konotayū's behalf, the chanter left to join the rival Toyotake Puppet Theater and the production had to close.[1] Even with its run cut short, there was no question in anyone's mind that *Chūshingura,* as the puppet play soon came to be called by everyone, was a new masterpiece. And that made it prime material to be stolen for the kabuki repertory.

Before the year was out, a kabuki *Chūshingura* was playing in

Osaka at the Arashi Theater next door to the Takemoto Puppet Theater.[2] This production failed, perhaps because it was hastily put together, but others soon followed. During the spring programs of 1749 four kabuki theaters staged *Chūshingura:* the Nakamura Matsubei Theater in Kyoto and the three major licensed theaters in the city of Edo—the Nakamura, the Ichimura, and the Morita. Audiences flocked to these performances, especially in Edo where one of the attractions must have been the opportunity to compare the different versions of the play.

Competition among theaters was always intense. When Edo's three theaters were all staging the same play, we can easily imagine that leading actors would have sought various ways to make their interpretations stand out from those of their rivals. We have descriptions of how Yuranosuke was played in each of the 1749 productions in Edo. Yuranosuke makes his first, intensely dramatic entrance the instant after Enya Hangan has plunged the dagger into his stomach in the act of committing *seppuku.* He appears at the back of the auditorium, on the rampway, or *hanamichi,* that leads to the stage. At the Morita Theater, the actor Yamamoto Kyōshiro

> entered with large and small swords in his sash and with much gesturing of his arms. He quickly took in the situation as he reached the middle of the *hanamichi* and, flinging his swords away, he prostrated himself at the edge of the stage, speaking all the while as he edged gradually closer.

At the Ichimura Theater, Bandō Hikosaburō I,

> dressed with long and short swords, with a lively bearing, trousers hiked up at the sides . . . and a riding crop pushed into his sash at the back, waited in the dressing room. Without warning, he burst through the *hanamichi* curtain, flung away the riding crop, yanked down his trouser hems, and leaped off of his horse. He dashed headlong to the edge of the stage. There he threw down his swords, fell back, and prostrated himself.

While at the Nakamura Theater, Sawamura Chōjūrō III

> entered while tying up his trousers. Only his short sword was tucked in his sash and he carried in one hand his long sword. Midway along the *hanamichi* he fell prostrate to the floor.[3]

The moment in the play is the same. The jōruri narrative and musical accompaniment to the entrance is the same. But each actor has conceived Yuranosuke as a different man. In Hikosaburō's strut-

ting we are given an impetuous Yuranosuke; Kyōshirō, edging closer, suggests Yuranosuke is a sensitive man who is deeply moved by
the sight of his master's disembowelment; and Chōjūrō is the man of
action carrying a sword ready for use.

In the same 1749 production at the Nakamura Theater, Ichikawa Danjūrō II acted the role of one of Hangan's retainers, Ōwashi
Bungo, in the bravura *(aragoto)* style that was the speciality of his acting family. He threw out completely the jōruri concept of the part.
He is described as entering the vendetta scene wearing a typically exaggerated *aragoto* costume—his face made up in the *kumadori* style
of bold stripes of red and white paint—and carrying an enormous
mallet with which he battered down the gate of Moronao's mansion.[4]
We can imagine that he introduced into the scene typical *aragoto*
acting elements—powerful poses *(mie),* roaring challenges to the
enemy, stylized flourishes of the mallet, and perhaps a battle sequence in which the outsized mallet would have been a novel and
amusing weapon.

What each of the actors did may not seem particularly significant. But these examples show the pattern which kabuki, in stealing
the jōruri play, would follow over the next century and more: a bit-
by-bit alteration of the original puppet play so that it would better
suit the nature of kabuki theater. For the fact is that while *Chūshingura* was a jōruri play well worth appropriating, kabuki actors never
intended to perform it exactly as it was done in the puppet theater.[5]
And even seemingly minor changes in role interpretations or in the
application of special kabuki acting styles would result, in the end, in
quite significant changes both in the text and in the staging of the
play.

When jōruri and kabuki came into existence in the early part of
the seventeenth century, they were almost totally different theater
arts, the one a narrative, vocal art casually illustrated by crude puppet
figures, the other a dance and first-person drama in which the actor's
physical presence was all-important. One was wedded to the word;
one to the human figure. The narratives of jōruri were bombastic and
ponderous; the dances of kabuki were gay—its earliest sketches,
about visits to the brothel quarters, were both erotic and amusing.
The material of early jōruri plays came from legend, myth, and history; early kabuki plays were based on scandalous doings of the day.
Nobility and samurai warriors peopled the narratives recited in jōruri;
rich merchants, dandies, prostitutes filled the kabuki stage. In its
maturity, kabuki developed as a first-person dialogue drama in which

the function of music was to underscore mood and to provide rhythmic accompaniment to entrances, exits, and fighting scenes. Kabuki dance plays were mimed to lyrics of extended songs, sung in many musical styles. Jōruri remained fundamentally a third-person narrative—as if a person were reading a novel—filled with verbal descriptions and commentary on the action. Of course the narrator *(tayū)* spoke or chanted the dialogue assigned to the puppet characters, yet the chanter was always an "outside" voice. He was the "interpreter" not the "actor" of the play. The small one-man puppets that were used from around 1600 until the 1730s had heads with fixed features and could not be moved in a realistic fashion. Since their expressive power was limited, the focus of jōruri performance on the vocal powers of the solo chanter was reinforced.

The original distinctiveness of the two theater forms is easy to overlook today, because later borrowings back and forth between them have moved the forms closer to each other. From today's perspective, the two arts are often interchangeably described. The confusion runs both ways. A standard American theater history text will credit the jōruri play *The Battles of Coxinga* to kabuki, while the Japanese National Commission for UNESCO will blithely list the entire kabuki repertory, with the exception of dance plays, as "classical jōruri plays of kabuki."[6] By what startling alchemy, one wonders, have the great kabuki plays like *Saint Narukami (Narukami Fudō Kitayamazakura), Sukeroku the Flower of Edo (Sukeroku Yukari no Edo Zakura), The Ghost of Yotsuya (Yotsuya Kaidan),* and *Benten the Thief (Shiranami Gonin Otoko)* been credited to the puppet theater? These are "pure" *(junsui)* kabuki plays, unknown on the puppet stage. The confusion becomes mystifying when we turn to Sakae Shioya's *Chūshingura: An Exposition,* the most complete analysis in English of the play and its historical surroundings. After pointing out the many misunderstandings that have plagued earlier works on *Chūshingura,* Shioya treats the play as if it were an original kabuki drama. The beauty of *Chūshingura* lies, he says, in the "peculiar Japanese form in which it is written, known as kabuki style," adding that this is natural since "all old plays were written in that style, that being the only style for plays in former days."[7] He describes elements of kabuki that lend charm to *Chūshingura* on the stage: the wooden clappers—whose beating "may jar upon our ears" but is nonetheless primitively effective, the posturing of the actors at the finale of a scene, the intonation of the actors' speech, and the rhythmic movements of fighting scenes.[8] No mention is made of the fact that *Chū-*

shingura was written as a puppet play, yet the text which he ex-
plicates is the jōruri text and the stage scenes he describes are from
puppet performances, not, except in a few cases, kabuki at all. In
spite of the obviousness of these misunderstandings, they are not ex-
ceptional.

If, then, jōruri and kabuki were so different in form originally,
how was it that *Chūshingura* was ever stolen by kabuki actors? In
order to understand this we need to discuss briefly how kabuki and
jōruri had moved closer in form and style in the time prior to 1748. It
is argued by Suwa Haruo and other Japanese scholars that, at least
from the Genroku period (1688–1705), kabuki was regularly borrowing from jōruri. A kabuki playbook *(eiri kyōgen-bon)* of 1697 reads,
"This text includes child roles, leading roles, sound effects *(hyōshigi)*, jōruri and *sekkyō* music, dance, and dialogue, leaving nothing
out . . . exactly as the actors speak the lines."[9] And it is noted that
the names of "jōruri singers" occur in the text of a 1699 performance
of *The Woman's Narukami (Onna Narukami)*, and that these were
musicians who played in the *Satsuma geki* style.[10] Jōruri, *sekkyō*, and
Satsuma geki are all types of narrative and musical styles that accompanied puppet performances. The terms can indicate either the plays
or the musical style. If these references are to the former, then kabuki
was undoubtedly being influenced in fundamental ways by the borrowings, for it would suggest that whole scenes from puppet plays
were being taken over into kabuki. But it also may be that what was
being referred to was the type of music that was played to accompany
a kabuki dance scene, in which case the borrowing was less significant. We know the actors Otowa Jirosaburō and Sawamura Chōjūrō
expressed disdain for acting in pieces "using jōruri" and both of
them refused, as long as they could, to appear in such plays.[11] The
implication is that kabuki plays, or at least acts in the plays, often incorporated jōruri elements. But whether this meant scenes taken
from jōruri or the acting style of the puppets or the chanting of the
jōruri narrative, we do not know.

It is also commonly held that Ichikawa Danjūrō I created the
bravura, or *aragoto*, acting style in kabuki after he had seen, as a
child, performances of a bombastic type of puppet play named, after
its hero, Kimpira jōruri. This is based on an account in *Hot-Blooded
Tales of the Kantō Region (Kantō Kekki Monogatari)* that describes
how the chanters Izumi Tayū I and II loved to perform in a powerful
style "beating time with a thick, two-foot metal rod. . . . The heads
of the puppets were twisted off, split down the middle, and smashed

to pieces, heedless of destruction. . . . The founder of *aragoto* acting, Ichikawa Danjūrō I, followed Tayū's example closely and the present Ichikawa Ebizō [Danjūrō II] continues that tradition.''[12] Until recently this passage had been accepted at its face value, but since it is an account written some seventy years after some of the events described, it is probably not to be taken literally.[13]

The form and content of kabuki plays were affected by jōruri examples in other ways. Kabuki programs gradually changed over from a variety format of independent scenes to multiact plays starting in 1664. At that time jōruri history plays were regularly written in five or six acts.[14] Probably stimulated by this model and the well-known example of the five-part division of a nō program as well, kabuki playwrights developed a standard dramatic structure of four acts (this was especially true in Edo). Suwa has compared kabuki and jōruri play synopses from the Genroku period and shows that, at least in some cases, the plays done in kabuki were similar in content to earlier jōruri plays.[15]

At the same time, jōruri also was borrowing from kabuki. In the process it gradually moved from a predominantly narrative art to a theater form in which the narrative element is reduced in importance and emphasis is placed on enactment of highly theatrical scenes *(miseba)*. We know that the soft kabuki acting style *(wagoto)* of the actor Sakata Tōjūrō and the prostitute-buying plays *(keiseikaimono)* he performed throughout his life were the basis for the love-suicide plays *(shinjūmono)* that Chikamatsu Monzaemon (1653–1725) later wrote for jōruri.[16] Over a period of twenty-four years Chikamatsu wrote more than thirty kabuki plays as vehicles for Tōjūrō.[17] During most of this time Chikamatsu was the chief playwright of the Mandayū Kabuki Theater in Kyoto, where Tōjūrō reigned supreme as actor-manager *(zagashira)*. Among his kabuki plays many were composed in *wagoto* style. The love-suicide play had a two-decade history in kabuki before Chikamatsu wrote his first jōruri play on the subject, *Love Suicides at Sonezaki (Sonezaki Shinjū)*, in 1703. Typically the hero is a young *wagoto*-style merchant, feckless and charming, and the woman he loves is a prostitute. In addition to the lovers' deaths, the one obligatory scene was a love scene set in the gaudy licensed quarters. Consequently, as Suwa remarks, the basic role types and scenes found in jōruri plays about commoners *(sewamono)*, whether love suicides or otherwise, had been first established in kabuki.[18]

We begin to encounter evidence of direct copying of jōruri

scenes in kabuki after the Genroku period. In 1714 the term *chobo* appears in connection with the kabuki adaptation of Chikamatsu's puppet play *Annals of the Gods (Tenjinki).* [19] Since *chobo* is a special kabuki term for the team of jōruri chanter and samisen player, and is not a puppet theater term, we can surmise that it indicates an acceptance of jōruri musicians as members of the regular kabuki troupe. The following year, Chikamatsu's exceptionally successful jōruri history play *The Battles of Coxinga (Kokusenya Gassen)* inspired a rash of kabuki imitations. The puppet play ran seventeen months, from the winter of 1715 through the spring of 1717, and by that summer ten kabuki troupes had brought out their own "Coxinga" productions. This number of "competitive performances" *(kyōen)* was unprecedented: three kabuki theaters in Kyoto and Osaka staged productions during the third month of 1717, and in Edo the three major kabuki houses opened Coxinga productions within days of each other in the fifth month. [20] Whole scenes from the puppet production at the Takemoto Puppet Theater may have been taken over. This is the opinion of Ihara Toshirō when he writes that "jōruri puppet plays were first performed in Edo kabuki" in these Coxinga plays. [21] The titles of some of the kabuki plays support this view, for they are identical with Chikamatsu's title (it was common in kabuki to alter titles to indicate some change in a well-known story), but lacking scripts we cannot say with certainty what the kabuki texts were like or how they were staged. The titles of others suggest they had little or nothing to do with Chikamatsu's drama. *The Prostitute's Coxinga (Keisei Kokusenya), Latter Battles of Coxinga (Kokusenya Gonichi Gassen),* and *Coxinga's Treasure Ship (Kokusenya Takarabune)* probably were wholly new plays that merely capitalized on the hero's name. In the Nakamura Theater production, *Coxinga's Treasure Ship,* the role of the hero, Watōnai (Coxinga's Japanese name), was played by Ichikawa Danjūrō II in his usual blustering *aragoto* acting style. In the play he called himself "Soga Gorō, later known as Watōnai," thereby linking the Coxinga story to the Ichikawa family's favorite kabuki hero, Soga Gorō. [22]

It was typical of kabuki play construction in Edo to weave together several story "worlds" *(sekai)* in a fanciful and playful way as Danjūrō did here. Prior to Danjūrō's great success in this role, "the truth is that there had always been an antipathy to adapting puppet plays" in Edo kabuki. [23] It may be that Danjūrō found the role especially congenial because the puppet hero's superhuman feats were compatible with Danjūrō's powerful acting style. [24] Without any doubt *aragoto* acting would suit Coxinga riding the tiger in the Bamboo Forest and smashing his way through Kanki's army to reach his captured mother. It also suggests that by this time minor borrowings back and forth had narrowed the gap between the two forms to the point where wholesale raids on each other's dramatic and theatrical territory would seem feasible. We can sense the jealousy the actor Otowa Jirosaburō felt toward this rival theatrical form and his feeling of self-protection for kabuki when he said he would not appear in plays that used jōruri techniques because, "from the beginning jōruri has modeled itself on kabuki, with even the puppets imitating kabuki actors. The natural result, now that kabuki is imitating puppet movements, is the decline of kabuki."[25]

A major hindrance to kabuki performers who found the plays of the puppet theater attractive enough to purloin intact during the Genroku period was the fact that the one-man puppet was limited in its expressive powers; as a consequence vocal narrative still made up a substantial part of a jōruri performance. This situation drastically changed between 1720 and 1734 when new techniques for manipulating the puppets in a more human fashion were developed. Puppets were made considerably larger, until they were about two-thirds life-size; fingers were jointed down to the last knuckle; and heads were carved with movable eyes, eyebrows, and mouth. Each of the new complex puppets was moved by a three-man team of manipulators. Instead of hiding below the stage, the puppeteers now moved out in full view of the audience, carrying their remarkably lifelike doll characters in front of them at chest level. The puppets could stand, sit, kneel, and move freely across the stage just like a person, either in an outdoor scene or in a realistically built room of a house or mansion.[26]

When the puppet was made to move like a human being, the visible behavior of the puppet characters in a scene became more like that of live actors playing a role in kabuki. This can be seen in a radically new staging approach that was used in the production of *The Summer Festival (Natsu Matsuri Naniwa Kagami)* at the Takemoto Puppet Theater in 1745. In place of the conventional padded puppet costume, which all figures previously wore, the young murderer Danshichi Kurobei was dressed in a real cotton kimono of the kind commonly worn in Japan during the hot summer months. All the movements of the character's body, arms, and legs showed through the thin material. As Danshichi was manipulated by the chief puppeteer Yoshida Bunzaburō and his two assistants, he was made to draw real water from a well in the murder scene. When Danshichi struggled to kill his father, both the puppets were drenched with water and their bodies and faces smeared with mud.[27]

New plays were written to capitalize on the increased expressive possibilities of the three-man puppets. The most famous of these, often called "The Three Masterpieces of Jōruri," were written in successive years: *The House of Sugawara (Sugawara Denju Tenarai Kagami)* in 1746; *Yoshitsune and the Thousand Cherry Trees (Yoshitsune Senbonzakura)* in 1747; and *Kanadehon Chūshingura* in 1748. They were composed jointly by the same team of writers for performance at the Takemoto Puppet Theater in Osaka, and they share many characteristics: they are all-day plays; their major scenes are built around a suicide or the forced killing of a beloved relative; they contain highly theatrical scenes; and their overriding theme is the demand of feudal obligation *(giri)* on members of the samurai class. If their texts are compared with those of Chikamatsu's jōruri plays, it will be seen that the proportion of spoken dialogue *(kotoba)* is much greater in this new generation of plays while the proportion of sung narrative *(ji)* is much less.[28] They are, in other words, more nearly first-person dramas than earlier puppet texts. The beautiful but very long descriptive passages for which Chikamatsu was justly praised have given way to carefully visualized actions which the puppets could now explicitly enact. To say, as some do, that these plays of the mid-eighteenth century cared nothing for the music, nothing for the chanting, but only for the puppets is, perhaps, stating the case too strongly.[29] Jōruri remained a unique fusion of music, chanting, and puppet manipulation. What is significant for our discussion is that the new plays placed their emphasis on aspects of performance that made the plays come ever closer to kabuki performance.

It is not an exaggeration to say that the most "kabuki-ized" of these new plays is *Chūshingura.* Almost alone among jōruri history plays, it contains no supernatural events. Scene after scene dramatizes what were in Japanese society recognizable people caught in understandable human dilemmas: a wife faced with an attempted seduction; a samurai provoked into carrying out a rash action; a loyal retainer offering a bribe to deflect anger away from his master; a young couple whose love brings them into disgrace; a painful death that must be endured with grace and courage; and a dozen other affectingly human situations. The focus in each scene is on the human personality of these tested and appealing people. Their nature and their emotions are conveyed primarily through the physical figure of the puppet and the words the character speak, as in kabuki.

When *Chūshingura* was first staged in 1748, the Ichiriki Brothel scene was produced in a radically new manner that emphasized the human personality of the puppet characters. Normally in jōruri the voices of all the characters in a scene are taken by a single chanter, but on this occasion six chanters were placed on stage. Each chanter was assigned a role, as is an actor: Takemoto Bunjitayū played Okaru; Takemoto Konotayū played Yuranosuke; Takemoto Tomotayū played Rikiya; Takemoto Masatayū played Heiemon; Takemoto Yuritayū played Kudayū; and Takemoto Shinanotayū played Bannai.[30] Consequently, each of the major characters in the scene had his or her own voice. The chanter "acted" the role and timed his character's speeches with those of the other chanters. There were opportunities to develop vocal interplay among characters and to create "builds" within the scene that were denied the single chanter. As we will see later, certain kabuki vocal techniques that depend upon characters overlapping their speeches were taken over in this scene because multiple chanters now could function as actors could.[31]

Indeed, the puppet premier of *Kanadehon Chūshingura* was indebted to previous kabuki productions of the *Chūshingura* story as well. In particular, puppet artists borrowed from the kabuki play *The Forty-Seven Great Arrows (Ōya Kazu Shijūshichihon)* that was first staged in 1726 in Osaka at the Arashi Sanemon Theater and was revived in the same city at the Ichiyama Theater in 1746. In the following year the actor Sawamura Chōjūrō III (known earlier in his career as Sōjūrō I) made a deep impression on audiences with his brilliant portrayal of Yuranosuke in a revised version of the play at the Nakamura Kyūtarō Theater in Kyoto. This production included the Ichiriki Brothel scene and it is reported that Chōjūrō's "movements and vocal inflections were exactly copied" by the puppet manipulators and chanters at the Takemoto Puppet Theater when they took over this scene for the 1748 *Kanadehon Chūshingura*.[32] Once *Kanadehon Chūshingura* opened, however, it eclipsed all earlier versions. It became the "standard" version against which all others were measured.

Let us now look at the manner in which kabuki stole from the puppet play and some of the major changes which were made in the purloined original. To begin with, the full puppet play, in all its eleven acts and eighteen scenes, was taken over more or less intact. The standard kabuki text today consists of the same number of acts and scenes (with the notable exception of dance additions which will be discussed later). In performing the play on the kabuki stage, actors took the lines of dialogue of the puppet script while the *chobo* team of jōruri chanter and samisen player, installed on the left side of the stage, sang and chanted narrative sections of that text. Actors copied the movement sequences, blocking patterns and gestures which had been worked out in puppet performance, and their timing was matched to the musical rhythms and the vocal patterns of the *chobo* team.[33] In short, the intent was to perform a puppet play using live actors. But even if the kabuki actors had wanted to reproduce the puppet production exactly, they would not have been able to, for in the last analysis the human actor and the inanimate puppet figure are not the same. Kawatake Shigetoshi notes that because of this fundamental difference, even jōruri samisen music and the chanting were altered when they were taken over into kabuki.[34]

And as we have seen, from the first kabuki actors deliberately set about to change the original. Although *Chūshingura* is one of the few jōruri plays that has regularly been revived in anything near its all-day form, it also has consistently been cut up into shorter versions the better to fit into the kabuki program. As the years passed this tendency became more pronounced. For example, although Acts VII and X were staged apart from the rest of the play in 1763 at the Araki Yojibei Theater in Osaka, and at the Kawarazaki Theater in Edo an 1804 version was made up of Acts V, VII, and IX, during those early years it was more usual for the play to be performed complete or at least up through Act IX or X. By the end of the nineteenth century, however, parts of *Chūshingura* were being shoehorned into a kind of concert program made up of independent plays that had become usual in kabuki at that time. Typical of this kind of program was the staging at the Shintomi Theater in Tokyo in December 1883 of the first four acts plus the last act of *Chūshingura* followed by an unrelated three-act domestic play, *Kawauchi Mountain (Kawauchiyama).*[35] It was considered important to vary mood, tempo, and artistic qualities throughout a day's program, but it was not considered necessary to continue any one story throughout.

These attitudes are reflected in the three-part program that was commonplace in nineteenth-century kabuki: the "first piece" *(ichibanme)* was a history play in four or more acts; a "between-the-acts" *(naka maku)* dance play followed; and the "second piece" *(nibanme)* was a domestic play in one, two, or three acts. The midsummer production at the Meiji Theater in 1895, for example, followed this format. *Kanadehon Chūshingura* (Acts I, III, IV, and VII) comprised the historical first piece; a dance play called *The Valley Battle (Hazama Gassen)* was the middle piece; and the program closed with a three-act domestic second piece with the fanciful title of *A Gallant*

Night-Blooming Cherry in the Licensed Quarter (Otokodate Kuruwa Yozakura).[36] It can be argued that precisely because the plays on such a program were not related they were likely to contain greater variety of characters and scene types, and hence greater artistic variety, than even the most skillfully made all-day play. A close parallel can be found in the standard arrangement of five independent plays in the nō program and, in the West, our juxtaposing varied types of musical compositions in a concert of classical music. So strong is the feeling for an appropriate "atmosphere" in kabuki that a bright dance piece may be added to conclude the day's program on what is considered the proper celebratory note, thus making a four-part program. It is not unusual in contemporary productions of *Chūshingura* to drop acts so that the day's performance can conclude with this kind of un-related dance number.[37]

In another variation, several scenes from *Kanadehon Chūshin-gura* might be used as a point of departure for the composition of a new work. The production *Chūshingura from Beginning to End (Maemote Chūshingura),* at the Kawarazaki Theater in 1833, consist-ed of twenty-two scenes, few of which bore much resemblance to the puppet original. It in turn contained a dance scene that inspired the playwright Kawatake Mokuami to write another version, *Collection of Beautiful Pictures of Chūshingura (Chūshingura Keiyo Gago).* He converted each scene of the original script into a dance scene, so that the play was performed as a dance from beginning to end. Just as Danjūrō II earlier had put Soga Gorō into the Coxinga story, actors and playwrights now took characters from *Chūshingura* and melded them with stories already in the kabuki repertory, often with startling results. In an 1828 production Honzō's delicate daughter Konami was transformed into a fierce *aragoto* figure to star in *A Female Wait a Moment (Onna Shibaraku).* The god Fudō, another *aragoto* hero, appeared in the fifth act of *Chūshingura* in 1836. Yuranosuke and other *Chūshingura* characters appeared in several versions of *The House of Sugawara.* There were kabuki versions of *Chūshingura* in which Kudayū and Yuranosuke commit *seppuku* and in which Kam-pei and Bannai reverse roles as lover and comic villain. The thief Sa-dakurō was the central figure in an eleven-act play tossed off by Tsuruya Namboku IV in 1821; near the end of the play, Sadakurō even takes Okaru as his wife![38] Interesting as these and other such plays are, they are too far from the original *Chūshingura* to concern us here. Instead, let us return to the changes that were made in per-formances that purported to be of the puppet play.

Several "kabuki" scenes were added to the jōruri play. The most extensive is the fugitive travel scene *(michiyuki)* written by Mimasuya Nisōji, the staff playwright of the Kawarazaki Theater for the 1833 production mentioned above. It is a dance scene accompanied by *kiyomoto* music. The author kept the dozen or so lines of Kampei and Okaru from the original jōruri text and reworked the scene to include three long sections of elegant dance—in which the lovers prepare to flee—and two contrasting fighting sequences between Kampei and the comic villain Bannai. Before this, kabuki performances of this scene had followed jōruri staging.[39] It is a popular scene and is included in most kabuki performances of *Chūshingura* today. The deeply emotional quality of the jōruri scene is transposed by the dance into gentle, wistful images of two young people in love: viewing the spring scenery, looking down the distant road, embracing fondly, helping each other prepare for the journey, walking hand-in-hand through the flowers. When Kampei tries to kill himself and Okaru stops him, their struggle for possession of the sword is shown in beautiful slow-motion dance. The fight between Kampei and Bannai's fighting chorus *(yoten)* is also dance *(shosadate)*. Eight or ten chorus members are dressed alike in colorful costumes covered with pink, red, and white flower designs. They carry blossoming cherry branches as weapons. They form geometric groupings on stage: they make single, then double lines through which Kampei gracefully weaves; they attack in twos and in fours; they flip in somersaults; they do cartwheels; they stand in formation on each others' backs; they strike at Kampei with their branches tracing pink arcs through the air; and in defeat they are whirled, tripped, and made to fall on their bottoms in unison. The lovers' dance, the spectacular fighting movements, the massed musicians seated in view on stage, the music itself, the bursting color of the spring setting—all contribute to create a special kind of kabuki beauty—elegant, brilliant, stylized—that is completely unlike the puppet performance.

The jōruri text also contains a dance scene, the bridal journey (Act VIII). In it Honzō's wife Tonase and daughter Konami travel to the home of Yuranosuke in preparation for Konami's wedding to Rikiya. This is sometimes performed in kabuki. But the Kampei-Okaru dance scene is far more popular (perhaps partly because it occurs about where the *naka maku* dance piece should in the all-day program whereas the jōruri dance scene seems too late in the play). Sometimes both dance scenes are performed, and a production of *Chūshingura* at the Kabuki Theater in 1959 included a third as well—a comic dance that showed a strutting Heiemon pursued by a swarm of bees. The latter rarely has been performed since it was created in 1791, and its revival in this generation is a good indication of how important dance scenes are in kabuki.[40]

Short dances and songs are also inserted in the Ichiriki Brothel scene to create an appropriately lively mood. A group of maids and several comic male geisha dance to entertain the supposedly drunken Yuranosuke. Music is provided by the standard kabuki offstage (geza) musical ensemble. Its bright rhythmic sound is quite unlike the heavy, "thick" sound of the jōruri samisen. In a reverse case of borrowing, current puppet performances of the Ichiriki Brothel scene often add this music, played on a kabuki samisen, to create the now well-known kabuki flavor for the scene.[41]

Kabuki productions of *Chūshingura* developed battle sequences choreographed from the more than two hundred cutting, piercing, parrying, and avoiding movements of swords and other weapons that are part of kabuki acting technique.[42] The dance battle in the fugitive travel scene is one of these. Even more spectacular are the battle scenes created for the final act of the play, the vendetta, that are only hinted at in jōruri performance. The act is picturesquely set in midwinter and at midnight. White snow blankets the ground, rocks, trees, and rooftops. Alternately, a pale moon shines through the clouds and swirling snowflakes engulf the groups of largely silent combatants. In the most elaborate productions this act has five scenes. Without breaking the action, the scenes come into view and disappear on the revolving stage, one of kabuki's most effective stage machines. In the first scene, Enya Hangan's loyal retainers mass before the gate to Moronao's mansion to begin the assault. (Danjūrō II's *aragoto* style of smashing down the gate is, alas, lost and not seen in performance any longer.) In the second, Hangan's men fight through various rooms of the mansion seeking Moronao without success. In the third, the action moves to the garden, where, in the falling snow, the retainers of Hangan meet those of Moronao in a series of spectacular sword fights. The bravest of Moronao's defenders dies falling from the garden's stone bridge into the waters of a pond. In the fourth, dawn is near and the men are desperate to find Moronao. Fighting continues into another part of the garden where Moronao is discovered hiding in a charcoal hut. He is dragged out, given the opportunity to commit *seppuku* with Hangan's dagger, and beheaded. In the fifth scene, Hangan's retainers, led by Yuranosuke, gather at Ryōgoku Bridge to celebrate their victory.[43]

The different natures of kabuki and jōruri are sharply contrasted in this act. There is a splendid virtuosity and boldness to the human actor's movements in the interlocking sequences of hand-to-hand combat and sword fights which even the three-man puppet cannot begin to match. On the other hand, long passages of narration in the jōruri conjure up vivid verbal images lacking in the kabuki: warriors "clamber up to the rooftops, their lanterns bright as stars"; Hangan's retainers "cry out rejoicing, as the blind turtle finding a floating log or the eye gazing upon the flower that blossoms but once in three thousand years"; and when Moronao is found "they all flash with courage as a flower sparkles with the dew."[44]

New comic sequences have been created for kabuki performances in addition to the humorous scenes already in the jōruri text. In the bribery scene that opens Act III, actors in the mid-1800s worked out a kind of vaudeville turn for Bannai that is almost obligatory in current performances.[45] The situation is as follows: Bannai is talking with Moronao when word comes that Wakasanosuke's retainer Honzō is seeking an audience with Moronao. Bannai has a fit of anger because Wakasanosuke insulted Moronao in the opening scene at Hachiman Shrine. So he coaches his ruffian followers to whip out their swords when he gives the signal "ahem" and to slice Honzō through. They rehearse the routine three or four times, as often as the audience finds it amusing. When Honzō arrives—carrying with him expensive bribes—Bannai's attitude immediately changes. But he inadvertently says "ahem" and the ruffians raise their swords. Bannai hastily calms them and is forced to apologize to Honzō. The routine is repeated; again, the number of times depends upon how skillful the actor playing Bannai is in amusing the audience. Adding this sequence creates a problem with the original scene. Bannai must take stage during the "ahem" routine, but he cannot do this with his master Moronao beside him (Moronao is the central figure in the bribery scene in jōruri). So Moronao is cleverly placed inside a closed palanquin where he cannot be seen but is still present, and his lines, such as "If I am with you, who could object?" are given to Bannai. In the past, Honzō has appeared on horse back in puppet performances, matching the narrative which says, "he has arrived at the mansion on a swift horse," but this is not done in kabuki.[46]

By the addition of such sequences and by being cut from serious scenes, Bannai has been built into one of kabuki's major comic roles.[47] Perhaps his funniest sequence is the derisive challenge to Kampei in the fugitive travel scene that begins, "Your stupid master, Enya Hangan. . . ." The speech in the jōruri text consists of just two phrases; in kabuki the speech has grown to thirty-two phrases. It is spoken in a vocal technique called *nori*—literally "riding" the rhythm of the jōruri samisen. Each phrase, marked by a comma in the translation, is fit into an eight-beat musical measure. Although the content of the speech is funny, its delivery is equally important, as in a Gilbert and Sullivan patter song. The speech is a delightful acting tour de force when it is precisely and rhythmically spoken and is accompanied by stylized gestures and exaggerated facial expressions. In fact, the vocal and physical patterns are so exact that anyone can remember it all quite easily after attending several performances. *Nori* is a jōruri vocal technique, but the jōruri version of *Chūshingura* does not use the technique for Bannai here. In this case it was a kabuki addition.

The Ichiriki Brothel scene contains a striking example of inserted kabuki humor. Heiemon has drawn his sword to kill his beloved sister Okaru, but he is moved by her pleas and cannot strike. He falls back weeping. In a puppet performance, Heiemon immediately goes on to relate to Okaru the story of the death of their father and of Kampei. And the two of them weep bitterly. But in kabuki a charming scene intervenes between the attempted killing and Heiemon's pathetic narrative. First, Heiemon lowers his sword and motions to Okaru to come close to hear his explanation. But she refuses, thinking he still intends to kill her. They quarrel, as brother and sister might do. She insists that he put away his swords. With much grumbling he does so. When she complains that she is frightened by his fierce face, he complains that "I can't help that, this is the face I was born with." She makes him turn his back to her, and as he poses, muttering testily, "What a nuisance," she at last feels safe to approach. She moves the swords far away and kneels beside him, saying, "Brother, dear, what is it you want?" Only now does Heiemon relate the awful account of Kampei's death. There is a friendly, affectionate humor to this scene. It appeals especially because of the contrast between it and the typical jōruri weeping and wailing and gnashing of teeth that follow, when Okaru learns of Kampei's suicide.

The original focus of jōruri on the chanted or sung word is still noticeable in mature jōruri performance. So too does the early emphasis upon the physical expressiveness of the actor's body continue today to affect the way kabuki plays are performed and organized. Actors can, of course, saddle a kabuki performance with absurdities in their quest to show themselves off in interesting ways. Actors have a terrible penchant for playing multiple roles in kabuki. *Chūshingura* is a favorite play in this regard because of the many excellent and varied roles that are spread through the long day's performance. It was a commonplace from the beginning for actors to play two or three roles in *Chūshingura*. It was a credit to the actor's versatility to be able to carry off the feat of portraying five or six characters. Examples of this are numerous. *Chūshingura* at the Kado Theater in Osaka in 1863 boasted Onoe Baisha in six roles, Kataoka Gatō in six roles as well, and Kawarazaki Gonjūrō in five.[48] As early as 1802 Ichikawa Danzō IV played seven roles in *Chūshingura*, a record that has been equaled a number of times but never, to my knowledge, surpassed.[49] In his seven roles in an 1828 production, Bandō Minosuke appropriated for himself the choice parts of Moronao, Yuranosuke, Hangan, Kampei, Kampei's father, Sadakurō, and Honzō.[50]

An actor could play several roles in one scene by wearing and discarding in rapid sequence special quick-change *(hayagawari)* costumes. Actors especially came to enjoy playing the thief Sadakurō and Kampei's father, whom he kills, in the highwayman scene (Act V), using quick-change. In a 1961 production, Jitsukawa Enjaku III (then Enjirō) changed from Sadakurō to the father and back again to Sadakurō without leaving the audiences' sight. And it was done in a perfectly natural way. His father, Enjaku II, and Danzō IV often used quick-change in this scene so that they could play not only Sadakurō and Kampei's father, but Kampei as well—three roles in this short scene.[51] Scenes came to be rewritten to accommodate the needs of quick-change, especially to prevent the simultaneous appearance on stage of two characters which one actor might be playing. One of the most drastic cases was when, due to the illness of other actors, Bandō Mitsugorō was forced to play both Hangan and Yuranosuke in Hangan's suicide scene in the summer production of 1803 at the Nakamura Theater in Edo. By using quick-change, Mitsugorō as Hangan was able to exit into an inner room to commit suicide and then moments later appear on the *hanamichi* as Yuranosuke rushing to meet his master.[52] The audience was deprived of seeing Hangan's suicide and the moving scene between master and retainer could not take place, but at least the production did not have to be cancelled.

Although quick-change is a theatrical trick, it need not be detrimental to an honest performance. The related practice of several actors dividing one role, however, is an absurdity that has no artistic justification. Yet, in performances today one is more likely than not to see Yuranosuke acted by, say, Matsumoto Kōshirō in Hangan's suicide scene and by Onoe Shōroku in the Ichiriki Brothel scene. Or Okaru will be played by Nakamura Utaemon in early scenes and by Onoe Baikō in late scenes. Even Bannai will be played by different actors in consecutive scenes. No attempt is made by the actors to interpret the role similarly, or even to look alike.

The overriding emphasis upon the person of the actor in kabuki is usually attributed—by Japanese commentators—to the desire to show off the actor's ''physical attractiveness'' *(nikutai miryoku)*. Undoubtedly a high degree of narcissistic egoism is involved in the kabuki acting profession. Yet, there is, it seems, more to it than this. Kabuki acting style is legitimately based on using the physical possibilities of the human body. Its aesthetic of performance is centered on projecting human character and feeling through the total physical form. Centering in the abdomen and the pelvis *(koshi)*, the actor uses breath control *(ki)* and deliberate phrasing of movements with exactly delineated pauses *(ma)* to create a powerful image of control on stage. The aims of these techniques are, in fact, not dissimilar to the focusing, centering, and breath control practiced in *aikidō*— literally the ''way of breath control''—and other Japanese martial arts. The fundamental posture of the kabuki actor on stage is one of repose. From this basic state of rest, which nonetheless contains within it great power, the actor moves outward in a limited number of clear-cut, sharp, and highly expressive actions. These actions may be of the arms, or stamps and cocking of the legs, or a sudden violent facial expression, or they may be combined. The significant fact is that they arise out of the power center of a settled, almost rigid torso, and when they occur they are perceived as radiating out from that powerful center.[53]

This is a very different concept of acting from that followed by the Western actor, who uses face and hands in great detail, but separated from the torso. And it is almost exactly opposite to the way the puppet moves in jōruri performance. Because the puppet is inanimate, as soon as it ceases to move it becomes completely inexpressive; it is then just an assemblage of wood and cloth, paint and strings. Therefore, the speaking puppet is in virtual nonstop motion: a hand gesture, a cock of the head, raising the eyebrows, settling the torso, looking over with the eyes, shifting the direction of the body, moving the head, adjusting the kimono, and so on, to match the dialogue or narrative from the chanter. In this sense, the movement sequence of the puppet is more like real life than the centered repose of the kabuki actor on stage. Kabuki repose is not the way people act in "real life," but represents a stylization of life. In brief, the jōruri movement pattern is continuous, detailed, even fussy, while the kabuki movement pattern is occasional, large in scale, clean, and strong.

When *Chūshingura* is performed by kabuki actors it is natural that their well-defined acting style would shape the dramatic material to suit that acting style. In many places details of puppet actions have been stripped away to fit the kabuki concept of performance. Two lines before the end of the jōruri text, the narrative describes Rikiya drawing his sword and killing Yakushiji and Bannai, lopping off the latter's legs with a single blow. This action is never performed in kabuki. Instead, the kabuki play will end with Yuranosuke and the massed retainers standing before Ryōgoku Bridge in a powerful group pose *(hippari mie)* as the curtain closes, or else moving in a silent procession down the *hanamichi* and out of sight. It is also common to cut lines from the jōruri text in order to free the actor for physical expression. An example that is often cited is Nakamura Nakazō I's portrayal of Sadakurō in a performance in 1766. In the jōruri text, Sadakurō has the largest number of speeches of any character in the highwayman scene, but Nakazō cut every line and acted the role completely in mime. His performance created a sensation and actors have followed this *kata,* or pattern, of playing the role ever since.[54]

Similarly, the gate scene which follows Hangan's suicide has been extensively reworked so that the actor playing Yuranosuke is able to give physical rather than verbal expression to the character's surging emotions. The basic action of the scene is simple: Hangan's retainers rush on to defend their deceased master's mansion, but they are intercepted by Yuranosuke and persuaded to retire. In jōruri this is accomplished directly: Yuranosuke takes out the bloody dagger with which Hangan has killed himself and explains that they will now gain vengeance. The retainers are overjoyed. They shout their agreement and retire to fight another day. But in kabuki, Yuranosuke gives the retainers no explanation of his intentions. He forces them back through his glowering physical presence and his threat to commit *seppuku* if they do not obey. He then poses in a fierce stance *(mie)* in which he glares them down. They go off unconvinced but cowed. The scene in jōruri ends with the retainers' exit; in kabuki, the conclusion of the scene may take up to fifteen minutes to perform and consists of a two-part solo mime by Yuranosuke. The first part is accompanied by jōruri singing, "The suicide blade, red with blood, cries out for revenge. . . . Burning tears rake his heart, tears . . . falling . . . falling . . . falling.'' During this Yuranosuke takes out Hangan's suicide dagger, licks his master's blood as an oath, gestures cutting off Moronao's head, and prepares to depart. In jōruri the accompanying narrative passage occurs in the previous scene, when Yuranosuke is prying the dagger from Hangan's death grip. The change in kabuki is effective. Because Yuranosuke is alone on stage he can express his deep emotions more extensively in mime than he can while under the watchful eyes of the shōgun's envoys in the jōruri version.

The second part begins with Yuranosuke crossing slowly from the main stage toward the *hanamichi,* the rampway that leads through the audience to the rear of the theater and is a unique feature of the kabuki stage. He does not speak, there is no narration. This seemingly simple cross is a major challenge for an actor. In silence and deep in thought, Yuranosuke takes one tentative step, then another. Three times he pauses and turns back, looking remorsefully at the mansion that is receding from view. Each thoughtful pose *(omoiire)* expresses a different combination of emotions: anguish at his master's death, chagrin that he arrived so late, sadness at leaving the mansion, fury at Moronao, determination to carry out the secret revenge. The melancholy cawing of crows is heard in the distance. A temple bell tolls. He reaches the *hanamichi* and there, overcome by grief, slips to his knees. He bows deeply toward the site of Hangan's death out of respect. He rises and begins to leave, stops, and turns back for one last glimpse of the mansion. Then, as music resumes, he strides with increasing determination off the *hanamichi* and out of sight. This marvelously effective closing sequence relies wholly on the actor's powers of physical expression and projection. We should note that this long, mimed sequence accurately expresses Yuranosuke's psychological state; it is not a case of self-indulgence by the actor. Because Yuranosuke cannot reveal his secret plan, his emotions remain repressed, and these repressed emotions sustain the scene through to its end. If he spoke out as he does in jōruri, the emotional tension he feels would be released and the scene would quickly end, as it does in jōruri. It is said that the basic acting *kata* for Yuranosuke in this scene was set by Nakamura Utaemon III in 1809 and was carried down into this century by Danjūrō IX. Before Utaemon's *kata,* it was usual for Yuranosuke to pose center stage, as in jōruri, as the curtain was closed in front of him.[55] The actor who thought of moving the narration about the blade to this scene was

Onoe Kikugorō I (1717-1783). The kabuki version of the scene is now often performed in puppet productions as well.[56]

Similarly, kabuki actors have changed the dramatic import of the sequence in the Ichiriki Brothel in which Rikiya delivers Lady Kaoyo's secret letter to Yuranosuke. This has been done by adding a few short lines of dialogue and by emphasizing mimed expression. The scene in jōruri is brief and to the point. Rikiya meets Yuranosuke, passes him the letter, and reveals its contents: "The enemy Moronao's petition to return to the country has been granted. Soon he will depart for home. She says that all the details are in her letter." And Rikiya leaves. In kabuki the scene is expanded to hint at, rather than tell about, the conspiracy. The whispered conference between father and son takes place at a garden gate that is placed on the *hanamichi*. This forces Rikiya to cross the long distance from the gate to the room where Yuranosuke is pretending to be drunkenly asleep and then cross back again, and Yuranosuke must follow. While crossing neither speaks. Rikiya shows his anxiety and alertness to danger by stopping several times and looking about. He crosses through the gate, kneels, and keeps watch on the road behind him. Yuranosuke approaches slowly, staggering drunkenly this way and that, covertly searching for spies that might be watching. Rikiya says only, "Soon, soon our enemy . . ." before Yuranosuke cuts him off by singing a snatch of a nō song. Yuranosuke staggers in a circle as he sings, once more looking about. Rikiya realizes his indiscretion; he covers his mouth with his hands and peers into the darkness in the opposite direction. Finally, when Rikiya firmly grasps the hilts of his swords and turns to leave, Yuranosuke calls him back saying enigmatically, "Be careful while passing through the quarter." Rikiya covers the hilts of his swords with his kimono sleeves and folds them out of sight against his breast. Then he delicately dances down the *hanamichi* and off. From Rikiya's actions we understand that Yuranosuke's message was, "If you walk proudly like a samurai you will be noticed and our plan will be discovered, so hide who you are and what you are doing."

What was a straightforward expository scene in jōruri has become a scene of delicately masked motives in which physical actions and reactions express unspoken meanings. Cutting off Rikiya's line, preventing an explanation of the letter, singing the nō lyric to throw any observer off the track, and hinting that Rikiya must deport himself in a surreptitious manner all add to the suspense of this short, but indelible, moment in the play. Again, we can note that these are not gratuitous changes based on the whims of the actors. They are excellently chosen means to convey the sense of secrecy and conspiracy which lies at the heart of the scene.

The *mie,* a strong physical pose, is unique to kabuki theater. There are hundreds of different *mie,* but typically the actor plants his feet in a firm position, sets his torso, cocks his arms outward, rotates the head, and freezes motionless for several seconds. The actor draws all of his energy inward, centers it in the motionless body, and in that "frozen moment" projects the full force of his character's physical presence out to the audience. In the strongest of *mie,* one eye is crossed over the other *(nirami)* for added force. The *mie* is then relaxed and the scene continues. The *mie* is used for those moments of highest dramatic tension in a scene. It is a remarkable acting technique. Rarely in world theater has motionlessness been used so effectively. (By way of contrast, the puppet, in the same moment of high emotion, will continuously shake its head; it dare *not* be motionless.)

Many high points in *Chūshingura* are expressed through *mie.* As the fiercest character in the play, Moronao shows his contempt for Wakasanosuke at the conclusion of the Hachiman Shrine scene by striking a *mie,* one leg forward on the steps, his arms whipped outward and then pointing at Wakasanosuke. His face contorts into a vicious sneer and he glares at his rival. In the Pine Room scene Moronao caps the taunts of his "tadpole" speech with an unusual seated *mie:* he leans back on his haunches, arches his back, points malevolently at Hangan with a fan held in his right hand while his left hand circles overhead and strikes the floor with a slap, cocks his head, opens his mouth, and crosses one eye over the other. The *mie* that Yuranosuke uses to stop the rampaging retainers in the gate scene is more restrained: he stands with feet together, draws himself up straight, runs his right hand up the edge of his vest, locks his head forward, and poses. Bannai has several *mie,* his bent knees and exaggerated head movements creating a comic effect. Kampei is a refined young hero *(nimaime),* so his *mie* during the group battle in the fugitive travel scene are small in scale and delicate.

It is a common staging technique to conclude a kabuki scene with characters posed in a group *mie (hippari mie)* as the curtain is closed. *Chūshingura* is staged with a number of these curtain tableaus. The Hachiman Shrine scene ends with Moronao and Wakasanosuke (and sometimes with Hangan as well) holding *mie* poses. We see Hangan clenching his fists and posing, surrounded by provincial lords, as the curtain closes on the Pine Room scene. The curtain tableau of the Ichiriki Brothel scene is especially elaborate: Yurano-suke mounts the steps and flicks his opened fan overhead; Okaru follows him, kneels by his side, and places her hands on his sash; Heiemon hoists the nearly dead Kudayū onto his back, plants his left foot forward, cocks his head, and poses. Each holds motionless as the curtain is closed. The effectiveness of the *mie* is heightened by the sharp sound of wooden clappers *(tsuke)* beating two or three times on a board placed on the stage floor. The curtain, as well, is opened and closed to sharp, penetrating clacks of another set of wooden clappers *(ki* or *hyōshigi).* Words, as a rule, do not support the *mie,* but aesthetically pleasing sound effects do.

Special curtains and the *hanamichi* are staging devices that help place a unique stamp on kabuki performances. When the main kabuki draw curtain is pushed open to begin the fugitive travel scene, we see behind it another light blue curtain *(asagi maku).* A phrase of music plays in the background as we look intently at the blank curtain. Then, one clack of the *ki* is heard as a signal. The blue curtain is released at the top and it falls to the ground. In an instant is revealed the full scene of Mt. Fuji—with acres of cherry trees bursting in bloom, and the lovers, Okaru and Kampei, posed with their faces hidden behind a straw hat. The audience feels an instant rush of excitement, which would not occur with a usual slow-moving curtain opening. At the end of the scene the draw curtain is pulled directly into the path of Bannai, who is running to catch Okaru standing on the *hanamichi.* He bumps into the curtain, spins around, bumps it again, spins again. Then with a good-natured laugh, he grabs the curtain in both hands and runs it closed himself. The main curtain is closed behind Yuranosuke when he moves onto the *hanamichi* in the gate scene. Since the mansion is no longer visible, the audience gives its full attention to Yuranosuke now kneeling in the midst of the audience. Isolating the character in this way, called acting "outside the curtain" *(maku soto),* is reserved for the single most important solo moment in any play.

One of the appeals of the *hanamichi* is that it encourages a feeling of intimacy by placing the character among the spectators. This is certainly true of Yuranosuke's scene on the *hanamichi* just described. Placing the conspiracy scene between Rikiya and Yuranosuke on the *hanamichi* heightens that feeling. When Okaru stands on the *hanamichi* in the rendezvous scene to tell of her errand, her youth and vulnerability seem more apparent. On the other hand, a sense of spectacle and sweeping action results when a group moves swiftly into a scene or out of it along the *hanamichi*. Bannai's fighting chorus marches on in a colorful parade, and then runs off pell-mell in terror when Kampei defeats them. Tadayoshi's exit in the Hachiman Shrine scene is turned into a formal procession: he walks down the steps of the platform on which he has been seated, stops center facing the audience, flicks out his sleeves, turns, crosses the width of the stage, and moves with deliberate steps down the *hanamichi,* followed by a dozen or more provincial lords and retainers walking at the same measured pace.[57] This is followed by equally deliberate mime sequences in which Hangan, Wakasanosuke, and Kaoyo, in turn, ask Moronao's permission to leave. There is no jōruri narration. There is no dialogue. The only sound is the slow beating of two drums and piercing notes of the flute from offstage kabuki musicians playing stately "Departure" ("Sagariha"). Why is this ten-minute scene, played without words, so effective? It is not difficult to see that we, as spectators, are encouraged to pay unusually close attention to the mimed actions precisely because they are not given a verbal explanation. We concentrate on what is happening because of the silence. And we are asked to interpret the actions ourselves. This is fundamentally different from the jōruri style of theater where the meanings of actions are constantly explained in the narrative and the spectator is not required to infer meaning for himself.

Another way to identify the different approaches of jōruri and kabuki to staging *Chūshingura* is to note some short jōruri sequences that have not found favor with kabuki actors. Here are three examples. First, Hangan's retainers in the vendetta are described in jōruri narration as killing Moronao as follows: "They leap and jump excitedly in the air. . . . Ecstatic with joy they even dance. . . . All together they strike the head, they bite it, weeping with happiness." The bloody head of Moronao is then washed and placed on a stand before a table dedicated to Hangan's spirit. A second example is from the Ichiriki Brothel scene. Heiemon is described in the jōruri narration as follows: "drawing his sword, he instantly leaps up, slashing Kudayū in strokes two and three inches long, until no part of his body is left uncut." The third example occurs in Hangan's suicide scene where the narration tells us that when Kaoyo views her husband, "she clings to his dead body, wailing, heedless of everything."[58]

What these passages have in common is that they describe intense emotional outbursts and actions that are violent, even grotesque. Normally, none of the actions described here are performed in kabuki, and by comparison the parallel kabuki scenes are models of restraint. In kabuki Hangan's men in the vendetta comport themselves with dignity. They do not leap for joy, nor bite Moronao's head; in fact, we do not see any retainer touch the head until it is wrapped in a white cloth. Heiemon does not use his sword on Kudayū; he does not even draw it. And although Kaoyo does weep in grief, she does so quietly, without approaching, let alone embracing, the corpse of Hangan. A high level of emotionalism is appropriate in the art of the puppet theater; it is through the infusion of powerful emotions that the puppet figures are brought to life. But it would seem that kabuki shies away from jōruri's extreme of emotional expression in favor of the actor projecting a physical image of control and stylized beauty through which the emotion, though still intense, is filtered.

Certain kabuki language and vocal forms have been written into the script for *Chūshingura* over the years, and a number of these can easily be identified in performance. A line of dialogue will be divided among several characters to show that they share the same thought. Usually the final phrase of the line is spoken in unison. In Hangan's suicide scene all the retainers feel as one when they say:

RETAINER: We, Lord Hangan's retainers, beg permission to see our
    master . . .
ALL RETAINERS: . . . one last time.

Or in the gate scene when they respond to Yakushiji's taunts:

RETAINER: Do you . . .
ALL RETAINERS: . . . hear that?

The vendetta concludes with a longer sequence of interconnected lines in which all the speakers share the same thoughts and feelings. The technique is called "passed-along dialogue" *(watarizerifu)*.

YURANOSUKE: Deep concerns like drifted snow, melt in the clear of
    day . . .
RIKIYA: . . . at last our long awaited, vengeance is achieved . . .
GOEMON: . . . together with the clearing, of the morning
    clouds . . .
AKAGAKI: . . . at the cock's crow announcing, dawn of a new
    day . . .
TAKEMORI: . . . our hearts filled to overflowing, rise with the rising
    sun . . .

GOEMON: . . . as we go together to . . .
ALL: . . . our Lord Hangan's grave.
YURANOSUKE: Shout victory together! Victory!
ALL: Victory![59]

It is easy to see why lines like these do not appear in jōruri texts. A single chanter would find it difficult to make the vocal distinction between the characters which the technique requires. And the single chanter cannot speak a unison line. Neither can he deliver the rapid, overlapped lines that are designed to "raise up" *(kuriage)* emotional tension between two characters, as in the "Your hand! My hand? Yes, your hand!" sequence between Moronao and Hangan in the Pine Room scene that has been added to kabuki performance. As wonderfully effective as these three short lines are in boosting the emotional temperature of the confrontation, the sequence would be unnatural in jōruri. (Only in a scene staged with multiple chanters, like the Ichiriki Brothel scene, are lines divided in jōruri.)

One of kabuki's most beautiful vocal techniques is heard when characters speak dialogue composed in phrases of seven and five syllables *(shichigochō)*. Narrative sections in jōruri, and songs in nō drama as well, are commonly written in lines of seven and five syllables, but because they are accompanied by music and are chanted or sung, the spectator in the theater is scarcely aware of their metrical pattern. However, in kabuki the passages of *shichigochō* are a part of the dialogue and are spoken in a gently rhythmic fashion that makes the seven-five metrical pattern clear to the listener. The great nō actor Zeami advised performers in the fourteenth century that strictly adhering to a regular seven-five syllable count would make a poem monotonous, and it is usual for *shichigochō* in kabuki to contain some irregular phrases of four, six, or eight syllables. *Shichigochō* is used for important sequences of passed-along dialogue in *Chūshingura*. One of the major objects of the technique is to give the speeches a formal beauty. The final lines in the vendetta just quoted are in *shichigochō*. When Heiemon speaks tenderly to Okaru in the Ichiriki Brothel scene, his speech is also in *shichigochō:* "Once you were a samurai, now a courtesan; combing out your silken hair, while the world has changed; precious sister how pitiful; totally unaware of the life you left behind!"

Improvisation is an important aspect of kabuki performance. But performers in jōruri cannot ever improvise because the timing of samisen, chanting, and puppet movement must be predetermined.

In *Chūshingura* we find many improvised sections indicated in the kabuki text by such terms as: "ad-lib" *(sutezerifu);* "appropriate business" *(yoroshiku atte);* "improvised business" *(iroiro atte);* and "actor's choice" *(mitate).* Nine such directions are found in the Ichiriki Brothel scene alone. The maids and the male geisha fill the time it takes them to come on or go off stage with a constant stream of ad-libbed chatter. Yuranosuke ad-libs lines such as, "I'll be back, girls. Don't go away. I'm going into the garden for some air"—really, anything he wants to say—to cover his cross to Rikiya at the gate on the *hanamichi.* Later with Okaru he keeps up a continuous, low-key flow of ad-libbing while he goes up the steps into the room and out through the curtain to see the brothel owner about her contract. When Heiemon draws his sword and Okaru flees onto the *hanamichi,* the printed kabuki text contains a few lines of dialogue followed by the stage direction "the actors ad-lib."[60] It is expected that the actors will make up the necessary lines to fill the time it takes Okaru to rise, cross through the gate, pick up Heiemon's swords, carry them out of reach, and return to kneel beside her brother. Okaru and Heiemon ad-lib in half a dozen other places in the scene as well (although this is not indicated in the text), usually to fill junctures between sections. One example occurs when Heiemon realizes Yuranosuke's intention to kill Okaru. In the printed text, he says simply, "Please forgive me," as he turns to the interior of the room and bows to Yuranosuke. In performance, however, Heiemon, tremendously excited, pours out a torrent of words, something like, "Indeed, forgive me. How could I have thought that my master. . . . Ah, it is too much. I was wrong, terribly wrong. Yes, I was. Forgive me, please. Forgive me. What a happy moment, dear sister. Wait until I tell you. Ah, just wait. It is such a splendid thing. It is. Your life, dear sister. You see. . . ." Simultaneously, Okaru ad-libs her uncomprehending reactions.[61] Ad-libbing is extremely effective in such a situation. Heiemon is agitated and Okaru confused, so the rapid, overlapping lines correctly express their state of mind. But it is difficult to carry off. *Sutezerifu* has to continue without hesitation or break to keep the scene moving forward; yet at the same time it should be casual, "throw away" patter that will not call attention to itself. One person's speech should meld perfectly into another's, neither cutting it off nor leaving a gap.

Bannai's "ahem" routine was once an ad-lib section, and it is usually called *sutezerifu,* but in fact it is now no longer actually improvised on stage as the lines in the situations just described are. Similarly, when Okaru tells Heiemon that his face is frightening and he replies that he can't help it because it is the face he was born with, these are *sutezerifu* lines that actors once created and theoretically they could be changed by actors today. In both cases, however, the lines worked so well they became traditional and are now rarely altered. The songs and dances which the maids and male geisha perform for Yuranosuke in the Ichiriki Brothel are "actor's choice." That is, the actor can decide which song or dance he will do. But once the choice is made, the scene is rehearsed and set (the maids also ad-lib chatter between the set numbers).

The kabuki text of *Chūshingura* also indicates numerous places in which the actor is to improvise appropriate actions—poses *(mie, kimari,* or *omoiire)*, reactions, and other stage business. At the conclusion of the fugitive travel scene, while Bannai is chasing Okaru and Kampei, the text reads, "during this Kampei and Okaru act as they wish."[62] In the gate scene some of Yuranosuke's mime is described in detail. Still, within the dagger sequence and during the cross to the *hanamichi,* the text twice indicates the actor is to improvise "appropriate business."[63] Battles are rechoreographed according to the needs of each production and this is indicated in the play text. The danced battle between Kampei and Bannai's fighting chorus will change, production by production, but in any case it is complex and made up of a score or more of movement sequences. The stage direction merely reads, "there is a dance battle as appropriate."[64] Heiemon's attempt to kill Okaru and her responses are laconically indicated by the direction "there is an appropriate stage fight between the two."[65] What we see on stage, however, may be Okaru falling back, Heiemon striking three times, Okaru dodging, Okaru rising and pushing Heiemon, Heiemon falling back and recovering, Heiemon raising his sword, Okaru throwing paper in his face, Heiemon falling back, and Okaru fleeing. These, and many other improvised scenes in *Chūshingura,* are all kabuki additions.

Over the years perhaps as much as one-third of the original jō-ruri chanting and samisen instrumental music has been replaced by kabuki styles of music. It is standard in kabuki performances for exits, entrances, and fighting scenes to be accompanied by the light-sounding *nagauta* samisen, nō drums and flute, the large kabuki drum *(ōdaiko),* and various gongs, bells, and other instruments played offstage right (and hence known as *geza,* or "offstage right" music).[66] We have noted before that when Tadayoshi leaves Hachiman Shrine and Hangan, Wakasanosuke, and Kaoyo take leave of

Moronao in pantomime, a dignified and somewhat suspenseful mood is created by *geza* drums and flute playing "Departure" ("Sagariha"). This musical pattern is taken from nō and is associated in the audience's mind, through long use, with the appearance or the departure of an imperial aristocrat. Offstage *nagauta* singers establish the atmosphere of the Gion licensed quarter as the curtain opens on the Ichiriki Brothel scene by singing the well-known courtesan's song "If You Play in the Flowers" ("Hana ni Asobaba"). The melody from this song, usually called "Dance Melody" ("Odoriji Aikata"), is played by the offstage *geza* samisen throughout the scene: when Heiemon appears, each time the maids and the male geisha rush on or off stage, quietly in the background under the dialogue, and for the closing curtain tableau. Yuranosuke's exit in the gate scene is accompanied by the melody "Farewell" ("Okuri Sanjū"), played solo by the lead samisen player in the *geza*.

In some performances the importance of this music is highlighted by bringing the samisen player onstage. After the curtain has been closed behind Yuranosuke, the right corner is pulled back to allow the drummers and flute player in the *geza* to see Yuranosuke through the slits cut in the scenery and to give the samisen player room on stage. He places his foot on a stool, rests the samisen on his raised knee, and begins to play. He starts with an elaborate introductory passage, rather like a cadenza in a concerto, which the audience invariably applauds. Only then does Yuranosuke begin his exit accompanied by the samisen and the unseen drums and flute.

In the vendetta almost all jōruri music has been replaced by offstage kabuki melodies and rhythms associated with fighting: members of Moronao's household flee across stage to "Triple Beat" ("Mitsudaiko") on the large drum; "Searching Melody" ("Shirabe Aikata") is played by the samisen as Hangan's retainers hunt for Moronao; samisen play "Ghastly Melody" ("Sugomi") during slow individual combats; and drums, flute, and samisen combine to play the lively "Chūya Aikata" during rapid group sword fights. These songs, melodies, and rhythmic patterns are part of the *geza* repertory of more than five hundred musical selections that are appropriate to one or another scene type, character type, or situation and may be called on, as desired, when *Chūshingura* is being performed in kabuki.[67]

Kiyomoto music accompanies the fugitive travel scene from beginning to end. *Kiyomoto* is one style of kabuki dance music (other important styles are *katōbushi, tomimoto* and *tokiwazu*).[68] Music and the lyrics for this scene were composed for the 1833 kabuki production and have been used ever since. The group of ten or more *kiyomoto* singers and samisen players sit on stage on a raised platform in full view of the audience. Although technically a narrative style of music, *kiyomoto* is noted for its sweet, melodious, and somewhat voluptuous sound, and hence it is especially appropriate for a dance scene between young lovers. *Kiyomoto* music is never heard in jōruri. Because offstage *nagauta*-style songs and melodies and *kiyomoto* dance music are heard in addition to the usual heavy, emotional jōruri music, the kabuki performance of *Chūshingura* encompasses a much wider range of mood than does the puppet performance of the play. Overall, the atmosphere is considerably lighter. It is interesting to note that the scene which is considered the most "jōruri-like" in kabuki performances does not use kabuki music at all. This is the scene of Hangan's suicide, the most serious scene in the play. The most suitable musical accompaniment for the preparations for Hangan's death, the suicide, and the mourning by Yuranosuke and Kaoyo is the original jōruri chanting and its somber samisen accompaniment.

In the Pine Room when Moronao confronts first Wakasanosuke and then Hangan we can see several processes working together to create a scene that is different in many respects from the jōruri original. Although the kabuki version of the Pine Room scene follows the jōruri text in general, there are many changes. Wakasanosuke takes as his own line the narrative comment that he wants to "cut in half that damned Moronao," and Bannai and Moronao both are given additional lines as they try to mollify the furious Wakasanosuke. Moronao's wonderfully funny comment, after Wakasanosuke departs, "A sword in a fool's hand makes the wise man cautious," is a kabuki addition. In kabuki, Honzō is not shown reacting with relief that Wakasanosuke is safe. Instead Moronao ad-libs a humorous bit in which he continues to bow obsequiously long after Wakasanosuke is gone. After Hangan's entrance, most of the short lines of narrative describing his and Moronao's actions are cut, and during their confrontation most of the jōruri samisen music is replaced by the *geza* stick drum *(taiko)* playing measured, suspenseful beats of nō-style "Slow Dance" ("Jo no Mai") behind the dialogue.

The major kabuki alteration occurs at the scene's climax. At the point where Hangan is called a "tadpole" a number of wholly new incidents are added that postpone the moment when Hangan draws his sword. First, Moronao expands on his taunting speech: he sneers that Hangan looks like a toad because his eyes are bulging so; he calls Bannai to come and look at the ridiculous sight; he strikes Hangan on the chest with his fan; he laughs that Hangan is a "samurai toad"; he pulls back and poses in a fierce seated *mie*. Next, Hangan responds and the two challenge each other in a *kuriage* sequence of short lines:

HANGAN: Then from the beginning, do you mean the insulting words you have said?

Surya, saizen yori no zōgon wa honshō de oiyatta ka?

MORONAO: Oh, I mean them. And if I mean them, what do you intend to do?

O, honshō da. Honshō naraba, omiya, dō suru no da?

HANGAN: If you mean them . . .

Honshō naraba . . .

MORONAO: If I mean them . . .

Honshō naraba . . .

HANGAN: Ahh!

Mū!

This can be compared with the jōruri original, which is shorter and does not contain a *kuriage* sequence:

HANGAN: Then your insulting words, just now, you can't mean them.

Surya, ima no akugon wa, honshō yo na.

MORONAO: You are tiresome, tiresome. And if I mean them, what will you do?

Kudoi, kudoi. Mata, honshō narya, dō suru?

HANGAN: I'll do this . . .

Kō suru . . .

At this point in the puppet play Hangan draws his sword and strikes Moronao; the kabuki scene is far from over, however. Hangan starts to draw his sword, but Moronao pulls back shouting furiously that he must stop or his house will be ruined. Hangan pauses. Moronao leans against Hangan's sword hilts, goading him again and again to draw, to kill him. Hangan apologizes, but when Moronao insultingly ignores him, he again reaches for his sword. There is another *kuriage* sequence, "Your hand! My hand? Yes, your hand! This hand . . . ," that concludes with Hangan apologizing a second time. Gloating in his victory, Moronao says he will instruct only Wakasanosuke. He tears up Kaoyo's letter and throws it in Hangan's face calling him a "provincial barbarian." He deliberately flicks first one trailing trouser leg in Hangan's face then the other, and he turns to leave. Hangan plants himself firmly on Moronao's trousers, jerking him to a stop. They exchange a third *kuriage* sequence, "Is there something you want? What I want is. . . . What you want is? . . . You!" At last Hangan whips out his sword and strikes Moronao, trying to kill him.

These added incidents are utterly gripping and they are true to kabuki performing style in that they depend upon the actor's physical expressiveness, as well as voice, for their effectiveness. In the final moments of the scene, Honzō and a number of provincial lords rush on to restrain Hangan. Honzō's speech in the jōruri text and Hangan's scream, "I'll cut you in two, damn you Moronao! Hands off, Honzō! Take your hands off me!" are cut. Instead, the scene ends on a curtain tableau: Hangan is surrounded and held tightly in a circle of restraining hands. His grasping fingers slowly clench. His chest heaves in anguish. The curtain is run closed while the *geza* drums and flute furiously play "Fast Dance" ("Haya Mai"). The final words of the jōruri narration are sung during the curtain, but in the din they are scarcely heard. In all, more than forty lines of text have been added or altered and a dozen new units of action added in kabuki performance of this act.

In considering the changes which kabuki actors and writers and choreographers have wrought in *Kanadehon Chūshingura* over the years, it is necessary to recognize the particular point of view from which such changes have been made. Through the first three hundred years of its history, kabuki was a contemporary theater form. It was simply "theater" in the Japanese context, always striving to be up-to-date. In spite of a strong tendency for acting families to develop and preserve their unique acting styles, such as the *aragoto* style of the Ichikawa family, each production was intended to be unlike any previous production. Even when a well-known play was performed, the aim was not to produce a "faithful revival," as a Westerner might assume, but rather to see what interesting variations could be rung on a familiar theme. It is this approach to kabuki drama which accounts for the fact that the most popular plays exist in many versions. There are more than a score of versions of the often-performed dance drama *Dōjō Temple (Dōjōji)*.[69] The *aragoto*-style play *Wait a Moment! (Shibaraku)* exists in countless versions deriving from the more than two hundred and twenty productions that the play has had since it was created in 1697 by Danjūrō I.[70]

While it is true that plays taken over from jōruri tend to be more unchanging than "pure" kabuki plays, nonetheless the prevailing inclination to make each kabuki production different affects these plays as well. The kabuki actor was happy to steal *Chūshingura* from the puppet theater, but he considered himself a creative as much as an interpretive artist, and if the original was worth taking in the first place it was worth the application of his creative imagination as well. For a rough parallel in American arts, we have to turn to the jazz musician. Working within a known musical idiom with other artists equally familiar with that idiom, he can improvise at will. And he would certainly consider it a sign of creative failure were he to perform a composition twice the same way. Today, of course, kabuki has become a classic theater form. Present-day actors rarely improvise, even in so-called ad-lib sections. When they perform *Chūshingura* they will reproduce the acting *kata* and follow the texts of scenes as they were developed by actors of the last century. But during the one hundred and fifty years—from 1750 to 1900—that kabuki remained a dynamic and changing theater form, kabuki artists constantly reworked *Chūshingura,* and in the process they ever more completely "kabuki-ized" their stolen jōruri prize.

Chūshingura is perhaps the most beloved kabuki play in the repertory today. It is performed, in full or shortened versions, in most theater seasons. Its famous scenes are known even by those who have but a nodding acquaintance with Japanese theater. And the best of the changes which have been created for kabuki are now so firmly identified with the play that they are often borrowed back in puppet performances. This is the best evidence, should any be needed, that far from being arbitrary or frivolous, most of the kabuki changes have served to increase *Chūshingura*'s effectiveness as a theatrical work.

NOTES

1.   Kawatake Shigetoshi, *Nihon Engeki Zenshi* (Tokyo: Iwanami Shoten, 1959), pp. 479–480.

2.   Ihara Toshirō, comp., *Kabuki Nempyō,* 8 vols. (Tokyo: Iwanami Shoten, 1956–1963), 3:30.

3.   Ibid., p. 41.

4.   Toita Yasuji, *Chūshingura* (Tokyo: Sogensha, 1961), p. 234.

5.   For a detailed study of another example of kabuki borrowing, see Stanleigh H. Jones, Jr., "Miracle at Yaguchi Ferry: A Japanese Puppet Play and Its Metamorphosis to Kabuki," *Harvard Journal of Asiatic Studies* 38 (June 1978): 171–189.

6.   Oscar Brockett, *The Theatre: An Introduction* (New York: Holt, Rinehart, and Winston, 1974), p. 307; and Japanese National Commission for UNESCO, *Theatre in Japan* (Tokyo: Ministry of Finance, 1963), pp. 85–169.

7. Sakae Shioya, *Chūshingura: An Exposition* (Tokyo: Hokuseido, 1956), p. 228.
8. Ibid., p. 230.
9. Suwa Haruo, *Genroku Kabuki no Kenkyū* (Tokyo: Kasama Shoin, 1967), p. 65.
10. Takano Tatsuyuki, ed., *Genroku Kabuki Kessakushū* (Tokyo: Waseda Daigaku Shuppanbu, 1939), 1:158.
11. Shuzui Kenji, *Yakusha Rongo* (Tokyo: Tokyo Daigaku, 1963), p. 110. Also in English, in Charles J. Dunn, ed., and Bunzō Torigoe, trans., *The Actors' Analects* (New York: Columbia University Press, 1969), p. 112.
12. Watsuji Tetsurō, *Nihon Geijitsushi Kenkyū* (Tokyo: Iwanami Shoten, 1959), p. 407.
13. As Watsuji points out, several events—separated in time by not less than sixty-two years—have been brought together in the single description, casting doubt on its accuracy. The stage debut of Danjūrō I was in 1673, while Danjūrō II took the name Ebizō in 1735. (Ibid., pp. 408–411.)
14. Suwa, *Genroku Kabuki*, pp. 43–46.
15. Ibid., pp. 55–64.
16. Chikamatsu's first kabuki play was probably written in 1684, by which time Tōjūrō had already played the important *wagoto* role of Izaemon at least five times. (Ihara, *Kabuki Nempyō* 1:132.)
17. See Takano Masami, *Chikamatsu to Sono Dentō Geinō* (Tokyo: Kodansha, 1965), pp. 93–101, for titles and dates of Chikamatsu's kabuki plays.
18. Suwa Haruo, *Chikamatsu Sewa Jōruri no Kenkyū* (Tokyo: Kasama Shoin, 1974), pp. 28–29.
19. Kawatake, *Nihon Engeki Zenshi*, p. 610.
20. Ihara, *Kabuki Nempyō*, 1:467–479.
21. Ibid., p. 473.
22. Kawatake, *Nihon Engeki Zenshi*, p. 517.
23. Ibid., p. 611.
24. Ibid., p. 517.
25. Shuzui, *Yakusha Rongo*, p. 110; and Dunn, *Actors' Analects*, p. 112.
26. Kawatake, *Nihon Engeki Zenshi*, p. 477.
27. Kawatake Toshio, *A History of Japanese Theater, II: Bunraku and Kabuki* (Tokyo: Kokusai Bunka Shinkokai, 1971), p. 50
28. Dialogue *(kotoba)* is not always delivered in a spoken style. Vocal technique can move through *iro* to *ji* in *kotoba* sections. See William P. Malm in the preceding chapter.
29. Kawatake, *Nihon Engeki Zenshi*, p. 481.
30. Otoba Hiromu, ed., *Jōrurishū* (Tokyo: Iwanami Shoten, 1965), 1:337. The chanters also divided minor roles and narration among themselves.
31. It was not unknown for a secondary chanter *(waki)* to be on stage with the chief chanter *(shite)* in the early 1700s. See, for example, pictures in Ando Tsuruo, *Bunraku: The Puppet Theater* (New York: Walker/Weatherhill, 1970), figures 77 and 80. *The Battles of Coxinga* contains one line, in Act IV, that is divided between the two chanters (see Shuzui Kenji, ed., *Chikamatsu Jōrurishū* [Tokyo: Iwanami Shoten, 1966], 2:278–279, or Donald Keene, trans., *Major Plays of Chikamatsu* [New York: Columbia University Press, 1961], p. 254).
32. Kawatake Shigetoshi et al., eds., *Engeki Hyakka Daijiten* (Tokyo: Heibonsha, 1960), 1:413.

33. Kawatake Shigetoshi believes that the 1749 kabuki productions of *Chūshingura* mark the first time a jōruri play was done more or less intact in kabuki *(History of Japanese Theater*, p. 51). Ihara cites a description of the 1748 production of *Yoshitsune and the Thousand Cherry Trees* at the Nakamura Theater to suggest it was the first: "In doing this new play, the chanter Sengatayū, the *shamisen* player Tsuruzawa Tomokichi along with two others, and six puppet manipulators led by Kiritake Monjūrō, were invited from the Takemoto Puppet Theater in Osaka [to guide] rehearsals" (Ihara, *Kabuki Nempyō,* 3:10).

34. Kawatake, *Nihon Engeki Zenshi,* p. 610.

35. See, for example, Ihara, *Kabuki Nempyō,* 3:533; 5:316, 326, 339, and 357; and 7:292.

36. Ibid., 7:467.

37. An example is the March 1967 program at the Kabukiza in Tokyo. The matinee performance consisted of Acts I, III, and IV of *Chūshingura* followed by the dance play *Black Hill (Kurozuka),* while the evening performance consisted of Acts V, VI, VII, and XI of *Chūshingura* followed by *The Lion Dance (Renjishi).*

38. These and other examples of kabuki versions of *Chūshingura* are described in Toshikura Kōichi, "*Kanadehon* no Hoka no Kabuki Kyakuhon," *Engekikai* 20, no. 12 (November 1962):50–53. Dates of *Chūshingura* performances, casts, and commentary for the 1800s can be found throughout Ihara, *Kabuki Nempyō,* vols. 6 and 7.

39. Toita Yasuji, *Kabuki Meisakusen* (Tokyo: Sogensha, 1959), 1:279.

40. Kabukiza *Program* (February 1959), p. 15.

41. This can be heard on the King album *Chūshingura* (KHA 55–56, 1976).

42. Bandō Yaenosuke, ed., *Tachimawari no Kata to Yōgo* (Tokyo: Kokuritsu Gekijō, n.d.), 3 vols.

43. Current productions draw upon scripts of a number of plays from the nineteenth century for dialogue and sequences in these scenes. See Toita, *Chūshingura,* pp. 233–234.

44. Otoba, *Jōrurishū,* pp. 378–380.

45. Uchiyama Mikiko, "*Kanadehon Chūshingura* no Enshutsu no Keifu," *Engekikai* 20, no. 12 (November 1962):119.

46. Onishi Shigetaka, "Bunraku no *Chūshingura,*" ibid., p. 139.

47. Bannai's appearance in the last act, the vendetta, is usually cut in kabuki performances.

48. Ihara, *Kabuki Nempyō,* 7:110.

49. Ibid., 5:316, 335, and 434; and 6:23, for example.

50. Ibid., 6:185.

51. Toita, *Kabuki Meisakusen,* p. 282.

52. Ihara, *Kabuki Nempyō,* 5:335.

53. See James R. Brandon, "Training at the Waseda Little Theater: The Suzuki Method," *The Drama Review* 22, no. 4 (December 1978), especially pp. 33–35 and 40, for a contemporary Japanese director's comments on the nature of kabuki acting.

54. Toita, *Kabuki Meisakusen,* p. 38; the scene ends with Sadakurō speaking a single line, "Fifty gold pieces."

55. Uchiyama, "*Kanadehon Chūshingura,*" pp. 118–119; and Ihara, *Kabuki Nempyō,* 5:435.

56. Toita, *Kabuki Meisakusen,* pp. 280–281.

57. The *hanamichi* exit is a recent *kata.* More often, perhaps, Tadayoshi's procession will exit stage left. See ibid., pp. 5 and 278.

58. Otoba, *Jōrurishū,* pp. 380, 349, and 318.

59. The vendetta is rarely the same in any two productions. The concluding lines of the play also may be quite different from one production to the next.

60. Toita, *Kabuki Meisakusen,* p. 69.

61. From performances at Toyoko Hall, February 1961 and the Kabukiza, March 1967.

62. Toita, *Kabuki Meisakusen,* p. 24.

63. Ibid., p. 35.

64. Ibid., p. 23.

65. Ibid., p. 68.

66. William P. Malm, *Japanese Music and Musical Instruments* (Tokyo: Tuttle, 1959), pp. 225–226, lists the major *geza* instruments.

67. See William P. Malm, ''Music in the Kabuki Theater,'' in James R. Brandon, William P. Malm, and Donald H. Shively, *Studies in Kabuki* (Honolulu: University Press of Hawaii, 1978), pp. 144–159, for a detailed discussion of the function of *geza* music.

68. Malm, *Japanese Music,* pp. 188–199.

69. Iizuka Tomoichirō, *Kabuki Saiken* (Tokyo: Daiichi Shobō, 1926), pp. 459–466.

70. Kawatake Shigetoshi, *Kabuki Meisakushū* (Tokyo: Kōdansha, 1936), 2:961–977, lists 210 productions from 1697 to 1936.

Act I, scene 1: In kabuki performance a puppet Stage Manager ceremoniously announces the entire cast of characters and the actors playing each role before the curtain opens to begin the play. The custom is derived from jōruri and reflects the puppet origin of the play. *(Photo: Don Kozono.)*

Act I, scene 1: The Hachiman Shrine in Kamakura. The voluminous sleeved robes, trailing trousers, and tall black hats are formal court dress. This striking color combination—black for Kō no Moronao (Bandō Mitsugorō VII), yellow for Enya Hangan (Onoe Baikō VII), and light blue for Momonoi Wakasanosuke (Ichimura Uzaemon XVII)—immediately identifies the scene as *Chūshingura*. This is the curtain *mie* pose: Hangan holds back an enraged Wakasanosuke, while Moronao glares down at them contemptuously. In shortened versions of the play Hangan is not in the scene. Kabukiza, Tokyo. *(Photo: Yoshida Chiaki.)*

Act I, scene 1: The Hachiman Shrine in Kamakura. The lavish staging is typical of kabuki productions. The shōgun's brother Tadayoshi (center) is attended by the governor of Kamakura,

Act I, scene 3: In the Pine Room of the shogunal mansion in Kamakura. Moronao (Onoe Shōroku II), leaning on the sword hilts of Enya Hangan (Onoe Baikō VII), taunts Hangan to draw and kill him. A kabuki addition to the script, not in the jōruri original. Kabukiza, Tokyo. *(Photo: Yoshida Chiaki.)*

Act II, scene 3: The gate of Hangan's mansion, following Hangan's death. Yuranosuke (Don Kozono) has persuaded the forty-some retainers still loyal to Hangan to retire peacefully from their master's confiscated mansion. Alone, he unwraps the bloody dagger with which Hangan has just killed himself and swears vengeance. Kabuki production in English, University Theatre, University of Hawaii, 1979; directed by Nakamura Matagorō. *(Photo: James R. Brandon.)*

Act II, scene 2: Hangan's suicide. Enya Hangan has removed his outer kimono revealing a white inner kimono appropriate for death. Rikiya places before him the wooden tray carrying the short dagger with which he will commit *seppuku*. The shōgun's envoys watch from the side: the puppet of Yakushiji, portrayed as a villainous character, has a ruddy face while the face of the sympathetic Ishidō is a refined white. Kabuki performance of this scene is similar. A jōruri performance at Aichi Culture Hall, Nagoya, 1965. *(Photo: James T. Araki.)*

Act II, scene 2: Ōboshi Yuranosuke (Matsumoto Kōshirō VIII), chief retainer of Enya Hangan (Onoe Baikō VII), arrives just after his master has plunged the dagger tip into his abdomen to begin his ritual death by *seppuku*. Hangan, in agony, looks down the *hanamichi* and therefore to the world outside, indicating to Yuranosuke that Yuranosuke is to take vengeance against Moronao after Hangan is dead. Retainers of Hangan prostrate themselves behind him. Kabuki production at the Kabukiza, Tokyo. *(Photo: Yoshida Chiaki.)*

Act II, scene 1: The fugitive scene *(michiyuki)* in kabuki is performed as a brilliant dance set in a romantic spring setting. Kampei (Nakamura Kanzaburō XVII) is accosted by members of the Fighting Chorus. Holding branches of cherry blossoms they delicately attack from either side in formalized fighting movements *(tate)*. Kabukiza, Tokyo. *(Photo: Yoshida Chiaki.)*

Act II, scene 1: In jōruri performance Kampei is attacked by the Fighting Chorus in a somber nighttime scene, just outside the gate leading to the Pine Room. Staves, instead of branches of cherry blossoms, are the weapons and the effect is, paradoxically, more realistic in puppet performance than it is in the danced kabuki version. Aichi Culture Hall, Nagoya, 1965. *(Photo: James T. Araki.)*

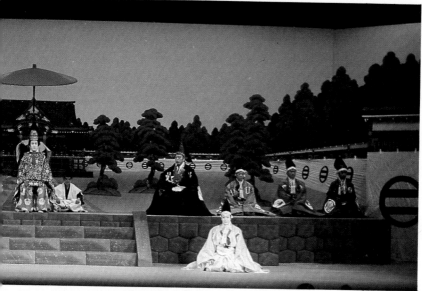

Kō no Moronao (to his left), and, in subordinate positions beneath and in front of him, Enya Hangan (in yellow) and Momonoi Wakasanosuke (in blue). National Theater of Japan, Tokyo. *(Photo: Don Kozono.)*

Act I, scene 3: The Pine Room. Enya Hangan, provoked beyond endurance, draws his sword and strikes Moronao on the forehead. Moronao staggers back as Provincial Lords rush on to restrain Hangan. A jōruri production at the Aichi Culture Hall, Nagoya, 1965. *(Photo: James T. Araki.)*

Act III, scene 1: The Ichiriki Brothel in Kyoto. Yuranosuke (Don Kozono) feigns dissipation at the Ichiriki Brothel in order to lull Moronao into complacency. He is called to the outer gate by his son, Rikiya (Penny Bergman). As they both carefully watch for spies, Rikiya passes to his father a letter from Kaoyo outlining Moronao's movements and a pledge from the faithful retainers to join Yuranosuke in the vendetta. Kabuki production in English, University Theatre, University of Hawaii, 1979; directed by Nakamura Matagorō. *(Photo: James R. Brandon.)*

Act III, scene 1: Yuranosuke, dressed in a sensuous purple kimono, urges Okaru to descend the ladder into the garden. A jōruri performance at the Aichi Culture Hall, Nagoya, 1965. *(Photo: James T. Araki.)*

Act III, scene 2: The vendetta. Yuranosuke (center), Rikiya (kneeling at his side), and the Retainers pose in the snow-covered garden of Moronao's mansion after carrying through their planned vendetta. Moronao's head, wrapped in a white cloth, is hoisted high on a spear. As fresh snowflakes fall, white against the deep blue of the winter night, the curtain closes. Kabuki production in English, University Theatre, University of Hawaii, 1979; directed by Nakamura Matagorō. *(Photo: Don Kozono.)*

The Forty-Seven Samurai
A Kabuki Version of *Chūshingura*

Adaptation by:	NAKAMURA MATAGORŌ II
	JAMES R. BRANDON
Translated by:	JAMES R. BRANDON
	JUNKO BERBERICH
	MICHAEL FELDMAN

BETWEEN September 1978 and March 1979 the professional kabuki actor Nakamura Matagorō II prepared a production of *Kanadehon Chūshingura* at the University of Hawaii to be performed in authentic kabuki style for an English-speaking audience. The translation that follows is the text that was used in this three-hour production. It includes stage directions and descriptions of costuming, music, and sound effects. Three English translations of the original jōruri text of *Kanadehon Chūshingura* have been published since 1876, Donald Keene's *Chūshingura: The Treasury of Loyal Retainers* being the most recent.[1] A translation of the kabuki text is nonetheless useful because of the many differences between it and the jōruri play. Since the translation was prepared for stage performance, it reads somewhat differently in style from previous translations.[2]

The translation consists of scenes normally performed in Japan when a shortened, three- or four-hour version of the play is staged: Acts I, III, IV, VII, and XI of the full-length kabuki text. The Hachiman Shrine scene (I) introduces many of the major characters and the main plot of the play is set in motion when Councilor Moronao attempts to seduce Enya Hangan's wife, Kaoyo. The short bribery and rendezvous scene (III, 1) introduces new characters and leads into the important Pine Room scene which follows. First, Kakogawa Honzō bribes Moronao to assist Momonoi Wakasanosuke; then the young lovers, Kampei and Okaru, meet for a tryst. In the Pine Room (III, 2) Moronao reads Kaoyo's poem rejecting his advances. He turns his fury against Hangan, taunting him until, provoked beyond endurance, Hangan draws his sword and tries to kill Moronao. Hangan's suicide scene (IV, 1) shows the immediate result of Hangan's rash at-

tack: he is ordered by the shōgun to die by *seppuku,* or ritual disembowelment. Hangan's chief retainer, Ōboshi Yuranosuke, arrives
just in time to receive his dying master's implied command to seek
vengeance. Immediately following this is the gate scene (IV, 2) in
which Yuranosuke prevents Hangan's impetuous young retainers
from defending the mansion. Alone, he swears vengeance over Hangan's bloody dagger. Yuranosuke next appears in a scene set in the
Ichiriki Brothel (VII). He pretends to have abandoned himself to debauchery. Secretly he plans the vendetta against Moronao with the
help of his son Rikiya and Kaoyo. Okaru, who has been sold to the
brothel, meets her brother Heiemon and both prove their loyalty to
the cause of the vendetta. In the play's final scene, the vendetta (XI),
Yuranosuke leads the loyal retainers of Hangan in a night attack on
Moronao's heavily guarded mansion. Moronao is captured and beheaded. They celebrate their victory. These are the obligatory scenes
which dramatize the main plot of Hangan's humiliation, death, and
vengeance.

The adaptation also includes the popular fugitive travel scene
(michiyuki) in which Kampei and Okaru flee to the countryside in
disgrace. The scene is not essential to the Hangan-Yuranosuke-
Moronao plot, but it prepares the audience for Okaru's later appearance in the brothel scene, and its colorful dance sequences, the
humor of the comic villain Bannai, and the spectacle of the cherry-
blossom battle provide a desirable contrast to the somber mood of
other scenes. In most modern productions the fugitive travel scene is
placed after Hangan's death, which has the effect of suggesting that
Kampei's flight is due to his master's death, thus casting a heavy
shadow on the lovers' delicate dance. We have followed the older
Osaka tradition of placing the scene after the Pine Room.[3]

Cuts that occur within scenes have been made in less important
sections wherever possible in order to preserve intact the major sections of a scene. Several introductory sequences, Kaoyo arranging
cherry blossoms prior to Hangan's entrance in the suicide scene, Bannai's comic ''ahem'' routine in the bribery scene, and Moronao's first
argument with Hangan and Wakasanosuke in the Hachiman Shrine
scene, for example, have been dropped so that the important scenes
which follow—Hangan's suicide, the rendezvous of Okaru and Kampei, and Moronao's confrontation with Wakasanosuke—can be
played out fully. The translation incorporates some changes made
specifically for this production: one helmet is examined by Kaoyo instead of four or five; a palanquin is not used; and portions of three

scenes of the vendetta are brought together into a single final scene. A three-hour adaptation such as this cannot show the full complexity of *Chūshingura,* but because so many acts in longer versions take up rambling subplots, it can convey the heart of the drama without too much loss.

Half a dozen lines of exposition have been added to the narration and dialogue. These provide information about actions that are not shown.[4] For example, Heiemon says that Okaru has sold herself to the brothel "hoping that with your contract price Kampei could contribute to the vendetta against Lord Hangan's enemy," thus describing her actions in Act VI that otherwise would not be known.

The aim of the translation was to create a text that would be, in performance, as faithful as possible to what might be seen and heard in a professional kabuki theater. This was a complex aim, of course, requiring that a number of aspects of text and performance be taken into account at the same time.

First, the emotional and intellectual states of mind that lie behind the words that the characters speak were sought out. The lines of dialogue are clues to these states of mind but in themselves are not necessarily the direct object of translation. To cite one example, when Heiemon gestures to Okaru to come close after he has tried to kill her she thinks Heiemon still intends to kill her and replies, *"iya ja wai na"* which means literally, "I hate it." This is a typical response by a young Japanese woman to a difficult situation. It is part pout and part defiance. It is a "cute" reply. And it is deliberately placed by kabuki artists (it doesn't occur in the jōruri text) in the middle of a scene of great pathos. It is intended to provide release; the audience is expected to react with warm, affectionate laughter. In brief, within the context of the scene the function of the line is more to express Okaru's flouncing, little-girl attitude than to convey the words "I hate it." In English, Okaru says that she thinks Heiemon still intends to kill her, "and I don't like that at all."

Second, there is much humorous wordplay throughout the text, some of it very bad punning, that cries out for English equivalents. When Kampei ridicules Sagisaka (Heron Hill) Bannai, for example, he reels off a string of bird images: "You are a funny bird, Sagisaka Bannai, a little chirping sparrow I could swallow in a bite. But instead of eating you, I will make you eat crow!" Our translation of Kaoyo's clever poem rejecting Moronao's advances, which is read in the Pine Room scene, does not reproduce the original images; rather it focuses on the spirit of wordplay lying behind them:

"A woman's love does, not lie in the hopeful eye, of her beholder;
Not beholden to lie I, aver never to lie with you."⁵

Third, dialogue in the play is characterized by a wide range of language levels. Moderate formality is expressed in a line such as Tadayoshi's "It is the shōgun, not I, who has summoned you here." More formal still is the shōgun's proclamation read at the beginning of Hangan's suicide scene: "Whereas, Enya Hangan Takasada, you have willfully committed an act of bloodshed against our chief councilor Moronao, and thereby have defiled the palace, know that your estates, large and small, are hereby confiscated and you are ordered to end your life by *seppuku*." Gruff Yakushiji speaks colloquially of Hangan's retainers "milling about like chickens with their heads cut off." Heiemon's lines to Okaru beginning "Once you were a samurai, now a courtesan," in the Ichiriki Brothel scene, are sentimental. Moronao's "blockhead, country bumpkin" to Wakasanosuke is a crude insult. Yuranosuke speaks in deliberate double entendre of Okaru's fear as she descends the ladder: "You're past the age to be afraid of a new position. Straddle it, open your legs, it'll all go smoothly."⁶

Finally, because the translation was written to be spoken in the theater, by actors approximating kabuki vocal conventions, attention was paid to line length and rhythmic patterns. As an illustration, Kampei and Bannai speak the following short, rhythmic lines at the conclusion of the *michiyuki* dance scene:

BANNAI:	*Kampei, matte!*	Kampei, wait!
KAMPEI:	*Nanzo yō ka . . . ?*	Bannai, you want . . . ?
BANNAI:	*Sono yō wa . . .*	Kampei, I want . . .
KAMPEI:	*Muuu?*	Hmm?
BANNAI:	*Nai.*	Nothing.
KAMPEI:	*Baka me!*	Simpleton!

The most patterned structure of language is found in lyric moments, such as the closing speeches of the finale or Heiemon's "Once you were a samurai, now a courtesan," just mentioned. These speeches are composed in phrases of seven and five syllables, phrase lengths common to Japanese poetry. Kaoyo's poem, a *waka*, is in 5-7-5-7-7 syllables. In kabuki elocution the final word of a powerfully spoken line is prolonged: taking as an example the last word of Tadayoshi's closing line in the Hachiman Shrine scene, *mekiki*, in performance it sounds like *me-ki-i-ki-i-i-i* (in translation: an-swe-er me-e-e-e). The kabuki pitch pattern is often an integral part of the written line and must be considered in translation as well. Thus, Okaru's plea to Kampei to spare Bannai's life during the *michiyuki* dance is spoken with an octave rise and fall on the third syllable and again on the next to the last syllable, *"mo-o YO-i wa-i NA-a"* (in translation: "so-o PLEASE just let him GO-o").

NOTES

1. Donald Keene, *Chūshingura: The Treasury of Loyal Retainers* (New York: Columbia University Press, 1971); Frederick V. Dickens, trans., *Chiushingura or The Loyal League* (New York: G. P. Putnam's Sons, 1876); and Jukichi Inouye, trans., *Chushingura or The Treasury of Loyal Retainers* (Tokyo: Nakanishi-ya, 1910) are translations of the full jōruri text. Sakae Shioya, *Chūshingura: An Exposition* (Tokyo: Hokuseido, 1956) is a detailed discussion of the play and the historical events it dramatizes.
2. The only translation of kabuki scenes from *Chūshingura* are in Donald Richie and Miyoko Watanabe, *Six Kabuki Plays* (Tokyo: Hokuseido, 1963). This contains the Hachiman Shrine, Pine Room, Hangan's suicide, and gate scenes as they were performed by Grand Kabuki in New York in 1960.
3. The fugitive travel scene followed the Pine Room scene in its first production in 1833 (Ihara Toshirō, *Kabuki Nempyō* (Tokyo: Iwanami Shoten, 1961), 7: 267). It also appears in this position in the standard kabuki text of *Chūshingura*, Toita Yasuji, ed., *Kabuki Meisakusen*, vol. 1 (Tokyo: Sogensha, 1959).
4. Originally the translators prepared more extensive additions. These were not kept, however, at the suggestion of the director, Nakamura Matagorō. True to kabuki attitudes about how the theater should work, he said that an audience should grasp the situation intuitively from the actions of the characters. The audience should not be told everything explicitly; verbal explanations are boring.
5. Dickens translates the poem, "Heavy the burden love doth lay; e'en when 'tis free from sin; let not thy heart, then, go astray; unlawful love to win" (p. 53); and Inouye more briefly as, "A husband's love my life doth shield, unneeded, all love else I spurn" (p. 36). Keene's translation is remarkably close in meaning and syllable count: "They would be heavy enough even without this new burden, these night clothes. Do not pile onto your robes, a robe that is not your own" (p. 58).
6. In their translations, Dickens and Inouye have rendered innocuous Yuranosuke's salacious comments. Inouye writes in his preface that among the few lines he has cut, those of "Yuranosuke and Okaru are too indelicate for translation." Keene gives a good idea of their bawdiness.

THE FORTY-SEVEN SAMURAI

Cast of Characters

TADAYOSHI, younger brother of the shōgun

KŌ NO MORONAO, chief councilor of the shōgun and governor of Kamakura

MOMONOI WAKASANOSUKE, a young samurai

ENYA HANGAN, a young provincial lord

KAOYO, wife of Enya Hangan

KAKOGAWA HONZŌ, chief retainer of Wakasanosuke

SAGISAKA BANNAI, retainer of Moronao

OKARU, in love with Kampei, and later his wife

KAMPEI, retainer of Enya Hangan

ISHIDŌ, the shōgun's representative at Hangan's death

YAKUSHIJI, envoy from the shōgun

GOEMON, elderly retainer of Enya Hangan

RIKIYA, son of Yuranosuke

ŌBOSHI YURANOSUKE, chief retainer of Enya Hangan

KUDAYŪ, former retainer of Enya Hangan, now Moronao's spy

HEIEMON, older brother of Okaru

SHIMIZU ICHIGAKU, Moronao's bodyguard

TAKEMORI KITAHACHI, retainer to Enya Hangan

Provincial Lords, Footmen, Retainers, Ladies-in-Waiting, Maids, Male Geisha, Fighting Chorus, Soldiers

Time and Place of Action

ACT I

SCENE 1: *Hachiman Shrine in Kamakura, 1338.*

SCENE 2: *Outside the gate of the shogunal mansion in Kamakura, the next evening.*

SCENE 3: *The Pine Room of the shogunal mansion in Kamakura, a few minutes later.*

ACT II

SCENE 1: *Along the road, near Mt. Fuji, the following morning.*

SCENE 2: *A reception room in Enya Hangan's mansion, the same day.*

SCENE 3: *The rear gate of Enya Hangan's mansion, immediately following.*

ACT III

SCENE 1: *The Ichiriki Brothel in Kyoto, eighteen months later.*

SCENE 2: *The garden of Moronao's mansion in Kamakura, several days later.*

ACT I

SCENE 1 *Hachiman Shrine*

[*Two sharp clacks of the hardwood* ki *signal offstage musicians to begin slow and regular drum and flute music, "Kata Shagiri" ("Half-Shagiri"). The deliberate pace of the music gradually accelerates. The lights in the auditorium dim slightly; the audience watches the kabuki curtain of broad rust, black, and green stripes. Very slowly, the curtain is pushed open by a* STAGE ASSISTANT *walking from stage right to left.* Ki *clacks intersperse every eighth, every fourth, then every second drum beat. Drumming and* ki *intermingle as the tempo rapidly increases during the last few feet of the curtain opening. The scene is a ceremonial audience before Hachiman Shrine in Kamakura. The shōgun's brother,* TADAYOSHI, *is seated on the center of a broad stone platform running across the back of the stage. He wears a subdued Chinese-style court robe with bloused trousers and a gold lacquered hat. On his left sits the highest local official of the government,* KŌ NO MORONAO. *A voluminous black robe with large sleeves and trailing trousers encase his body and a high black hat increases his height. Six* PROVINCIAL LORDS *kneel behind them on the platform. Kneeling on the ground before them are two samurai officials,* MOMONOI WAKASANOSUKE *and* ENYA HANGAN, *dressed, respectively, in powder blue and yellow robes of the same exaggerated cut as* MORONAO's, *and* HANGAN's *wife,* KAOYO. *She wears a silk embroidered kimono and outer robe of deep blue. Two* FOOTMEN *sit on the ground cross-*

Act I, scene 1: The Hachiman Shrine in Kamakura. Tadayoshi (Catherine N. Lee) occupies the place of honor in the center of the platform. Kō no Moronao (Dale Ream) sits to his left; attending him are a group of Provincial Lords. In less exalted positions are Enya Hangan (Tony Soper), kneeling in front of Moronao, and Momonoi Wakasanosuke (David Reinke) and Lady Kaoyo (Susan Stuart), kneeling next to the box containing the helmet which is to be presented to the shrine. Kabuki production in English, University Theatre, University of Hawaii, 1979; directed by Nakamura Matagorō. *(Photo: James R. Brandon.)*

legged to the right. The heads of all the characters are dropped forward limply on their chests, in imitation of puppets before they have been brought to life. Two ki *clacks signal the music to stop and the action of the scene to begin.*]

STAGE MANAGER [*rhythmic, prolonged calls from offstage right*]: Hear ye, hear ye, hear ye, hear ye, hear ye, hear ye . . . hear ye!

[*Deep, thick chords of a jōruri, or puppet-style, samisen are heard from the small room above the set stage left. The team of jōruri* SAMISEN PLAYER *and* NARRATOR *are not seen, but they can see the action on stage through the thin bamboo blind that hangs in front of them. The* NARRATOR *constantly shifts his vocal style between a kind of half-spoken chanting and singing. His tones are rich and full and unabashedly project the extremes of human emotion. Each syllable is precisely uttered. Sharp samisen chords punctuate the end of a chanted phrase; they become melodic under sung passages. A syllable can be clipped or staccato, or it can be prolonged into a lengthy obligato, spread over many samisen chords, so that the narrative line compresses or expands in time in order to best project the theatrical needs of the moment.*]

NARRATOR [*chants*]: "A banquet laid out before your eyes! Without eating of its food, never will you be able to know its taste!" Likewise, a country in peace . . . its able retainers will hide their gallantry and chivalry. [*Sings.*] Take our story as an example . . . witness here and now . . .

SECOND STAGE MANAGER [*calling from offstage left*]: Hear ye, hear ye, hear ye, hear ye . . . hear ye!

STAGE MANAGER [*calling from offstage center*]: Hear ye, hear ye . . . hear ye!

NARRATOR [*chants*]: Ashikaga government chief Takauji has Kyoto as the headquarters of his reign, his power expanding far. The time is the closing of February, thirteen thirty-eight. The place is Kamakura in the east, at Hachiman Shrine, now completed in its awesome grandeur. [*Sings.*] Gathered here to celebrate a battle fought and won are lords of distinction, in their solemn moments. [*Chants.*] Acting as government proxy, Ashikaga Tadayoshi has just arrived from the capital . . . of Kyoto!

[*At the mention of his name,* TADAYOSHI *raises his head, opens his eyes, and elegantly flicks open his sleeves: puppetlike, he has been "brought to life."*]

Here in Kamakura, he is received by the shōgun's official, Kō no Moronao! The officers of the reception are: Momonoi Wakasanosuke Yasuchika, Moronao's target of displeasure for his rough manners, and Hakushu's castle lord, Enya Hangan Takasada. [*Sings.*] Among these men, a single flower, Lady Kaoyo, wife of Hangan.

[*Each character, as named, comes to life, showing his or her personality through the simple actions of lifting the head, opening the eyes, and adjusting the trailing kimono sleeves:* MORONAO'*s evil nature—seven abrupt head jerks ending in a fierce* mie *pose with eyes crossed, arms extending aggressively forward as two loud beats of the wooden* tsuke *call attention to the pose;* WAKASANOSUKE'*s impetuosity—five strong movements of the head, sudden opening of the eyes, each arm flicked out inde-*

pendently; HANGAN's *composure—three smooth head movements, gentle eye opening, and both sleeves elegantly adjusted;*
KAOYO's *modesty—no movement at all except for the slow raising of the head. Narrative shifts to song.*]

Moronao casts amorous eyes at this rare beauty. Loyal men,
bowing low . . .

[MORONAO *leers openly at* KAOYO. *Then everyone places their
hands on the floor and they make a ceremonious, deep bow to*
TADAYOSHI. *Narrative returns to chanting.*]

As Tadayoshi speaks, all listen in reverence!

[*All lift their heads and listen respectfully.*]

TADAYOSHI [*clear, unaffected voice, looking straight ahead*]:
    Attend, Lady Kaoyo!

KAOYO [*bowing*]: My lord.

TADAYOSHI: It is the shōgun, not I, who has summoned you here.
    You served the emperor Godaigo when he bestowed upon the
    warrior Yoshisada the imperial battle crown. Now, with prayers
    commemorating our victory in battle, my brother the shōgun
    wills that this battle crown be dedicated to the shrine of Hachi-
    man, god of war. If you can, confirm that this, and no other, is
    the one! Come, come! Answer me, answer me!

KAOYO [*bowing*]: My lord.

NARRATOR [*chants*]: Attendants carry forth the precious battle
    crown, bending down to open up the heavy wooden chest. Lift-
    ing up the battle crown . . . is it the one of fame? [*Sings.*]
    Though gazing closely at the battle crown held high, she will
    only speak when she is certain . . . and then, floating famous
    fragrance of the crown well known . . .

[*The two* FOOTMEN *place a large wooden chest center and remove its lid. They bring out a samurai helmet. Its golden fit-
tings gleam in the light.* KAOYO *moves forward the better to
observe it, kneels, and noticing its special perfume, nods deci-
sively.*]

KAOYO: This is the very crown Yoshisada wore in battle, I can say
    with certainty.

NARRATOR [*chants*]: Saying these words, Kaoyo bows deep in reverence.

[*She bows. A* FOOTMAN *places the helmet at* TADAYOSHI'*s feet. With the second* FOOTMAN, *he carries off the chest.*]

TADAYOSHI: Enya Hangan! Momonoi Wakasanosuke! In conjunction with the dedication, all ceremonies are placed in your care. Consult Lord Moronao. Kaoyo, you may go!

KAOYO [*bowing*]: My lord.

NARRATOR [*chants*]: Kaoyo has now been freed of her demanding task, waiting as his lordship . . . into the palace goes!

[TADAYOSHI *rises; a* STAGE ASSISTANT *takes off the stool he has been sitting on. Without looking to the right or left, he walks with a dignified gait down the steps. He stops and poses. Drum and flute play stately exit music.* TADAYOSHI *flicks open his sleeves, turns, and moves slowly off left.* PROVINCIAL LORDS *rise and follow, their formal court trousers trailing behind them.* FOOTMEN *bring up the rear. They exit. The music continues in the background as* HANGAN, WAKASANOSUKE, *and* KAOYO *play out in silence their petitions to* MORONAO *for permission to depart. To* HANGAN'*s polite bow of request* MORONAO *nods condescendingly.* HANGAN *rises, and with unruffled composure, goes off left, carrying the helmet with him, to be deposited in the shrine.* WAKASANOSUKE *bows brusquely, scarcely bothering to conceal his contempt for* MORONAO. *In response,* MORONAO *deliberately and disdainfully averts his gaze. Moving to where he is in* MORONAO'*s line of sight again,* WAKASANOSUKE *bows a second time, more brusquely still. Again* MORONAO *ignores him and looks away. Trembling with fury,* WAKASANOSUKE *moves directly in front of* MORONAO *and bows a third time.* MORONAO *looks over his head as if the young samurai were not there.* WAKASANOSUKE *leaps up in rage, strikes back his sleeve, and rushes off left. Music stops.* MORONAO *laughs soundlessly, then looks expectantly to* KAOYO, *who bows politely, rises, and starts to move away.* MORONAO *rises, a* STAGE ASSISTANT *removing the stool on which he has been sitting. He stops* KAOYO *with an unctuous, but clearly threatening, command.*]

MORONAO: One moment, Lady Kaoyo! I wish to have a word with you. I believe that you and I share in common an unspoken passion, for the art of writing poetry. Will you accept from me this poem, composed with loving care, your reply to which I will not be displeased to receive from your own lips, Kaoyo, my lady.

NARRATOR [*chants*]: From his sleeve to her sleeve, a love letter from Moronao! [*Sings.*] Saying not a single word, she throws it aside.

[*Crossing to her,* MORONAO *looks around to see that no one is watching. He passes a love letter into* KAOYO's *sleeve. She takes it out, and looking at the salutation, knows immediately what it is. Coldly she drops it to the ground.* MORONAO *scoops it up and tucks it away in the breast of his kimono.*]

MORONAO [*insinuatingly*]: Casually you cast my letter to the ground, but you will not cast down my intentions that easily. Until you accept my love, I will track you, chase you, wear you down. In the palace your husband is my puppet, to rise or to fall in his duties, solely on Moronao's will. Kaoyo, my lady . . . well? Do you not agree?

[*He glances about again, then moves behind her and enfolds her in a rough embrace. She discreetly tries to free herself: their bodies sway back and forth.*]

NARRATOR [*sings*]: In her heart are angry words but Kaoyo refrains. Dear Lady Kaoyo, tears in her eyes.

[*Without warning* WAKASANOSUKE *strides on. Taking in the situation at a glance, he turns his back.*]

WAKASANOSUKE: Ahem! Ahem! [*Furious,* MORONAO *breaks away.* WAKASANOSUKE *moves beside* KAOYO.] Lady Kaoyo, Lord Tadayoshi dismissed you long ago. If you linger, you are risking his displeasure. Go! Do not stay a moment longer!

KAOYO: Yes, good Lord Wakasanosuke, with your permission, I shall take my leave.

NARRATOR [*sings*]: Burdened with care, to her mansion . . . Kaoyo returns.

[KAOYO *bows and moves quickly onto the* hanamichi, *the rampway which extends from the stage, through the audience, to the rear of the auditorium. She stops at the "seven-three" position, that is, the position seven-tenths of the distance from the back*

Act I, scene 1: The attempted seduction of Lady Kaoyo (Nakamura Utaemon VI) by Moronao (Nakamura Kanzaburō XVII) is explicitly portrayed in Kabuki performance. Kabukiza, Tokyo. *(Photo: Shochiku.)*

of the auditorium and three-tenths from the stage. She poses, puts her hands inside her kimono sleeves, then regally moves down the hanamichi. *She passes out of sight as the narration ends.*]

MORONAO [*snarling*]: No one summoned you! You are insolent, Wakasanosuke! Kaoyo was entreating me, in private audience, to guide Hangan in his palace duties. That is how even the mighty must grovel before the shōgun's chief councilor. And who are you? A country rustic, a nobody. So low a single word from Moronao would send you tumbling into the streets to beg for your food! And you call yourself a samurai? A samurai? [MO-RONAO *strikes* WAKASANOSUKE*'s chest with his heavy fan.*] You . . . a sa–mu–rai? [*On the last three syllables,* MORONAO *strikes* WAKASANOSUKE*'s chest, sword hilt, and chest again.* WAKASA-NOSUKE *falls back.*] B-b-blockhead country bumpkin!

NARRATOR [*chants*]: You dare to meddle, little man? Moronao's re-venge! Bursting in hot anger, Wakasanosuke . . . here in the sacred shrine before his Majesty, a moment of patience is all I need! One more word decides my life, death may be my fate! Wakasanosuke now holds himself in!

[*To the narration:* WAKASANOSUKE *poses with hand on the hilt of his sword; he notices he is in a sacred shrine and falls back; his hand trembles; he nods with determination, throws his fan into the air, and lunges forward as if to draw his sword.* MORONAO, *slaps his fan against* WAKASANOSUKE*'s sword arm and glares at his young opponent in alarm and rage. At that moment a cry is heard from off stage announcing the return of* TADAYOSHI.]

VOICES OFF [*in unison*]: Bow down!

MORONAO [*snarling*]: Bow down, I say!

[MORONAO *strikes* WAKASANOSUKE*'s sword arm viciously with his closed fan.* WAKASANOSUKE *drops to one knee, glares at* MO-RONAO, *and poses with his hand on his sword.* MORONAO *rushes up the platform steps, suddenly pivots back to face* WAKASANO-SUKE, *flips open his sleeves, and poses in a fierce* mie. MORONAO *crosses his eyes and glares to two loud beats of the* tsuke. WAKA-SANOSUKE *restrains himself; his chest heaves. The curtain is run closed to accelerating* ki *clacks. A single* ki *clack marks the end of the scene and signals the offstage drum and flute to play "Sa-gariha" ("Departure") as the scene is changed.*]

SCENE 2 *Bribery and Rendezvous*

[*Two* ki *clacks: the curtain is run open. Ki clacks accelerate, then fade away. The scene is the rear gate of the shogunal mansion in Kamakura where the state ceremonies are to be held. It is night. Pale blue light floods the stage. One* ki *clack signals action to begin.*]

Act I, scene 1: Momonoi Wakasanosuke is infuriated when Moronao snubs his departure courtesies. In a difficult and impressive puppet gesture, Wakasanosuke angrily flicks out the large sleeves of his robe in preparation to bow a final time. Jōruri performance at the Aichi Culture Hall, Nagoya, 1965. *(Photo: James T. Araki.)*

NARRATOR [*chants*]: Chief retainer of Wakasanosuke, [*sings*] Kakogawa Honzō comes in with a tray full of gifts, a self-assigned task.

[HONZŌ, *carrying a tray of silks as a bribe for* MORONAO, *comes onto the* hanamichi. *He stops at the seven-three position, looks toward the gate, and poses.*]

HONZŌ: Bannai. Master Bannai.

[BANNAI, *a comic villain, enters from inside the gate.* HONZŌ *moves quickly onto the stage, places the gifts on the ground, and kneels respectfully before* BANNAI.]

BANNAI [*officiously*]: Someone calls me. Who is it, who is it? [*Notices* HONZŌ. *Starts.*] State your business, I am a busy man!

HONZŌ [*bowing obsequiously*]: I am Kakogawa Honzō, chief retainer of Momonoi Wakasanosuke.

BANNAI [*chuckles delightedly*]: The bluebird Wakasanosuke and his friend, the yellow canary Enya Hangan, are country chickens.

What a cackling they will make in the palace. Oh, my master, Lord Moronao, will pluck them clean!

HONZŌ [*carefully watching* BANNAI'*s expression*]: That is the matter on which I have come, good Bannai. My master is young and untutored in the intricacies of palace etiquette. Only with Lord Moronao's generous guidance will he be able to carry out his important duties. Taking this opportunity, I express my gratitude for your master's favor.

[HONZŌ *bows low.* BANNAI *turns front with a self-satisfied smirk on his face.*]

BANNAI: Everyone needs a chief councilor's favors. But your Wakasanosuke was rude to my master. Go back where you came from, go back, go away! [BANNAI *strikes a pose: feet together, head up, right fist extended toward* HONZŌ.]

HONZŌ: What you say is true, still please accept these gifts on behalf of Wakasanosuke and his grateful followers.

Act I, scene 2: At the gate of the shogunal mansion leading to the Pine Room. Wakasanosuke's chief retainer, Kakogawa Honzō, presents a list of gifts—really bribes—to Moronao's retainer, Sagisaka Bannai, intended to alleviate Moronao's anger against his master. In jōruri, Bannai is portrayed by a comic puppet with wide brows and squashed face. Aichi Culture Hall, Nagoya, 1965. *(Photo: James T. Araki.)*

[HONZŌ *bows toward the gifts of silk. He looks about, to be sure they are unseen, then takes out a wrapped package of gold coins. Moving forward on his knees to* BANNAI*'s side, he drops the package into the open kimono sleeve.*]

Carry my message to Lord Moronao. Do what is necessary, good Bannai. Will you do so, Bannai? Bannai? [HONZŌ *tugs lightly on* BANNAI*'s sleeve.*]

NARRATOR [*chants*]: Wondering, Bannai takes it in his hand!

[BANNAI *flicks* HONZŌ*'s hand away and in doing so strikes the heavy coins. He clutches his fingers in pain, then wonders what his hand hit. He sneaks a look at the coins. He reacts with delighted surprise.*]

NARRATOR [*sings*]: Money talks words of power!

BANNAI [*effusive, his attitude completely changed*]: Well, well, Kakogawa Honzō, how nice of you to come. [*He squats and bows to* HONZŌ.] You have come at the right moment: the ceremonial rooms are being prepared. Come, come! [BANNAI *picks up the tray of gifts, rises, and gestures for* HONZŌ *to follow him.*]

HONZŌ [*bowing carefully*]: I am a person of no importance, I do not dare enter the palace.

BANNAI [*proudly*]: If Lord Moronao is with you, who would dare object? Come, I will show you the rooms.

HONZŌ: I will enter then, most gratefully.

BANNAI: Then come along. Come along!

[BANNAI *poses.* HONZŌ *bows. They cross toward the gate: three times* BANNAI *turns back, chuckling and bowing, to beckon* HONZŌ *forward. At the gate* BANNAI *stops short.*]

Master Honzō, the threshold is high.

NARRATOR [*sings*]: Moronao is happy. Honzō bought the life of Wakasanosuke. His scheme now is accomplished. Together they go.

[BANNAI *steps carefully over the foot-high threshold of the gate and goes inside, followed by* HONZŌ.]

NARRATOR [*a nō song, as if part of the entertainment inside the mansion*]:

"At the end of the journey we have reached Takasago Bay;
At the end of the journey we have reached Takasago Bay.''

[OKARU, *a beautiful young girl in her late teens, enters on the*
hanamichi. *She wears a maiden's trailing kimono with long
sleeves, in a purple arrow pattern. She holds a lacquered letter
box in her right hand. She stops at the seven-three position,
looks toward the gate, and poses.*]

OKARU: My Lady Kaoyo urgently sends this letter to her husband,
Lord Enya Hangan. How fortunate that I, her favorite, was allowed to bring it. Dearest Kampei, I cannot bear to be apart
from you a single moment.

[*Offstage musicians play nō-style drum and flute music in the
background.* KAMPEI, *a young samurai, enters from the gate followed by a* RETAINER. *They wear black kimono under stiff vests;
their divided skirts are folded up to their knees, showing that
they are on guard duty.* KAMPEI *is in the service of* HANGAN *and
is* OKARU*'s lover.* OKARU *sees him and runs to meet him.*]

KAMPEI: Okaru, is it you?

OKARU [*coquettishly*]: Dearest Kampei, I missed you so.

KAMPEI [*flustered and worried about meeting her while he is on
duty*]: But why are you here at the palace gate, at night, and all
alone?

OKARU: I've come for Lady Kaoyo. "Meet Kampei and tell him he is
to ask my husband to deliver this letter to Lord Moronao''—
those were her very words. [OKARU *passes him the letter box.*]

KAMPEI [*unsure*]: I am to deliver this directly to Lord Hangan?

OKARU: Yes, dearest Kampei. [*She smiles invitingly at him.*]

KAMPEI: Wait for me, Okaru. [*He turns to go.*]

OKARU [*she holds his sleeve*]: Kampei!

KAMPEI: I should take it to our master myself. I should be with him.
It is my duty not to leave his side in the palace. I . . .

[*He is irresolute. He tries to leave; she tugs gently, persuasively
at his sleeve. He looks into her pleading eyes. He decides. He
turns to the* RETAINER.]

Take this immediately to Lord Hangan.

RETAINER: I will. [*The* RETAINER *takes the letter box, bows, and crosses into the gate.*]

OKARU: I want to be with you so. Now that we are here, together . . .

KAMPEI: You are flushed with excitement, Okaru!

OKARU [*taking his hand in hers*]: Please come. I don't care!

NARRATOR [*sings*]: Seizing fast her lover's hand . . . she leads him away!

[*She presses against him boldly, folding her arm over his. They pose: a sharp* ki *clack emphasizes the moment. Offstage drum and samisen resume in the background. They look excitedly into each other's eyes and then hurriedly cross into the darkness of the trees beyond the gate. The curtain is run quickly closed to accelerating* ki *clacks. Music ends. Soft, intermittent* ki *clacks mark time while the scene is changed.*]

SCENE 3 *Pine Room*

[*Two* ki *clacks: the curtain opens. The scene is a large reception room of the shogunal mansion called the Pine Room because of the designs painted on the gold sliding doors extending across the full stage. A single* ki *clack: action begins.*]

NARRATOR [*chants*]: Utter indignation, for Moronao is late! Impatiently waiting in the palace . . . Wakasanosuke!

[WAKASANOSUKE *rushes onto the* hanamichi. *He drops to one knee at the seven-three position, resolutely slaps his thigh, and poses, waiting for the arrival of* MORONAO. *A sliding door left opens. Rapid drum and flute music.* BANNAI *ushers* MORONAO *on stage, bowing obsequiously. He carries a small paper lantern to light the room. Without a word,* WAKASANOSUKE *leaps to his feet, slips his sword arm free of the restricting formal vest, and rushes to attack* MORONAO. BANNAI *momentarily is able to block* WAKASANOSUKE'*s path, but then is hurled to the floor as* WAKASANOSUKE *pushes past.* MORONAO *falls to his knees. He clasps his hands together pleadingly.* BANNAI *throws his arms around* WAKASANOSUKE'*s lower leg, holding him fast. Music stops.*]

MORONAO: There you are, there you are, Lord Wakasanosuke, good Wakasanosuke. Your early arrival makes me ashamed, ashamed, so very ashamed. I was rude to you at Hachiman Shrine. I was. [WAKASANOSUKE *edges forward as if to draw.*] Now, now, now, you have every right to be angry. But have pity on a foolish old samurai. I throw my sword at your feet. I clasp my hands and apologize. Bannai, Bannai, you too, bow, apologize to Lord Wakasanosuke.

NARRATOR [*sings*]: Flattering, and what is more, detestable words so sweet. Taken aback completely, Wakasanosuke wonders what has happened. There is nothing he can do . . .

[MORONAO *bows his head low to the floor.* WAKASANOSUKE *cannot believe his eyes, seeing the proud councilor abasing himself. He kicks* BANNAI *away, slips his sword arm inside his vest, and strides past* MORONAO. MORONAO *circles to avoid him, crawling on his hands and knees indecorously.* WAKASANOSUKE *turns back, spitting out his words.*]

WAKASANOSUKE: Contemptible samurai! [*He strides off stage left.*]

MORONAO: I was wrong, I was wrong, I apologize, I apologize, I . . .

Act I, scene 3: The Pine Room of the shogunal mansion. Honzō's bribes have had their intended effect: Moronao (Ichimura Uzaemon XVII) obsequiously throws his sword at the feet of Wakasanosuke (Onoe Tatsunosuke). Bannai (Ichikawa Nedanji) desperately clings to Wakasanosuke to stop him from drawing. Kabuki performance at the National Theater of Japan, Tokyo. *(Photo: Don Kozono.)*

[Eyes fearfully on the ground, MORONAO *continues.* BANNAI *registers comic shock, seeing his master bowing and speaking to no one. He scurries forward on his hands and knees. He pulls* MORONAO's *sleeve. Music stops. Their eyes meet.* BANNAI *nods in the direction of* WAKASANOSUKE's *exit.* MORONAO *sees that he is alone and sighs with relief. Recovering his dignity, he sits up.*]

MORONAO: Bannai, that stupid young puppy meant, I think, to kill me. "A sword in a fool's hand makes the wise man cautious."

BANNAI [*bowing*]: Oh yes, my lord, how true.

NARRATOR [*chants "Jo no Mai" ("Slow Dance") drum and flute music*]: Who has planned this mischievous fate? [*Sings.*] Enya Hangan . . . innocent of this all, proceeds to Moronao. [*Chants.*] Moronao . . . seeing his victim!

[Simultaneously, BANNAI *arranges his master's sword and the lantern and exits stage left while* HANGAN *appears on the hana-michi, carrying in his left hand the letter box given by* KAMPEI's *retainer. Nō-style "Jo no Mai" drum and flute music continues in the background.*]

MORONAO [*ominously*]: Late, late, late! You're late, Hangan!

*[*HANGAN *bows slightly and hurries on stage. He kneels, bowing again.*]

HANGAN: I humbly beg your pardon for being a few moments late. I come ready for your instructions. First, however, I have been asked by my wife to place this letter in your hands. [*He moves forward on his knees, places the letter box on the floor besides* MORONAO, *moves back, and bows respectfully.*]

MORONAO [*feigning ignorance*]: Hmm, hmm. A letter from Lady Kaoyo? To me? [*Opens the box and removes the letter card.*] Ah, I understand. My poetic skill is renowned. No doubt she wishes me to place the touch of my pen upon her heartfelt words, to correct any blemishes. There is time before the cere-monies. Sit and be at ease. [*He reads.*] "A woman's love does, not lie in the hopeful eye, of her beholder; not beholden to lie I, aver never to lie with you." [*Music stops.* MORONAO *again.*] "Not beholden to lie I, aver never to lie . . . with you."

NARRATOR [*chanting rapidly*]: After weighing the words . . . Kaoyo has rejected my love and this is the proof! This must mean that Hangan has found out my intention! [*Sings.*] Anger and humiliation . . . but pretending ignorance.

[MORONAO *looks straight forward, his face frozen in humiliated rage, his right hand slowly closing into a rigid fist that crushes his brocade silk robe. Masking his emotions he turns toward* HANGAN. *Drum and flute music resume.*]

MORONAO: Hangan, was this poem shown to you?

HANGAN [*bows politely*]: I have not seen it until this moment, your Excellency.

[*Reassured that* HANGAN *is not party to* KAOYO'*s insult,* MORONAO *proceeds to deliberately humiliate him.*]

MORONAO: Is that so? Well, the lord of little Hakushu castle has a clever wife. She can dash off a subtle poem like this. A woman so talented and famous for her beauty must be a source of great husbandly pride. Such a superlative creature in fact, that her infatuated husband, not bearing to be separated from her, finds his sacred duties at the palace . . . wearisome!

[MORONAO *casually turns his back to* HANGAN, *idly playing with his fan.*]

NARRATOR [*chants*]: Moronao is filled with spiteful words of insinuation. Riding on his frustration . . . any may be his prey. Hangan is perplexed at the burst of displeasure. [*Sings.*] Gushing anger, he holds it down, holds it in!

[HANGAN *starts. He almost turns to confront* MORONAO, *but then suppresses his anger. He pretends to smile, as if sharing* MORONAO'*s joke. Ominous drum beats continue in the background.*]

HANGAN: Ha, ha, ha, ha. I see my lordship is in a playful mood. He has, perhaps, been drinking and is feeling in good humor. Yes, surely my lord has been drinking. Ha, ha, ha, ha.

MORONAO [*dangerously, facing* HANGAN]: What is that? When have you seen me drinking? You, who have never offered me as much as a cup of wine? Whether I, Moronao, choose to drink or not, nothing keeps me from *my* duty! The one who's been drinking is you, Hangan. You've come from a drinking party with your charming wife, she pouring for you, and you pouring for her! Isn't that why you come to the palace late?

[HANGAN's face tightens. MORONAO *notices and turns away with a malicious look in his eye.*]

Isn't there a story about a stay-at-home like you, helpless beyond his front door? I seem to recall . . . ah, yes, the "Tadpole in the Puddle." There once was a young tadpole that lived in a tiny puddle. He knew no other place between heaven and earth, and so he thought his puddle the most wonderful home in the world. One day a compassionate person passed by, just like Moronao, who, taking pity, lifted him from his stagnant pool and released him in the waters of a broad river. [*Arms out,* MORONAO *deliberately strikes* HANGAN's *chest with his heavy fan.*] Well, the tadpole was out of his depth, dropped suddenly into the great world from his shallow one. Completely at a loss, willy-nilly he went this way, and willy-nilly he went that way. [*Pointing with fan.*] And in the end he ran headfirst smack into a bridgepost. [*Strikes* HANGAN *full in the chest with his fan.*] And shivering and quivering, and shivering and quivering, the little tadpole expired. [*Twirling his fan in limp fingers.*] The tadpole is . . . you! [*Looks full into* HANGAN's *straining face.*] Oh? I do believe the young tadpole has lost his tail and is turning into a toad. [HANGAN *turns and glares furiously at* MORONAO.] Yes, with your eyes bulging out, Hangan, you look exactly like a toad. Ha, ha, ha, ha! This Moronao has lived many years, but this is the first time I've seen in the palace a toad wearing clothes. Oh, come here, come here, Bannai, Hangan's turning into a toad. Hangan *is* a toad, a sa–mu–rai toad! [*Drum beats stop. Silence.* MORONAO *deliberately strikes* HANGAN's *chest, sword hilt, and chest with his fan.*] Ha, ha, ha, ha, ha!

NARRATOR [*chants*]: Toad! Devil talk! Demon words!

[MORONAO *rears back, points contemptuously at* HANGAN *with his fan, rotates his head, and poses in a* mie *to two loud* tsuke *beats. Music stops.*]

Hangan can no more take the vile old man!

HANGAN [*slowly, with dangerous, suppressed fury*]: Do you dare compare Enya Hangan Takasada, castle lord of Hakushu . . . to

Act I, scene 3: Moronao (Ichimura Uzaemon XVII) taunts Hangan (Onoe Baikō VII) by telling the tale of the tadpole who "shivering and quivering, and shivering and quivering" lost his way in the river and expired. Kabuki production at the National Theater of Japan, Tokyo. *(Photo: Don Kozono.)*

Act I, scene 3: Moronao deliberately provokes Hangan, striking him on the chest with his fan while he taunts, "Hangan is a toad, a toad, a samurai toad!" Jōruri production at the Aichi Culture Hall, Nagoya, 1965. *(Photo: James T. Araki.)*

a toad? You cannot possibly mean the words you have said! Have you gone out of your mind . . . Councilor Moronao! [HANGAN *pivots to face* MORONAO, *slapping his thigh for emphasis.*]

MORONAO [*darkly*]: Watch yourself, Hangan! Remember I am councilor of the shōgun. No one calls me insane. You are ludicrous!

HANGAN: You have been deliberately insulting me? Do you dare tell me that!

MORONAO [*insinuatingly*]: Indeed, I dare. And if I dare, who are you to complain?

HANGAN [*drawn out*]: If you dare . . .

MORONAO [*leaning in insolently*]: If I dare . . . ?

HANGAN: Hmm!

[HANGAN's *patience snaps. He rises on one knee, his hand on his sword.* MORONAO *instantly parries* HANGAN's *sword arm with his closed fan.*]

MORONAO [*commandingly*]: The palace! [MORONAO *slaps* HANGAN's *sword arm away and the two men pull back:* MORONAO *fearfully,* HANGAN *furious.*] The palace! The palace! It is the palace! Don't you know the law? Draw your sword in the palace and your house will be destroyed! Don't you know that! [*Drum beats resume.* MORONAO *slaps his fan commandingly on the floor.* HANGAN, *anguished that he must restrain his rage, folds his arms tightly over the hilts of his swords and slowly sinks back onto his haunches.* MORONAO *notes this and is emboldened to continue his provocation.*] Hm, since you know . . . then go ahead, kill me. Well . . . draw . . . draw . . . draw your sword. Come, kill me! Kill me . . . Hangan!

[MORONAO *forces himself bodily against* HANGAN *and leans against* HANGAN's *swords. They pose. Burning with humiliation,* HANGAN *abases himself in order to fulfill his ceremonial duties. He backs away and bows low.*]

HANGAN: A moment, a moment, Lord Moronao, I beg your indulgence. Without thinking I spoke out of turn. I implore you, instruct me in my duties for the ceremony. I will do as you say. Humbly, I beseech you, your Excellency.

[*Music stops.* HANGAN *looks up from his bow.* MORONAO *smugly turns away, avoiding his gaze.* HANGAN's *patience snaps a second time: his hand leaps for his sword. Instantly* MORONAO *reacts.*]

MORONAO: Your hand!

HANGAN: My hand?

MORONAO [*with all his authority*]: Yes, your hand!

HANGAN: This hand . . .

[*He hesitates, looks at his trembling hand, then drops his hands to the floor and bows in defeat.*]

. . . humbly begs your forgiveness.

MORONAO [*savoring his victory*]: So, you apologize, do you? Very well, very well. Soon instructions in great detail for today's ceremony . . .

HANGAN [*looks up hopefully*]: . . . will be given to me?

MORONAO [*viciously*]: No, not to you! To Wakasanosuke! [HANGAN *is stunned, motionless. In silence* MORONAO *casually rises, tears* KAOYO's *letter card in two, and throws the pieces in* HANGAN's *face.*] There is no educating a provincial barbarian.

[MORONAO *deliberately turns his back and kicks his left and right trailing trouser legs in* HANGAN's *face.* HANGAN *rears back. Chuckling,* MORONAO *starts to leave.*]

HANGAN: Moronao! Wait!

[HANGAN *steps on* MORONAO's *trailing trouser leg.* MORONAO *is brought up short. He tugs at the trouser; it is held fast.*]

MORONAO: [*deadly calm*]: Be careful. You'll soil my trousers. Hop. Hop, hop, hop. [MORONAO *turns to leave, but cannot move.*] So, you won't hop away, little toad? Can there be something else you want?

HANGAN: What I want is . . .

MORONAO: What you want is . . . ?

[HANGAN *quietly slips his sword arm free of the stiff vest.* MORONAO *turns and thrusts his sneering face toward* HANGAN.]

Act I, scene 3: Hangan (Nakamura Utaemon VI) is prevented from pursuing Moronao, and Moronao escapes. In kabuki performance a dozen Provincial Lords surround him as the curtain closes. Honzō, the first to seize and hold Hangan, is unseen except for his hands under Hangan's arms. Performance at the Shimbashi Embujō, Tokyo, 1958. *(Photo: James T. Araki.)*

Act I, Scene 3: In jōruri, Hangan is flanked by two puppet figures. Honzō, instead of holding Hangan, can be clearly seen standing behind him. Aichi Culture Hall, Nagoya, 1965. *(Photo: James T. Araki.)*

HANGAN [*a scream*]: You!

[HANGAN's *short sword flashes out of its sheath and gashes* MO-RONAO's *forehead. Drum and flute play furious "Haya Mai" ("Fast Dance").* MORONAO *staggers and falls.* BANNAI *rushes on to help his master flee.* HANGAN *leaps to his feet and is about to finish* MORONAO *with a second blow when* HONZŌ, *who has been hiding behind a decorative screen stage right, rushes out and seizes* HANGAN *from behind.*]

NARRATOR: "Hold me not! My foe is there!"

[*Six* PROVINCIAL LORDS *run on from right.* HANGAN *struggles to get free, but he is encircled and held fast. In desperation he hurls his sword after the disappearing enemy. A single sharp clack of the* ki. *The sword falls short. He reaches out with both hands after* MORONAO *and poses: his fingers curl into fists and his chest heaves with sobs of mortification. But* HONZŌ *and the* PROVINCIAL LORDS *hold him fast. To gradually accelerating* ki *clacks the curtain is run closed. Offstage musicians play "Shagi-ri." A single* ki *clack concludes the act.*]

ACT II

SCENE 1 *Fugitive Travel*

[*The large drum beats melancholy "Yama Oto" ("Mountain Pattern"). To accelerating* ki *clacks the curtain is slowly pushed open. A sky-blue curtain fills the stage. A single* ki *clack: the blue curtain drops and is whisked away by black-robed* STAGE ASSISTANTS *to reveal a colorful springtime scene in the country. Snow-covered Mt. Fuji is seen in the background, pink cherry blossoms bloom everywhere.* OKARU *and* KAMPEI *stand center, their faces hidden behind a straw hat. A temple bell tolls in the distance.* Kiyomoto *music begins from off stage.* KAMPEI *lowers the hat and we see the lovers dressed for traveling: kimono skirts raised and a bundle over* KAMPEI's *shoulder. They mime in slow dance movements to the* kiyomoto *lyrics the story of their disgrace and flight.*]

KIYOMOTO SINGER: Oh, you who flee, do you not see yon green field, a veil of new green?

[*They look at the flowers at their feet, to the left and the right. They look into each other's eyes, then pose gazing into the distance. Singing ends; samisen continues in the background. Facing upstage, they pass their sandals and* KAMPEI's *hat and bundle to two* STAGE ASSISTANTS. *They turn front and kneel center stage.* KAMPEI *places his long sword on the ground beside him.*]

KAMPEI [*melancholy*]: Giving myself over in love to you, I failed our master when he needed me, and now we are fugitives fleeing in the dead of night I know not where. When I think of it, I no longer have the heart to live. Say prayers over the grave of this dishonored samurai. Okaru . . . farewell.

[KAMPEI *takes his short sword from his sash and is about to draw the blade. Gently she seizes it and prevents him.*]

OKARU: No, I won't have you saying that again. I am to blame that you were not beside Lord Hangan. I cannot live without you. If you die then so must I. But rather than praising your spirit, people will say we died as lovers frequently do. Please, live, dearest Kampei. Live . . . in love . . . for me.

[KAMPEI *tries to draw the sword again. She pulls one way, he the other.* KAMPEI, *irresolute, allows her to take the short sword. She places it beside her, away from his reach.*]

KIYOMOTO SINGER: " 'Twas then my heart went astray. It was when you, yes, you made me love, oh, so imprudently. Blame my imprudent heart that spoke to me thus: 'So easy it is to die, but you must live, live on.' "

[KAMPEI *takes up the long sword to kill himself. Again, she gently holds the scabbard so that he cannot draw. They rise and move left, then right, in a delicate struggle for the sword. Allowing himself to be persuaded, they pose with the sword held firmly in her hands. He looks away, wiping his falling tears. She takes the sword and places it out of his reach. They kneel side-by-side.*]

KAMPEI: Your tenderness overwhelms me. [*Nods with resolution.*] We will flee across the mountains to your father's home.

OKARU [*smiling, relieved*]: You make me so happy.

KAMPEI: In time I know I can find a way to atone for deserting my master. Come, let us go.

OKARU [*meekly*]: Yes, Kampei.

KIYOMOTO SINGER: Now for travel they prepare, but who should confront them! [KAMPEI *rises and poses facing front.*]

BANNAI [*off, at the rear of the* hanamichi]: Hey, hey! Here we go!

FIGHTING CHORUS [*also off*]: Haaa!

[*Loud beats of the big drum. Strong accelerating* tsuke *pattern as* BANNAI *runs onto the* hanamichi *followed by eight of his men, the* FIGHTING CHORUS. BANNAI *has his kimono tucked up to his knees, and a cord holds back his sleeves. His makeup has become ludicrous: bat-shaped eyebrows, drooping eyes, and a tiny blue-gray mustache. The* FIGHTING CHORUS *is dressed identically in red leggings and arm coverings and red and white patterned kimono that stop at their knees. Each carries a branch of cherry blossoms as a weapon.* BANNAI *stops at the seven-three position.* KAMPEI *escorts* OKARU *to the left, out of harm's way, and stands calmly.*]

BANNAI [*a comic challenge*]: Hey, hey! Kampei!

[*He stamps forward with two steps, each accented by two* tsuke *beats. He and his men march on stage. The men, alert for their master's call, kneel upstage in two rows.* BANNAI *faces front, with a supercilious look. He speaks in a special rhythmical pattern,* nori, *in which each dialogue phrase fits into an eight-beat samisen musical phrase. He accompanies the tale with comic gestures.*]

Your stupid master, Enya Hangan, Takasada and, my honored master, Councilor Moronao, met in the palace while, chittering chattering, chittering chattering, your master Hangan, flew into a snit. Taking a teensy sword, he whipped it out, he made a slash. He is a traitor, locked up in his residence, boxed up like a criminal. Ha ha ha . . . ha ha ha . . . haha haha hahaha! Hangan has been hauled away! I'll catch you like a chick! I'll pluck you like a duck! I am claiming Okaru! Well? Well? Well, well? [*Accelerating.*] Well, well, well, well, well! Kampei! Your goose is cooked! Give her . . . to me!

[BANNAI *stands on tiptoe, holds his sword hilts threateningly, and cocks his head in comic* mie *to two beats of the* tsuke.]

KIYOMOTO SINGER: "Give her to me," yells Sagisaka Bannai. Kampei bursts out with mocking laughter.

KAMPEI [*laughs, then speaks in rhythmic* nori *phrases*]: You are a funny bird, Sagisaka Bannai, a little chirping sparrow, I could swallow in a bite. [*Rapidly.*] Kampei's fiery gaze could fry you to a crisp! But instead of eating you, I will make you eat crow!

[KAMPEI *slips his fists out of the breast of his kimono, allowing the black outer kimono to drop. An inner kimono of brilliant crimson color is revealed. He stamps aggressively forward, then poses with arms outstretched, head cocked in a* mie, *to two* tsuke *beats.* BANNAI *tumbles to the ground terrified.*]

KIYOMOTO SINGER: Glaring and with arms outstretched, Kampei stands before him!

BANNAI [*weakly*]: Help!

[Kiyomoto *samisen and drums play instrumental music as the eight members of the* FIGHTING CHORUS *attack* KAMPEI. KAMPEI *waves half of them past him until he stands center in a* mie *position. Four men face him from either side, holding their cherry branches as if they were swords. They strike at him right, left, right. He forces them back. They fall away. They pose in a* mie *to two* tsuke *beats.* KAMPEI *now fights his opponents in a series of group combats that are executed in delicate, controlled dance patterns. Rhythmic drums and samisen support the action.*]

KIYOMOTO SINGER: Cherry, cherry blossoms! A name, oh, so beloved.

[*One man on each side strikes at* KAMPEI *with the cherry branch. Three times* KAMPEI *avoids, then seizing the tips of the branches, he whirls them in a circle and presses them to their knees. He poses in a* mie. *Flicking the branches away, the men are hit on the forehead; they retreat.* KAMPEI *nonchalantly dusts off his hands.*]

"No, no, you can't have her," and why should that be?

[*One man on each side seizes* KAMPEI's *arms. They struggle right, left, right.* KAMPEI *flicks them forward onto their knees. They try to seize his feet, he backs up. They rush in to encircle him. He avoids, then casually taps them on the back. They do a cartwheel and fall prostrate on the ground.* KAMPEI *poses in a* mie.]

So tender, so fine, so frail, never to be won by you!

[*Four men form a square around* KAMPEI. *Two-by-two they attack, but he pivots to avoid them. Six men strike with their cherry branches.* KAMPEI *drops to his knees, deftly knocks the wind*

out of them with an open-hand blow, and, with a sweeping ges-
ture, knocks them off their feet. They fall on their bottoms in
unison.]

Delightful, though she's only to be seen. How can you ever feel
true love, if she won't play with you!

[*The* FIGHTING CHORUS *retires upstage.* BANNAI *pulls* OKARU *by*
the sleeve. Foolishly flirting, he touches his cheek to her hand.
KAMPEI *pushes him away, and when* BANNAI *tries to get past to*
OKARU, *blocks his way.* BANNAI *slips under* KAMPEI'*s sleeve, but*
is caught and held by the nape of the neck. BANNAI *struggles*
free, strikes at KAMPEI, *is kicked to his knees, and finally is*
grasped by the ear, lifted, and spun around. BANNAI *is near*
tears in frustration and humiliation. Trying once again, he raises
his fist, but KAMPEI *turns and casually pushes* BANNAI *to the*
ground. KAMPEI *stamps forward and poses in a strong* mie *to two*
tsuke *beats.*]

BANNAI [*plaintively*]: Take him!

[*Large drum and* tsuke *beats. The* FIGHTING CHORUS *attacks in*
unison: KAMPEI *passes them off right and left as he strides from*
stage left to right; he turns and passes unharmed between them
as they strike at him with their cherry branches. One man, com-
ing from hiding, strikes at KAMPEI *from behind.* KAMPEI *kicks*
him to the ground, places his foot on his back, and poses in a
strong mie *to two beats of the* tsuke. KAMPEI *kicks the man away*
and attacks. Booming drum accelerates. The FIGHTING CHORUS
retreats. They run pell-mell down the hanamichi *and out of*
sight. KAMPEI *poses in a powerful ''stone-throwing''* mie *to two*
beats of the tsuke. BANNAI *sneaks up.*]

BANNAI: Kampei, here I come!

[BANNAI *raises his sword to strike.* KAMPEI *catches his wrist,*
spins him around, forces him to his knees, and raises the sword.]

KAMPEI [*bantering*]: Shall I cut your ears off? [*Terrified,* BANNAI
covers his ears with wildly trembling hands.] Shall I cut off your
nose? [BANNAI *covers his nose.*] Or shall I simply kill you?

OKARU: Killing him would bring more trouble. So, please, just let
him go.

Act II, scene 1: Usually in kabuki, Kampei's fight with Bannai is staged as a comic, stylized dance. The scene is bright daylight. The surroundings are beautiful. Bannai is dressed as a comic character. Kampei (Kathryn Yashiki); Bannai (Kati Kuroda); Okaru (Elizabeth Wichmann). English-language production, University Theatre, University of Hawaii, 1969; directed by Nakamura Matagorō. *(Photo: Don Kozono.)*

BANNAI [*foolishly, imitating* OKARU'*s inflections*]: So, please, just let him go! [BANNAI *clasps his trembling hands together in prayer.*]

KIYOMOTO SINGER: Oh, how he prattles on, that bird, Sagisaka! Smoothing his ruffled feathers, slowly, then faster, flirts with death, and yet to live, away he flies!

[KAMPEI *nods agreement. He casually rolls* BANNAI *across the stage away from* OKARU. *He poses facing front.* BANNAI *rubs his throat, then noticing* KAMPEI *is holding his sword, meekly gestures a request that it be returned. Contemptuously,* KAMPEI *tosses the sword on the ground.* BANNAI *leaps back in terror. Gathering his courage, he snares the sword with his foot, then suddenly turns and raises the sword as if to strike. A fierce glance from* KAMPEI *deflates him completely. He turns and escapes off right, lifting his legs high in the air in a "stork walk."*]

KAMPEI: He deserved to die. But his death would be a crime to add to my disloyalty.

[*A cock crows in the distance. They both look up into the sky. They speak in melancholy, poetic tones.*]

Already it is dawning . . .

OKARU: . . . on the peaks of the mountains . . .

KAMPEI: . . . the eastern light glows . . .

OKARU and KAMPEI [*in unison*]: . . . lighting trailing clouds.

[*They pose together center stage, absorbed in their own melancholy.*]

KIYOMOTO SINGER: They fly away at daybreak, like the crows that cry, "caw, caw." So dear to each other, in love, in love.

[*A* STAGE ASSISTANT *passes to* OKARU *the hat, bundle, and swords. Dutifully,* OKARU *helps* KAMPEI *adjust the bundle and slide the swords into his sash. They put on their sandals. A temple bell tolls. They move apart, pose, then move back-to-back.*]

Though they must hasten to depart, their minds are filled with woe. Who would doubt their loyalty if they proved the guilt they feel? Away they go.

[*They look into each other's eyes. Restraining tears,* KAMPEI *puts on a manly bearing, takes* OKARU *by the hand, and turns to begin their long journey.* BANNAI *sneaks up behind them. He holds* OKARU *by the waist.*]

BANNAI: Okaru is mine, all mine!

[KAMPEI *moves to block* BANNAI, *passing* OKARU *to safety on the* hanamichi. *He pushes* BANNAI *away and turns to join* OKARU.]

BANNAI: Kampei, wait!

KAMPEI [*turning back at the seven-three position*]: Bannai, you want . . . ?

BANNAI [*posing*]: Kampei, I want . . .

KAMPEI: Hmm?

BANNAI [*deflated*]: Nothing.

KAMPEI: Simpleton!

[*A loud* ki *clack:* BANNAI *collapses to the ground. Drum booms loudly.* KAMPEI *takes* OKARU's *hand and slowly they exit down the* hanamichi. *Kiyomoto samisen plays plaintive chords and* ki *clacks accelerate as the curtain begins to close.* BANNAI *is in the path of the curtain. He retreats before it, then, realizing it is hopeless, seizes the curtain with both hands and, grinning happily, prances across the stage, closing the curtain and disappearing from sight. A single* ki *clack: drum and flute play lively "Shagiri" to close the scene.*]

SCENE 2   *Hangan's Suicide*

[*Two* ki *clacks: the curtain is slowly opened to the rachetlike sound of an old-fashioned clock. The scene is a large, formal room in* HANGAN's *mansion. Sliding doors that make up the rear wall are painted powder blue and covered with silver crests of* HANGAN's *clan. Tatami matting covers the floor.* HANGAN, *dressed in a simple kimono and vest so pale a blue-gray that it verges on white, kneels center. He faces two envoys from the shōgun,* ISHIDŌ *and* YAKUSHIJI, *who are sitting stage left on*

Act II, scene I: Kampei (Ichikawa Danjūrō XI) consoles Okaru (Onoe Baikō VII) on the *hanamichi* at the conclusion of the battle with the Fighting Chorus. Bannai (Matsumoto Kōshirō VIII) cannot follow them; his path is blocked by the closing curtain. Resigned, he seizes the curtain and runs it closed. Kabukiza, Tokyo. *(Photo: Shochiku.)*

high stools. They wear dark kimono, vests, and trousers. ISHIDŌ*'s sympathetic manner contrasts sharply with* YAKUSHIJI*'s derisive attitude.* GOEMON, *a senior retainer of* HANGAN, *kneels upstage. Silence.* ISHIDŌ *rises and faces* HANGAN. *He takes from the breast of his kimono a large folded letter. He holds it reverently to his forehead.*]

ISHIDŌ: Hear the shōgun's command. [*Removing the letter from its envelope, he reads.*] "Whereas, Enya Hangan Takasada, you have willfully committed an act of bloodshed against our chief councilor, Moronao, and thereby have defiled the palace, know that your estates, large and small, are hereby confiscated and you are ordered to end your life by *seppuku.*"

[ISHIDŌ *gravely holds the open letter in front of him, so* HANGAN *can read the order with his own eyes. After glancing at it,* HANGAN *bows respectfully.*]

HANGAN [*with perfect control*]: In all respects I accept the shōgun's command.

NARRATOR [*chants*]: From the adjoining room, knocking on the door . . .

[*A* RETAINER *knocks on the sliding door. He speaks in a faint, muffled voice, suggesting tears.*]

RETAINER [*off*]: Goemon, Goemon. We, Lord Hangan's retainers, beg permission to see our master . . .

RETAINERS [*off, quietly in unison*]: . . . one last time.

GOEMON [*bowing to* HANGAN]: My lord, your retainers wish to see you.

HANGAN: Tell them not until Chief Retainer Yuranosuke has arrived from our province.

GOEMON [*facing the door*]: You heard our lord. You may enter when Yuranosuke arrives, not before.

RETAINERS [*scarcely audible*]: Ahhh.

NARRATOR [*sings*]: Their plea, not granted . . . no one dares utter a single word. In the room, silence prevails. [HANGAN *rises and retires upstage, where he kneels with his back to the audience.*]

GOEMON [*quietly, facing offstage right*]: Proceed.

RETAINERS [*faintly, off*]: Yes.

[*In complete silence arrangements are made for* HANGAN'*s death by ritual disembowelment.* RETAINERS, *dressed in somber blue and gray kimono, vests, and split trousers, swiftly and unobtrusively enter. They place two tatami mats center to make a six-foot square platform. They cover it with a pure white cloth. Sprigs of green, in small bamboo holders, are placed at the four corners. With downcast eyes, the* RETAINERS *slip quietly away.* GOEMON *bows to* HANGAN *indicating that the place of suicide is ready.* HANGAN *rises, slowly pivots front, and crosses down to the cloth seat. Unconsciously his gaze drifts to the* hanamichi: *he is waiting for the arrival of his chief retainer,* YURANOSUKE, *and does not want to die before passing to him his last instructions. His right foot touches the cloth. He remembers it is obligatory to step into the place of suicide with the left foot. He glances at the envoys to see if they have noticed: they are gazing straight ahead. He deliberately steps onto the cloth and slowly kneels.*]

NARRATOR [*chants*]: Rikiya proceeds with the saddest order. [*Sings.*]
The master's suicide blade weighing heavy on his heart . . .

[YURANOSUKE's *son,* RIKIYA, *enters from up left. He carries a
plain wooden tray bearing the short dagger with which* HANGAN
*will kill himself. The long sleeves of his black kimono and a del-
icate forelock of hair indicate he is a youth, not yet grown to
manhood. He places the tray on the floor before the envoys for
their verification. He bows.* ISHIDŌ *and* YAKUSHIJI *look at the
blade, then nod to each other that it is satisfactory.* ISHIDŌ *nods
gravely to* RIKIYA.]

NARRATOR: Before Lord Hangan he lays the blade.

[RIKIYA *places the tray on the cloth before* HANGAN, *bows low,
and then looks up for instructions.* HANGAN *looks gently into*
RIKIYA's *eyes and with a single head movement indicates that*
RIKIYA *is to leave: a boy so young should not have to witness
seppuku.* RIKIYA *politely shakes his head: until his father arrives, he must fulfill his father's duties.* HANGAN *repeats the
order to leave; again* RIKIYA *shakes his head. Impressed by the
boy's loyalty,* HANGAN *nods that he may stay.* RIKIYA *bows
gratefully, rises, backs away, and takes a place beside* GOEMON.]

NARRATOR [*sings*]: Taking off, in hushed silence, his outer clothes to
expose his death robe . . . securing the seat of death.

[HANGAN *prepares himself for death with calm deliberation. He
slips off the vest, letting it drop to his waist. He tucks the ends
under his legs so as to hold his body in place after he has died.
He drops the outer kimono to his waist and tucks it in as well.
Beneath he is wearing a pure white kimono appropriate for
death, an indication to the envoys that he was prepared to die
even before they brought the shōgun's command. He places his
hands firmly on his thighs and looks intently down the* hanamichi.]

HANGAN [*softly but urgently*]: Rikiya.

RIKIYA [*bowing*]: Yes.

HANGAN: Yuranosuke . . . ?

RIKIYA: Yuranosuke . . . [*He looks down the* hanamichi *for a sign
that his father has arrived.*]. . . has not as yet arrived.

NARRATOR [*sings*]: Proper steps for suicide, he lifts the tray and bows. [*Chants.*] Waiting no longer, the blade in his hand.

[HANGAN *prepares the dagger. He lifts the tray to his forehead respectfully. He ceremoniously takes the dagger in his right hand and a sheet of white paper in his left. He wraps the paper around the blade until only its tip is bare. He is now able to grasp the blade low for extra leverage. He holds the blade at ready on his thigh. The tip points to his stomach. Outwardly calm, his voice betrays his anxiety.*]

HANGAN: Rikiya, Rikiya!

RIKIYA [*bowing*]: Yes.

HANGAN: Yuranosuke . . . ?

RIKIYA: Yes! [RIKIYA *bows and rushes to the end of the* hanamichi. *He falls to his knees, looks to the right, the left, then straight ahead, searching for sight of his father. His lip trembles, he is close to tears.*] Yuranosuke . . . [*He rushes back and throws himself on the floor before* HANGAN.]. . . has not as yet arrived!

HANGAN [*calmly*]: Tell him that I regret . . . not seeing him one last time. [HANGAN *nods that* RIKIYA *may retire and pivots slightly toward* ISHIDŌ.] Lord Ishidō, I ask that you witness and report my death.

NARRATOR [*sings*]: Here at last the time has come, the blade is aimed. Hangan . . . thrusts it in . . . thrusts it deep!

[HANGAN *places the tray behind him. He rises slightly on his knees, looking one last time down the* hanamichi *for* YURANO-SUKE. *He holds the dagger under the ribs on his left side. With a sudden jerk he thrusts the blade into his stomach. Involuntarily his body drops forward and his head falls. Rapid narrative shifts to chanting.*]

Running at a desperate speed, the awaited person comes! Here at last is Ōboshi Yuranosuke! A frantic gaze at his master: "Is he still alive?" Overcome by the sight, he falls on his knees!

[YURANOSUKE *bursts onto the* hanamichi, *running frantically, all decorum cast aside. He wears a formal gray kimono, vest, and trousers pulled up for travel. Reaching the seven-three position, he sees his master in the midst of suicide. He reels, falls back, then slowly sinks to his knees.*]

ISHIDŌ [*rising*]: Is it Ōboshi Yuranosuke?

YURANOSUKE: It is.

ISHIDŌ [*urgently*]: Approach, approach quickly!

[YURANOSUKE *attempts to rise, but his legs will not function. He weeps unashamedly. To gain control of himself, he reaches inside the breast of his kimono to pull tight the inner cloth binding his waist. With great effort he pushes himself up from the floor and moves unsteadily to* HANGAN's *side. He falls to his knees and bows deeply.*]

NARRATOR [*chants*]: The men of Hangan, all, till now forbidden . . . but no longer! They come rushing in!

[*Ten* RETAINERS *enter swiftly from up right. They are barefooted and carry no swords. They fall to their knees in a row upstage and, following* YURANOSUKE's *lead, bow deeply to their master* HANGAN. YURANOSUKE's *eyes remain downcast and* HANGAN, *in pain, does not yet look up.*]

YURANOSUKE: Ōboshi Yuranosuke kneels before my lord.

HANGAN [*weakly*]: Yuranosuke?

YURANOSUKE: I am here.

HANGAN: At last you've come.

YURANOSUKE: All that I could ever ask is to be at your side in these last moments . . .

HANGAN: Ah, it makes me content as well. [*Slowly their gazes meet.*] You have heard, have you not . . . everything . . . everything . . . ?

[*His voice trails off in pain.* YURANOSUKE *edges closer, looking meaningfully at* HANGAN.]

YURANOSUKE: Yes!

HANGAN [*rousing himself*]: I am humiliated . . . !

YURANOSUKE [*interrupting*]: No words can express such feelings as I hold. Nothing remains now but for me to assure you a just end.

a

b

Act II, scene 2: Enya Hangan (Onoe Baikō VII) kills himself by *seppuku:* (a) kneeling on white mats, he removes the upper garment of his death robes; (b) he wraps the dagger in white paper so that he can firmly grasp it low on the blade; (c) he is about to plunge the tip of the blade into the left side of his stomach; (d) having

c

d

pulled the blade from left to right across his stomach, near death and in great agony, he raises the dagger to cut his jugular vein. Kabuki production at the National Theater of Japan, Tokyo. *(Photos: Don Kozono.)*

HANGAN [*meaningfully*]: One thing remains.

NARRATOR [*chants*]: Gripping tight the blade, cutting straight across in disembowelment. [*Sings.*] Such moments of agony . . . exhaling his breath . . .

[HANGAN *cuts his stomach across from left to right. Although the pain is excruciating and his lips tremble and his breathing grows labored,* HANGAN *maintains the stoic decorum expected of a samurai until the blade reaches its final point just under the right ribs. Then breath seems to leave him. His body sags. He braces his left hand on his thigh.*]

HANGAN [*faintly*]: Yuranosuke . . . Yuranosuke . . . come close . . .

YURANOSUKE: Yes.

[HANGAN *is near death.* YURANOSUKE *slides forward urgently. Knowing* HANGAN *cannot speak openly because the shōgun's envoys are present, he searches his master's face for some command.*]

HANGAN: Take this blade . . . to remind you . . . do not forget. Re-ve-n . . . [YURANOSUKE *starts.* HANGAN *must not say "revenge" out loud.* HANGAN *catches himself.*] . . . remember me.

[*Weakly* HANGAN *looks into* YURANOSUKE'*s face, then down the* hanamichi. YURANOSUKE *follows* HANGAN'*s gaze. Master and retainer look deeply into each other's eyes.* YURANOSUKE *understands that in spite of his master's seeming calm acceptance of the death sentence,* HANGAN *passionately desires vengeance against the enemy outside the mansion, that is,* MORONAO.]

YURANOSUKE [*passionately*]: I swear!

[YURANOSUKE *slaps his chest for emphasis and bows deeply.* HANGAN *knows that* YURANOSUKE *understands. He is now free to die. He smiles.*]

HANGAN: Ha ha. Ha ha. Ha, ha, ha, ha . . .

[*The laugh fades. With ebbing strength,* HANGAN *pulls the blade from his stomach. He gasps.*]

NARRATOR [*chants*]: Aiming the blade at his throat . . . one slash across. Breathing his last breath, lifeless he crumples.

[*Weakened hands, trembling violently, lift the blade upward. He tilts his head. His neck is exposed. A quick slash and the jugular vein is cut. His body rises upward in three spasms of breath. His eyes flutter closed. He falls limply forward, dead. Silently* ISHIDŌ *rises. A* STAGE ASSISTANT *whisks his stool off stage.* ISHIDŌ *places the shōgun's letter on his open fan and places them on* HANGAN's *body. He moves stage right and kneels beside* YURANOSUKE.]

ISHIDŌ [*quietly*]: Yuranosuke, Yakushiji now assumes authority over Hangan's estates. Hangan's retainers are hereby denied the rank of samurai and are disbanded. I will report to the shōgun that the death of Hangan is accomplished. You have my deepest sympathy, Yuranosuke.

NARRATOR [*sings*]: Ishidō, the envoy, expresses sympathy. His sad assignment is over.

[ISHIDŌ *rises facing the line of* RETAINERS. *He raises his arms in a gesture of condolence. The* RETAINERS *look up, then bow respectfully. Slowly* ISHIDŌ *walks to the seven-three position on the* hanamichi. *At a signal from* YURANOSUKE, RIKIYA *moves forward to see him out.* ISHIDŌ *turns back.*]

ISHIDŌ: There is no need. There is no need.

NARRATOR: He prays silently.

[ISHIDŌ *folds his hands and, with downcast eyes, walks slowly down the* hanamichi *and out of sight.*]

NARRATOR [*chants*]: Yakushiji holds them in contempt!

[YAKUSHIJI *rises brusquely. The* STAGE ASSISTANT *takes away his stool.*]

YAKUSHIJI: Now that he's dead, I'm master here! Cart the corpse away, while I settle in. Show me the way! [*He starts to go, then turns back.*] It's a sad time, isn't it! Ha, ha, ha, ha!

[YAKUSHIJI *strides off left, shown out by a* RETAINER. *Complete silence.* YURANOSUKE *moves in to attend to his master's body. He straightens the legs and brings kimono and vest up over the torso. He moves closer and tries to take the dagger from* HANGAN's *hand. In death* HANGAN's *fingers hold it tightly.* YURANOSUKE *falls back weeping. He gently massages his master's hand until the fingers are warmed, softened, and the dag-*

ger slips from their grasp. YURANOSUKE *places the dagger carefully into the breast of his kimono. He backs away. He and the* RETAINERS *bow expectantly.*]

NARRATOR [*singing plaintively*]: Lady Kaoyo enters from another room. Her hair so long and black, oh, so beautiful, now pitiful, it is no more. She will pray as a nun, till her end.

[KAOYO *and four* LADIES-IN-WAITING *enter from the left, walking with downcast eyes. They are dressed in pure white kimono and hold Buddhist rosaries. The last* LADY-IN-WAITING *carries a small tray on which rests the cloth-wrapped remains of* KAOYO*'s long hair. They kneel left. The* MAIDS *bow deeply.*]

KAOYO [*quietly*]: Yuranosuke. When I think of why my husband had to die, and that I was the cause . . .

YURANOSUKE [*firmly*]: My lady, please understand our heartfelt feelings. All of us, each retainer offers his deepest condolence.

[YURANOSUKE *bows to* KAOYO, *then nods to* GOEMON. GOEMON *and the* RETAINERS *rise and move in a circle around their master.*

Act II, scene 2: The dagger is grasped tightly by Hangan's hand even after death. When Ōboshi Yuranosuke (Nakamura Kanzaburō XVII) attempts to remove it he finds, to his surprise, that he must forcibly peel back each finger in order to release the blade. Kabuki production at the National Theater of Japan, Tokyo. *(Photo: Don Kozono.)*

Silently, they take up the white cloth, the tatami mats, tray, and sprigs of green. They exit upstage right. HANGAN *moves off behind the cloth. In an instant all sign of the suicide is removed.*]

KAOYO: Yuranosuke.

YURANOSUKE: Yes, my lady.

KAOYO: I offer my lock of hair.

[*The* LADY-IN-WAITING *places the tray with the hair center stage.* YURANOSUKE *sees it and weeps.* KAOYO *turns to show her close-cropped head.*]

NARRATOR [*prolonged, melancholy singing*]: Kaoyo is left behind, her grief is so . . . o . . . o . . . She yearns to go to the temple . . .

[*She rises, as if to follow her husband, but* YURANOSUKE *stops her with a commanding gesture.*]

YURANOSUKE: My lady!

[*She falls back weakly. A single* ki *clack. They move into a pose:* YURANOSUKE *picks up the tray with one hand and forces her back with the other;* KAOYO *faces front, lifts the rosary to her eyes, and sobs silently. Ki clacks accelerate as the curtain is slowly walked closed.*]

SCENE 3   *Outer Gate*

[*Two* ki *clacks signal drum and flute to play "Toki no Taiko" ("Time Drum"). The curtain is pushed quickly open. The scene is outside the massive outer gate of* HANGAN'*s mansion. No one is on stage.*]

NARRATOR [*chanting rapidly*]: Farewell to Hangan. Now his body lies alone. The young retainers run back from the temple! They no longer can hold the shame inside!

[*To loud, accelerating* tsuke *beats,* RIKIYA *leads a band of* RETAINERS *onto the* hanamichi. *They urge each other on with shouts of "Kill them!" "They won't have our lord's mansion!" "We'll fight them!" "Lord Hangan was unjustly killed!" At the same time* YURANOSUKE *and* GOEMON *come out of a small door in the gate.* GOEMON *rushes up to the* RETAINERS *with out-*

stretched arms, shouting, "Stop, stop!" YURANOSUKE *roughly pushes* RIKIYA *to the ground.*]

YURANOSUKE [*furious*]: What, you too, Rikiya? What are you thinking of, trying to attack the mansion? We are no longer samurai. We cannot fight Yakushiji's men. [*Drops to one knee, hand on the hilt of his short sword.*] If you do not stop, I shall commit *seppuku* on this very spot! Do you want to be my seconds, all of you?

RETAINERS: No, but master . . .

YURANOSUKE [*implacably*]: Then will you stop when I tell you?

RETAINERS: Yes, but . . .

YURANOSUKE: It will achieve nothing to die now!

[*The* RETAINERS *cannot disobey. Grumbling and rebellious, they begin to fall back.*]

NARRATOR [*chants*]: Behind the gate is heard . . . Yakushiji's voice!

YAKUSHIJI [*off*]: Hey, men, there's a sight. Newly hatched ex-samurai, milling around like chickens with their heads cut off! It's enough to make you laugh!

YAKUSHIJI'S MEN [*off*]: Ha, ha, ha, ha, ha!

FIRST RETAINER: Do you . . .

RETAINERS: . . . hear that?

[*Furious, they turn to storm the gate, hands on the hilts of their swords.* YURANOSUKE *springs into their path and blocks the way.*]

YURANOSUKE: Have you forgotten our late lord?

RETAINERS: No, but . . .

YURANOSUKE: Not now! Go back, go back! Go back I tell you!

[YURANOSUKE *draws himself up commandingly. He runs his hand up the edge of his vest and poses in a furious* mie. *Two* tsuke *beats.*]

NARRATOR [*sings*]: "Go back," he commands!

YURANOSUKE [*almost in a scolding tone now*]: Back, back, back.

[YURANOSUKE *waves them away. They fall back grudgingly, then turn and stride off down the* hanamichi. YURANOSUKE *watches them leave. He is alone. Silence. He sighs with relief. The hand at his breast slides down until it accidentally touches the dagger. He slowly drops to his knees and takes it out. He unwraps the covering purple cloth. The blade tip is red with* HAN-GAN's *blood.*]

NARRATOR [*sings*]: The suicide blade, red with blood, cries out for revenge . . . cries out for revenge! Burning tears rake his heart, tears . . . falling . . . falling . . . falling . . . falling . . .

[*Gazing at the blade,* YURANOSUKE's *chest heaves. He covers his eyes to hide the tears.*]

Hangan's last words of vengeance imbedded deep in Yuranosuke. [*Chanting.*] We know indeed the motive of Yuranosuke, his revenge to be noted for many ages . . . forty-seven loyal men immortalized!

[*He wipes blood from the blade onto his palm and then deliberately brings his hand up to his mouth. He licks the blood as an oath of vengeance. Music stops. Silence.* YURANOSUKE *begins his long pantomime of departure. He carefully wraps the dagger in the purple cloth. He holds it to his forehead respectfully. He places it in the breast of his kimono. He rises and stands. He slaps the dust from his knees. He adjusts his trousers. He folds both hands inside his kimono sleeves. He rests his hands on the hilts of his swords. He half-closes his eyes, regretting deeply that he must abandon his master's mansion. A temple bell tolls in the distance. Pensively, he begins to walk away from the gate. The gate recedes, indicating* YURANOSUKE *has covered a long distance. He turns back. A crow caws in the distance. He resumes the painful separation. A crow caws a second time. A second bell tolls. He stops, stricken with the finality of parting. Then, he moves onto the* hanamichi. *Once more he turns back and, as if he has no heart to continue, slides to his knees. A temple bell tolls. Plaintive, tentative chords of the samisen begin. He rises, begins to walk away, looks sadly over his shoulder for one last glimpse, then resolutely turns and strides down the* hanamichi *and out of sight. Music crescendoes and ki clacks accelerate: the curtain is run closed. Drum and flute play rapid "Shagiri" to end the scene.*]

ACT III

SCENE 1 *Ichiriki Brothel*

[*Two* ki *clacks: the curtain is pushed open to offstage singing of "Hana ni Asobaba" ("If You Play in the Flowers"). The scene is the Ichiriki Brothel in the Gion licensed quarter in Kyoto. Two pavilions are set in a garden. Lying on his side in the larger room, stage center, is* YURANOSUKE. *He is feigning sleep, his face covered with a half-open fan. He wears an elegant purple kimono and matching cloak. Curtains are at the back and a stone water basin is left. Three steps lead down into the garden. Paper-covered sliding doors conceal the interior of the smaller pavilion, stage left. It is several feet higher off the ground than the center pavilion.*]

NARRATOR [*singing briskly*]: The mountains and the moon. From the eastern mountains, just a few miles, breathless from running fast, the young man . . . Rikiya.

[RIKIYA *enters on the* hanamichi. *A purple scarf covers his head and serves as a partial disguise. His black kimono is hiked up at the sides, to free his legs for running. He stops at a garden gate set on the* hanamichi *at the seven-three position. He looks back to see if he is being observed, then swiftly passes through the gate, closing it.*]

Entering the brothel garden . . . there lies Yuranosuke, pretending to be drunk. Taking caution to wake his father in secrecy, he walks softly in, stepping close to him. The sword guard speaks!

[RIKIYA *sees his father. He mounts the steps, kneels, and makes a ringing sound by striking sword guard against sheath.* YURA-NOSUKE *gestures* RIKIYA *away with a sleepy movement of the fan.* RIKIYA *crosses swiftly back through the gate, closes it, looks around to be certain they are not being observed, and kneels to wait for his father. Offstage samisen play tentative chords.* YURANOSUKE *rises. He staggers as if drunk, ad-libbing, "That was heady wine. I need some air. Don't go away, girls. I'll be in the garden." He looks through the curtains to see if anyone is watching. He crosses to the gate, stumbling several times in order to have the chance to look carefully in all directions. He stands swaying, fan before his face. He speaks guardedly.*]

YURANOSUKE: Rikiya, do I hear the sound of urgency in the echo of your sword?

RIKIYA: Yes, Father. I bring a secret message from Lady Kaoyo. [RIKIYA *brings out a letter from his right sleeve and passes it to* YURANOSUKE, *who puts it immediately into the breast of his kimono without examining it.*]

Act III, scene 1: Rikiya calls his father, Yuranosuke, to the gate of the brothel garden. He carries a secret letter from Kaoyo warning that Moronao is about to escape.
Rikiya wears a cloth over his head to hide his identity; Yuranosuke feigns drunkenness as part of his ruse to allay Moronao's suspicions. The three-man system of puppet manipulation can be seen with Yuranosuke: the chief puppeteer is unhooded;
the middle puppeteer moves the feet; and the outside puppeteer manipulates the
left hand of the puppet. Jōruri production at the Aichi Culture Hall, Nagoya, 1965.
(Photo: James T. Araki.)

YURANOSUKE [*carefully*]: Did she say anything to you?

RIKIYA [*rising on his knees urgently*]: Soon, soon our enemy . . .

YURANOSUKE: Rikiya! "Soon at night our enemy, flees like plovers o'er the sea. . . ."

[*Music swells. To cover the slip of his son's tongue,* YURANO-SUKE *sings a well-known passage from a nō play. He staggers in a circle looking to see if anyone has heard* RIKIYA's *remark. Simultaneously,* RIKIYA *pivots in the opposite direction, looking for eavesdroppers.* YURANOSUKE *gestures for* RIKIYA *to come closer;* RIKIYA *whispers* KAOYO's *message in his father's ear. The curtains in the room center part.* KUDAYŪ *peeks out. He is a gray-haired former retainer of* HANGAN, *now secretly working for* MORONAO. *He wears a plain brown kimono and cloak. He watches for a moment, then slips away.*]

YURANOSUKE: Send a palanquin for me tonight. Tell the others to be ready. Go, go!

NARRATOR [*sings*]: No time left for hesitation . . . to the eastern hills, homeward now . . .

[YURANOSUKE *sharply gestures with the fan.* RIKIYA *bows, rises, and holding firmly onto the hilts of his swords, begins to leave.*]

YURANOSUKE: Rikiya!

RIKIYA [*returning and bowing*]: Yes.

YURANOSUKE: Be careful while passing through the quarter. Then hurry! Go now!

RIKIYA: Yes!

NARRATOR: Rikiya returns home.

[RIKIYA *realizes his mistake; he is holding his swords ready to draw, thus calling attention to himself. He hides the hilts with his sleeves. Swiftly, carefully, he hurries down the* hanamichi *out of sight. Offstage samisen play* "Odoriji Aikata" *("Dance Melody"). Four* MAIDS *and a male* JESTER *enter through the curtain, ad-libbing,* "Yura, where are you?" "Come drink with us." "Don't leave us, Yura." YURANOSUKE *pretends drunkenness again.*]

FIRST MAID: Yura, Yura, are you here?

YURANOSUKE: Hmm. You've come to get me? I'm a lucky man. Come close all of you, let's amuse ourselves. Come, sing and dance for me.

[YURANOSUKE *sits on the steps. The* MAIDS *and the* JESTER *kneel in the garden in a semicircle around him.*]

SECOND MAID: Very well . . .

ALL: . . . let's begin, let's begin!

[*Lilting music of offstage samisen, drum, and bell accompanies various dances and songs. These are extemporized by the performers from production to production.* MAIDS *and* JESTER *ad-lib comic banter throughout.*]

MAIDS [*clapping as they sing*]: "What will it be like, what will it be like? If you don't be careful, we will make you drink. Ah, what will it be like, what will it be like?"

[JESTER *and* THIRD MAID *rise and move center. They do a game of* jan-ken-po, *"scissors-paper-stone." He loses. She laughingly pushes him. He falls in a heap on the ground. The* MAIDS *rise and form pairs.*]

FOURTH MAID: Come, let's dance!

ALL: "First your left foot, then your right, tap, tap, tap;
Around we go, back again;
Are you ready, one, two, three!"

[*They circle left, then right, touching palms of their outstretched hands. They turn their backs to each other and bump bottoms on the count of three. With peals of laughter they recover their balance. The* JESTER *and* YURANOSUKE *laugh and applaud.*]

YURANOSUKE: Very good, very good!

FIRST MAID: How about a game, Yura dear?

JESTER: Blind man's bluff!

SECOND MAID: You be It!

ALL: Yes, yes!

[YURANOSUKE *tries to wave them away, but they playfully surround him and put a cloth over his eyes. They twirl him around in the center of the garden, and move left, laughing and clapping in time to their song.*]

ALL: "Yura, Yura, over here;
Listen to our clapping hands."

YURANOSUKE [*sings*]: "I'll catch you all, soon enough you'll see."

[*He stumbles in their direction. They easily avoid his outstretched arms and flee to the other side of the garden.*]

ALL: "Yura, Yura over here;
Come and catch us if you can."

YURANOSUKE: "I'll catch you all, and make you drink with me."

[*They duck under his arms. When he turns back to continue pursuit, they take him by the hands and, still singing and clapping, lead him off to the inner room with his blindfold still in place. They are no sooner off than* KUDAYŪ*'s head pops through the curtain on the other side of the stage. Samisen music stops.* KUDAYŪ *peers about intently. He slips into the room.*]

KUDAYŪ: That letter Rikiya gave to Yuranosuke . . . the rumor of a vendetta must be true! He has not forgotten; they are plotting, just as I thought. When I tell Moronao, what will be my great reward? If, of course, it's true. I'll spy him out! Here's a perfect place to hide.

[*He sees a hiding place. He removes a board under the veranda, opening a space for him to crawl in. He hides behind the steps.* YURANOSUKE *enters alone from upstage, pretending to be drunk.*]

YURANOSUKE: I'll be back . . . don't wait, girls . . . in a minute, I'll be back.

[*Samisen music resumes. He looks around. Seeing he is alone, he drops his pretense. He rinses his mouth with water from the stone basin. He spits it out. It falls on the unsuspecting* KUDAYŪ. *He takes out the letter from* KAOYO *and holds it respectfully to his forehead. He begins to read, slowly unrolling the letter until it reaches the ground. At the same time the paper doors slide open to reveal* OKARU *in the small room left.*]

She wears the elaborate hairstyle and clinging kimono of a courtesan.]

NARRATOR [*sings*]: Evening breeze, brings a courtesan, Kampei's wife Okaru, away from her love. Someone has sent a love letter, "I wish it were for me." Okaru from a room above, tries to see the words. Too far in the evening dusk, the letters are not clear to read. Thinking of a way out, a mirror in her hand, she leans back . . . mirror held up high, reflection of the letter. Under the floor a spy, Kudayū waits . . . the trailing letter glows in the moonlight. [*Chants.*] Who could know someone is reading words of confidence?

[*The three form a tableau:* YURANOSUKE *is engrossed in reading the secret letter;* OKARU *views the letter backwards in a mirror; and* KUDAYŪ, *spectacles on his nose, reads the bottom portion, line-by-line, as it comes down to him. Narrative shifts to singing.*]

Okaru, unaware that her hairpin has loosened! [*Chants.*] It drops to the floor! Surprised by the sound above, he quickly hides the letter . . . Yuranosuke! Underneath Kudayū smirking at his game. [*Sings.*] Okaru pretends nothing has happened here.

[YURANOSUKE *quickly resumes his drunken role. He begins to roll up the letter, but not before* KUDAYŪ *rips off the part he has been reading.* OKARU *puts down the mirror, picks up a fan, and turns to* YURANOSUKE.]

OKARU [*languidly*]: Yura dear, is it you?

YURANOSUKE: Hmm, Okaru? So close at hand, what are you doing?

OKARU [*in poetic form of seven and five syllables*]: Yura dear, it's all your fault, I drank too much wine; my head is whirling round and I can scarcely see; I have come to sober up, wafted by the evening breeze.

[YURANOSUKE *reaches the end of the letter. He feels the ragged edge. Startled, he looks quickly at the letter, then puts it away in the breast of his kimono. He takes out a piece of tissue paper and wads it up, covering his action by improvising conversation with* OKARU.]

Act III, scene 1: One of the elaborate stage compositions designed to show off the physical dexterity of the puppets that is typical of jōruri stagecraft. Kabuki productions closely follow such jōruri compositions as in the letter-reading sequence: Yuranosuke (Don Kozono) reads the secret letter by the light of a veranda lantern; beneath the veranda Moronao's spy Kudayū (Howard Noh) peeks at the bottom section; and in the room opposite Okaru (Elizabeth Wichmann) deciphers it—from its reversed image—in her vanity mirror. Okaru leans backward in a common female-puppet pose. English-language kabuki performance, University Theatre, University of Hawaii, 1979; directed by Nakamura Matagorō. *(Photo: Don Kozono.)*

YURANOSUKE: Hmm. Wafted by the evening breeze, you say? Wafted by the evening breeze? Ah!

> [*He drops the wad of paper to the ground.* KUDAYŪ, *thinking it is part of the letter, snatches it and stuffs it into his kimono breast.* YURANOSUKE *falls back, supposedly in a drunken stupor, but actually wanting to ponder what to do next. He decides. Soft samisen plays "Odoriji Aikata" in the background.*]

Hm. Okaru, there is something I want to talk to you about. Come over here.

OKARU [*rises as if to leave her room*]: Very well, I'll come around and visit you.

YURANOSUKE [*coming down into the garden*]: No, Okaru, if you go that way the maids will catch you. They will force on you more wine. Ah, a ladder. Fortune smiles. Climb down this way and you won't be seen. [*Places a ladder against* OKARU's *pavilion. Bantering.*] Descend for me, Okaru!

OKARU [*coquettishly on the ladder*]: I've never climbed a ladder before.

YURANOSUKE: You've climbed other things.

OKARU: I'm not used to this strange position. It frightens me.

YURANOSUKE: You're past the age to be afraid of a new position. Straddle it, open your legs, it'll all go smoothly.

OKARU: Don't be naughty, Yura. I tell you it frightens me. It's swaying like a boat.

YURANOSUKE: Never mind, I'll throw in my anchor. That will hold you down. Where shall I put it? [*He tries to lift her skirt with his fan. She brushes his hand away.*]

OKARU: You mustn't peek, Yura.

YURANOSUKE [*singing*]: "I adore your crescent moon, glistening in its secret grotto." Ha, ha, ha.

OKARU [*pouting*]: If you talk that way, I won't come down.

YURANOSUKE: Don't prattle like a virgin. You're a courtesan in the Gion brothel. I'll take you from behind. [YURANOSUKE *embraces her from behind.*]

OKARU: Oh, stop it.

YURANOSUKE: Then come, come.

OKARU: I am, I am!

[*Laughing, she slips off the final rung of the ladder and moves away from* YURANOSUKE. *She kneels right, fanning herself.* YURANOSUKE *glances at her sharply, then resumes the drunken pose. He stoops to retrieve the dropped hairpin and crosses to give it to her.*]

YURANOSUKE [*casually*]: Just now, Okaru, did something catch your eye?

OKARU: I . . . nothing.

YURANOSUKE [*coaxing*]: Come now, didn't you see, didn't you see . . .

OKARU: . . . your interesting letter . . .

YURANOSUKE: . . . from up above?

OKARU [*lightly*]: Hmm, yes.

YURANOSUKE: And you read it all?

OKARU: Oh, you do go on.

> [*Covering his concern, he pretends to stumble. He recovers his balance, singing a nō song which both hides and expresses his feelings.*]

YURANOSUKE: "Fate conspires to bring, my life to this crisis. . . ." [*Mimes striking a nō drum.*] Ya, tum, tum, tum! Ha, ha, ha!

OKARU [*turns to him, laughing*]: What in the world do you mean?

YURANOSUKE: It means that of all the women in the world, I have become enamored of you. Come live with me, Okaru.

OKARU: Stop it. You're such a tease!

YURANOSUKE [*grandiloquently*]: I will redeem your contract with the master of the brothel and take you away.

OKARU: I don't believe it. You're making fun of me.

YURANOSUKE: I'll prove it's not a lie. Be my mistress for just three days, and after that, Okaru, your spirit will be free to go where it will.

OKARU [*taking him seriously for the first time*]: For three days?

YURANOSUKE: On my sacred oath as a samurai. Live with me for three days. I'll find the master and buy your contract now. Well, is it agreed?

> [OKARU *looks carefully at him to see if it possibly can be true. They pose. She bows low.*]

OKARU: I am grateful, Yuranosuke.

YURANOSUKE: Can it make you happy to be redeemed . . . by this Yuranosuke?

OKARU: Oh, yes!

YURANOSUKE: Such radiance shines in that happy face.

[*They pose: she looks at him with gratitude; flicking open his fan, he covers his face to hide his stricken expression.*]

YURANOSUKE: Don't go away now. I'll be right back.

OKARU: Three days? Yes, Yuranosuke. I'll be here.

[*Off stage, sad "Yo ni mo Inga" ("Nighttime Fate") is sung quietly. They lightly ad-lib to cover his exit. Still pretending to be drunk, he staggers up the steps. He turns back several times. He passes through the curtains in search of the master of the house. When he is gone she kneels center stage, trembling with excitement.*]

OKARU: How happy I am! I must write to dearest Kampei that I am coming home! And to Mother and Father, to tell the wonderful news!

[*She hurries up the steps into the center room, brings out a writing box and roll of letter paper, kneels, and begins to write a letter home. Song ends.*]

NARRATOR [*chants*]: Now appears . . . Heiemon!

[*Offstage samisen briskly play "Odoriji Aikata." A young samurai strides on from the right into the garden. His hair is severely drawn back and his plain kimono suggests poverty. It is* HEIEMON, OKARU's *older brother, in search of both* YURANOSUKE *and* OKARU. *He looks around, then seeing a woman in the room, enters and sits behind her. He speaks brusquely, almost rudely.*]

HEIEMON: Sorry to trouble you, Miss, but I am looking for a young woman, from my hometown of Yamazaki, by the name of Okaru, brought here a year ago . . .

[*Hearing her name* OKARU *turns. They recognize each other.*]

Sister!

OKARU: Heiemon! Oh! I feel ashamed for you to see me here!

[OKARU's *demeanor completely changes: in the presence of a male family member who is her elder, she becomes submissive, gentle, a little girl seeking approbation. She hides her face. She rushes down the steps, and falls to her knees.* HEIEMON, *though stern, acts protectively toward her. He rises and poses on the steps.*]

HEIEMON: What is there to feel ashamed of? When I returned home Mother told me you had sold yourself to this brothel, hoping that with your contract price Kampei could contribute to the vendetta against Lord Hangan's enemy. You have willingly sacrificed yourself for your husband and for Lord Hangan. I am proud of you, Okaru! [*He poses at the top of the steps: right foot forward, right arm extended protectively in her direction.*]

OKARU [*hesitantly, looks up at him*]: Then you're not going to scold me?

HEIEMON: Scold you? I am filled with admiration, filled with admiration!

[*He crosses down the steps and kneels. He sits proudly, sword placed on the ground beside him.*]

OKARU: I'm happy that you think kindly of me. [*Becoming excited.*] Oh, there are so many things I want to ask my dear big brother. I don't know where to begin . . . how is Kam . . .

HEIEMON [*uneasy*]: Kam . . .?

[*OKARU is embarrassed to have asked about her husband first. She changes the subject.*]

OKARU: Come . . . tell me, how is Mother?

HEIEMON: Set your mind at ease. Mother is well.

OKARU: And Father? Nothing troubles him, I hope?

HEIEMON [*uncomfortably*]: Hm . . . Father . . . he is at rest . . . he is at rest.

OKARU [*modestly*]: And what of Kampei?

HEIEMON: Kampei? Ah . . . well . . . he is as well as can be.

OKARU: You set my heart at ease. [*Bubbling.*] Oh, I forgot . . . be happy for me, Brother. Tonight, without warning, Yuranosuke offered to buy out my contract.

HEIEMON: Yuranosuke did that? [*Trying to understand how such a thing could be.*] Ah, then he's become your patron?

OKARU: Nonsense. We have only drunk together two or three times. And Heiemon, it's almost too good to be true. After three days he will let me come home.

HEIEMON: Hm? Then you told him you are Kampei's wife?

OKARU: How could I, a prostitute, tell him that and bring disgrace to Kampei and to my parents?

HEIEMON [*facing front*]: Hm! Then he is no more than a whoremaster! [*He slaps his thigh in anger.*] He has no intention of avenging Hangan, our lord and master!

OKARU: Oh, no, Brother, he has. He has. Listen . . .

NARRATOR [*sings*]: In whispers, the content of the letter is revealed.

[OKARU *and* HEIEMON *rise. He leans forward. She whispers in his ear. They pose for a moment, then break apart and kneel.*]

OKARU: . . . so you see?

HEIEMON [*shocked*]: Then you read it all?

OKARU: Yes, and after reading it, his eye met mine, and flirting, he looked me up and down, up and down, and then began to talk of taking me away.

[OKARU *mimes his flirting by pressing the backs of her index fingers together, right on top of left, then left on top of right.* HEIEMON *is puzzled. He tries to understand her words, miming as she did.*]

HEIEMON: What? After reading it, flirting, he looked you up and down, up and down . . . [*He slaps his thigh for emphasis.*] Ah! Now I understand!

OKARU [*laughing*]: You startled me.

HEIEMON [*facing the inner room, he bows low*]: Forgive me, Master Yuranosuke, I misjudged you! I was wrong, forgive me!

OKARU: Dearest Brother, what in the world are you doing?

HEIEMON: [*turns and looks into* OKARU*'s eyes*]: Dear Sister. There is something I must ask of you. Okaru, do now exactly as I say.

OKARU: You sound so very stiff and formal. What must you ask of me?

HEIEMON: What I must ask of you is . . .

OKARU: What you must ask of me is . . . ?

HEIEMON: Okaru, let your brother take your life!

> [*He springs to his feet and whips out his long sword. She falls back. Rapid "Odoriji Aikata." To double beats of the* tsuke, *he slashes at her right, left, right. She avoids. She rises and pushes him away. He turns to strike; she distracts him with a shower of tissue paper drawn from her breast and thrown in the air. She runs to the* hanamichi; *he follows. She closes the gate between them. They pose in a* mie *to two loud* tsuke *beats: on the ground, she holds up her hands imploringly; he stands with legs together, the sword directly overhead as if to strike. Music stops.*]

OKARU [*appealing to him*]: What am I supposed to have done wrong? You have no right to just do as you please. I have my husband and both my parents to care for. Forgive me if I have spoken out of turn. I clasp my hands and beg you to spare me!

NARRATOR [*sings*]: Seeing his sister's clasped hands . . . a brother's love overwhelms the dutiful heart. He can only cry.

> [*He tries to but cannot strike his sister. He falls back distraught, turns upstage to face away from her, holds the sword behind his back, and weeps unashamedly. When the narration is finished, he turns to face* OKARU. *He is contrite. Slow offstage "Odoriji Aikata" resumes in the background.*]

HEIEMON: I was wrong, Okaru, not to explain. Come, come over here.

> [*He waves her to him. She flounces.*]

OKARU: No, I will not come near you.

HEIEMON [*sternly*]: When your elder brother calls, why don't you come?

OKARU [*sweetly*]: If you want to know, I'll tell you why: I think you still intend to kill me, and I don't like that at all!

> [HEIEMON *notices the long sword in his hand. He puts it on the ground and pushes it toward her.*]

HEIEMON: Ah, this. There is nothing to stop you now. So come, come!

OKARU: Yes, there is. Something else.

[*She points at the short sword in his sash. Annoyed, he pushes it toward her.*]

HEIEMON: There, now. Come over here!

[*She rises and is about to cross through the gate. She looks at him and stops.*]

OKARU: Your face is so frightening.

HEIEMON: I can't help that. This is the face I was born with.

OKARU: Well then, please turn around.

HEIEMON: What a nuisance. Like this? Like this?

[*Grumbling, he turns his back. He poses with arms stretched out to either side.*]

OKARU: Now, don't look. Keep your face turned away. [*She cautiously goes through the gate, picks up the swords, and puts them out of his reach. She kneels behind him, placing her hands on his sash. Music stops. She poses.*] All right, here I am. Brother dear, what is it you want? [*He turns to face her. He places his hands protectively on her shoulders. They pose.*]

HEIEMON [*voice filled with emotion, he speaks in poetic form of seven and five syllables*]: Once you were a samurai, now a courtesan; combing out your silken hair, while the world has changed; precious Sister how pitiful, totally unaware of the life you left behind!

[HEIEMON *breaks away and kneels left.* OKARU *moves close.*]

OKARU: Totally unaware . . . of what, Heiemon?

HEIEMON: Soon after you left home last year, one rainy night, Father was . . .

OKARU [*frightened*]: Father was . . . ?

HEIEMON [*choked scream*]: . . . struck down by a robber and slain by his sword!

OKARU [*falls back slackly*]: That cannot be true.

HEIEMON: You must be strong, Okaru. You look forward to leaving here and being with your husband . . .

OKARU: Yes . . . Kampei . . . what about Kampei?

HEIEMON: Kampei . . .

OKARU: Kampei . . . ?

HEIEMON [*a terrible scream*]: Cut open his stomach and is dead!

> [*He mimes the suicide and collapses, weeping.* OKARU *falls back, shocked, hardly able to breathe.*]

OKARU: Kampei . . . oh . . . no. What shall I do? What shall I do?

HEIEMON: I know, I know, I know . . .

> [*They speak alternately, then faster and faster, until they are speaking at the same time. Then their grief-stricken voices fade away.* OKARU *crawls to her older brother and puts her head on his lap. She weeps pitiably. At last* HEIEMON *gains control of himself. He gently disengages himself.*]

HEIEMON: Don't you see? Yuranosuke is not a man to be infatuated, and he did not know you were Kampei's wife. Okaru, you were wrong to have read that secret letter. Yuranosuke's loyalty is clear. He cannot risk letting you live and he intends to buy your contract . . . just to kill you! Rather than dying at someone else's hand, let me be the one to take your life. Let me prove to Yuranosuke and his followers that though I am a mere foot soldier, my spirit is as loyal as theirs. Let me serve our late master. Give me your life, dear Sister!

NARRATOR [*sings*]: The tragedy is disclosed! Okaru is prepared!

> [HEIEMON *is agonized by the conflict between his duty to* HANGAN *and his love for* OKARU. *He beseeches her with clasped hands.* OKARU *willingly prepares to sacrifice herself. Gently she opens his hands.*]

OKARU: It is my karma not to meet my beloved husband and father again. There is no reason for me to live.

> [*She crosses to get the swords, returns, and places them before him.*]

Brother dear, please end my life now.

[*She turns her back, clasps her hands in prayer, and drops her head forward, exposing her neck to his sword.*]

HEIEMON: Admirable resolve. Namu Amida Butsu. Praise Buddha the Merciful.

[*He stands. He unsheaths the sword. He raises it to strike.* YURA-NOSUKE'*s voice is heard from behind the curtain.*]

YURANOSUKE [*off*]: Wait, wait! Stop at once! [*He enters.*] Your behavior is admirable, both of you. I acknowledge your loyalty. Heiemon, I hereby permit you to accompany us on our journey to the east.

[HEIEMON *and* OKARU *move right and kneel respectfully.* HEIE-MON *is excited by* YURANOSUKE'*s acceptance of him into the vendetta group.*]

HEIEMON: Then you are ready? And I may go with you? Okaru, Sister, do you hear? I am forever grateful.

[HEIEMON *bows to* YURANOSUKE. YURANOSUKE *comes down the steps.*]

YURANOSUKE: Okaru, for your loyalty, your husband, Kampei, will be admitted to our league. And since he was unable during his life to kill even a single enemy, let your action, Okaru, serve as his apology to Lord Hangan in the afterlife . . . here and now . . .

[YURANOSUKE *takes* HEIEMON'*s long sword and places it in* OKARU'*s hands. He guides her to the veranda. They pose.*]

NARRATOR [*chants*]: Thrusting deep through the dark of the hiding place. The hateful spy, Kudayū, a fatal blow in his shoulder, rolls and turns in deadly pain!

[*They thrust the sword under the veranda. Double* tsuke *beats.* KUDAYŪ *cries out.* HEIEMON *drags the mortally wounded* KUDAYŪ *into the garden and throws him to the ground.* YURANOSUKE *kneels, and holding* KUDAYŪ *by the scruff of the neck, strikes furiously with closed fan.*]

YURANOSUKE: Kudayū, you wretch! Traitor! More than forty of us day and night have shed tears of agony. We have parted from our children, deserted our parents, and sold our wives into prostitution—all in order to avenge our Lord Hangan's death. And you, who enjoyed wealth and honor in his service, have betrayed your master and become Moronao's spy! Fiend! Demon! You are a monster!

NARRATOR [*sings*]: As if to grind him into the ground, Yuranosuke . . . his burst of anger cannot be gratified!

[*He strikes him five times to sharp* tsuke *beats. Then contemptuously he pushes him away. Bringing his hand to his eyes,* YURANOSUKE *openly weeps. Just then the* MAIDS *cry out offstage. Rapid "Odoriji Aikata." Instantly* YURANOSUKE *reverts to his pose as a drunken brothel patron. He rises, staggering. The* MAIDS *enter and kneel in a semicircle in the center room.*]

FIRST MAID: Master Yuranosuke, Master Yuranosuke . . .

SECOND MAID: . . . your palanquin has arrived.

YURANOSUKE: You've come for me?

ALL: We will see you out.

[YURANOSUKE *crosses up the steps and stands at the top. He gestures for* OKARU *to join him there and for* HEIEMON *to pick up the nearly dead* KUDAYŪ. *Music stops.*]

YURANOSUKE: Heiemon. Take our drunken friend to the Kamo River. Let him drown his sorrows . . . in the waters there!

[YURANOSUKE *flicks open his fan and raises it overhead.* OKARU *kneels beside* YURANOSUKE, *placing her hands on his sash.* HEIEMON *drapes* KUDAYŪ'*s limp body over his shoulder. A single sharp clack of the* ki. *They freeze in a group* mie *pose.* Ki *clacks accelerate, drum beats speed up, and off stage "Odoriji Aikata" crescendoes as the curtain is slowly pushed closed.*]

SCENE 2   *Vendetta*

[*Two sharp* ki *clacks: large drum softly beats "Yuki Oto" ("Snow Sound"). The* ki *clacks accelerate to accompany the opening of the curtain. The scene is the garden of* MORONAO'*s mansion in Edo. It is night. Snow is falling. Rocks, trees,*

Act III, scene 1: In jōruri performance the Ichiriki Brothel scene concludes with Heiemon lifting Kudayū overhead and posing. The curtain is then closed. This feat of
strength, so easy for the puppets, cannot be duplicated by kabuki actors; in kabuki,
Heiemon merely throws Kudayū's right arm over his shoulder and leans the dying
man's weight against his body. Aichi Culture Hall, Nagoya, 1965. *(Photo: James T.
Araki.)*

> *ground, and small bridge across a pond are covered with a man-
> tle of white. Soft, rapid* tsuke *beats. Several* WOMEN *from*
> MORONAO's *household rush on from the left. They are wearing
> nightclothes. Frightened and confused they urge each other to
> flee. They disappear. Drum and* tsuke *beats crescendo. Two* RE-
> TAINERS *with drawn swords rush on from the right. They pose.*]

MORONAO'S RETAINER: I am Riku Handayū, retainer of Moronao.
Name yourself!

HANGAN'S RETAINER: Akagaki Genzō, loyal to Enya Hangan. Let
me pass!

[*They pose. Another two* RETAINERS *run on from the left.*]

MORONAO'S RETAINER: You will burn in hell before you touch Lord
Moronao!

HANGAN'S RETAINER: I, Katayama Genta, will take his head for Lord
Hangan! Stand aside!

[*Large drum pattern of triple beats, "Mitsudaiko," and loud continuous* tsuke *beats. The paired opponents fight: they slash and parry with their long swords. In the end* HANGAN's *men gain the upper hand;* MORONAO's *men turn and are pursued off stage. Drumming changes to quiet "Snow Sound."* SHIMIZU *enters on the* hanamichi. *He is a famous swordsman hired by* MORONAO *as a bodyguard. A woman's kimono is draped over his head as a disguise, to allow him to reach the side of his master without being detained by* HANGAN's *men. He stops at the seven-three position.*]

SHIMIZU: The war drum. Yuranosuke has come at last. But he will not succeed. The moon shall see the severed heads of forty-seven rōnin before it witnesses the death of Lord Moronao!

[SHIMIZU *rushes on stage. He meets* TAKEMORI, *one of* HANGAN's *men. They circle each other warily.* SHIMIZU's *swords are seen.*]

TAKEMORI: Stop! Who are you?

SHIMIZU [*dropping the kimono to his waist*]: I am Shimizu Ichigaku, protector of Lord Moronao.

TAKEMORI: And I am Takemori Kitahachi! I've come for Moronao's head!

SHIMIZU: Then you must take mine first.

TAKEMORI: Come, fight! Fight!

[*"Mitsudaiko" drumming, loud* tsuke *beats, and "Chūya Aikata" samisen music accompany the battle.* TAKEMORI *attacks, rushing past* SHIMIZU. SHIMIZU *throws tiny daggers at* TAKEMORI, *who falls to the ground to evade. One of* HANGAN's *spearmen rushes on from the right, forcing* SHIMIZU *away from* TAKEMORI. SHIMIZU *is attacked from both sides. He slips free and runs onto the bridge over the pond. He is attacked by spear and sword simultaneously.* TAKEMORI *reaches under his guard and stabs* SHIMIZU *in the chest. A second slash, down his back, sends* SHIMIZU *toppling into the water of the pond and out of sight. Drum crescendoes. A loud whistle is heard off left. It signals* MORONAO's *capture.* MORONAO *is dragged on by several of* HANGAN's *men. He is thrown to the ground. He wears nothing except a white sleeping kimono. He is unarmed.* YURANOSUKE,

RIKIYA, GOEMON, HEIEMON, *and other retainers enter. They surround* MORONAO, *watching him carefully.* YURANOSUKE *kneels beside* MORONAO *politely.*]

YURANOSUKE: We allow you to die, Moronao, by your own hand . . . with this blade.

[*He unwraps* HANGAN's *suicide dagger and respectfully places it before* MORONAO, *offering him the opportunity to die with honor, instead of being killed.* MORONAO *is shaking with fright. He picks up the dagger as if to kill himself, then lunges at* YURANOSUKE. *Seizing* MORONAO's *wrist,* YURANOSUKE *turns the dagger against* MORONAO *and plunges it into his breast.* MORONAO *cries out once, then falls back dead. The* RETAINERS *form a ring around* MORONAO, *hiding him from view.* TAKEMORI *raises his sword and with a single stroke cuts off* MORONAO's *head. Two loud* tsuke *beats. It is wrapped in a white cloth and held high at the end of a spear.* MORONAO *moves off stage unseen behind a black cloth held by a* STAGE ASSISTANT. *The* RETAINERS *rise triumphantly.*]

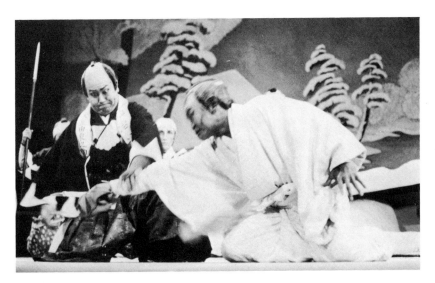

Act III, scene 2: Moronao (Norris Shimabuku) has been found hiding in a coal shed in his garden. Captured, he has been offered the use of Hangan's dagger with which to commit honorable suicide. Instead he lunges at Yuranosuke (David Furumoto) attempting to kill him. He is disarmed and beheaded. English-language kabuki production, University Theatre, University of Hawaii, 1979; directed by Nakamura Matagorō. *(Photo: James R. Brandon.)*

Act III, scene 2: A number of different concluding sequences are possible for *Chū-shingura*. Often seen in jōruri performances, Rikiya is allowed by his father, Yurano-suke, to be the first among the Retainers to offer incense to Lord Hangan's spirit. Ai-chi Culture Hall, Nagoya, 1965. *(Photo: James T. Araki.)*

Act III, scene 2: Commonly in kabuki, Yuranosuke takes the wrapped head of Moro-nao under his arm and, at the lead of the band of loyal Retainers, marches off, down the snow-covered *hanamichi,* to Sengaku Temple. There he will lay the head as an offering on the grave of their master. Yuranosuke (Matsumoto Kōshirō VIII) poses with two Retainers just before departing. Kabuki performance at the Shimbashi Em-bujō, Tokyo, 1958. *(Photo: James T. Araki.)*

YURANOSUKE: You have fought bravely, all of you. Your years of hardship, endured without thought of self, have brought success to our cherished plan. What joy Lord Hangan's spirit must feel for your deeds. On his behalf I thank you.

GOEMON: And now, let us bring Moronao's head to our master!

[*Spoken lightly, the lines are in poetic phrases of seven and five syllables.*]

YURANOSUKE: Deep concerns like drifted snow, melt in the clear of day . . .

RIKIYA: . . . at last our long awaited, vengeance is achieved . . .

GOEMON: . . . together with the clearing, of the morning clouds . . .

AKAGAKI: . . . at the cock's crow announcing, dawn of a new day . . .

TAKEMORI: . . . our hearts filled to overflowing, rise with the rising sun . . .

GOEMON: . . . as we go together to . . .

ALL: . . . our Lord Hangan's grave.

YURANOSUKE: Shout victory together! Victory!

ALL: Victory!

[*Single* ki *clack: offstage drum and samisen play "Taka no Hara" ("Hawk Plain") slowly, gradually accelerating until the scene is over. Each person turns to those next to him, nods, wipes tears of gratitude, grips an elbow, or places a hand on a shoulder. Then their thoughts return to their master,* HANGAN, *and all of them stand silent, posed in mingled happiness and grief. The curtain closes to rapidly accelerating* ki *clacks. The offstage musicians play "Shagiri" indicating the play is over.*]

Contributors

James R. Brandon is professor of Asian theater at the University of Hawaii. He has translated and directed kabuki plays over the last twenty years. He is the recipient of fellowships from the Ford Foundation, the JDR 3rd Fund, Fulbright-Hays, the National Endowment for the Humanities, the Japan Foundation, and the American Institute for Indian Studies. In 1977 he received the University of Hawaii's Regent's Medal and Award for Distinguished Research for his work in Asian theater. Among the books he has written and edited are *Two Kabuki Plays, Traditional Asian Plays, Theatre in Southeast Asia, On Thrones of Gold: Three Javanese Shadow Plays, The Performing Arts in Asia, Kabuki: Five Classic Plays, A Bibliography of Asian Theater, Brandon's Guide to Theater in Asia, Studies in Kabuki: Its Acting, Music, and Historical Context* (with William P. Malm and Donald H. Shively), and *Sanskrit Drama in Performance.*

Donald Keene, professor of Japanese at Columbia University, has written and edited numerous books on Japanese literature and theater, including *The Japanese Discovery of Europe, Japanese Literature: An Introduction for Western Readers, Anthology of Japanese Literature, Modern Japanese Literature, Living Japan, Bunraku: The Art of the Japanese Puppet Theater, Nō: The Classical Theater of Japan, Landscapes and Portraits,* and *World Within Walls.* He has translated works of both classical and modern Japanese literature, including *Major Plays by Chikamatsu, Essays in Idleness, Chūshingura, Twenty Plays of the Nō Theatre,* and novels and plays by Dazai Osamu, Mishima Yukio, and Abe Kōbō, among others. He was awarded the Kikuchi Kan Prize in 1962 and received the Order of the Rising Sun in 1975.

William P. Malm is professor of musicology at the University of Michigan School of Music and director of its Stearns Collection of Musical Instruments. He lectures and writes on ethnomusicology, particularly the theater music of Japan. His publications include *Japanese Music and Musical Instruments, Nagauta: The Heart of Kabuki Music, Music Cultures of the Pacific, the Near East, and Asia,* and *Studies in Kabuki: Its Acting, Music, Historical Context* (with James R. Brandon and Donald H. Shively). Among his honors are the Henry Russel Award for Teaching (Michigan 1966) and the Ernst Bloch Professorship in Music (Berkeley 1980). Other areas of research include popular music, computer cataloguing of musical instruments, and holography.

Donald H. Shively is professor of Japanese history and literature and director of the Japan Institute at Harvard University. He is also editor of the *Harvard Journal of Asiatic Studies*. He is especially interested in the relationship of literature and drama to the social and cultural history of eighteenth- and nineteenth-century Japan and has written extensively on this period. He has contributed to and edited numerous publications and is the author of *The Love Suicide at Amijima: A Study of a Japanese Domestic Tragedy by Chikamatsu Monzaemon,* and *Studies in Kabuki: Its Acting, Music, and Historical Context* (with James R. Brandon and William P. Malm). His current research interests include the social and cultural history of Japanese cities in the seventeenth and eighteenth centuries.

Index

ⓧ *Production Notes*

This book was designed by Roger Eggers and typeset on the Unified Composing System by the University of Hawaii Press.

The text and display typeface is Garamond No. 49.

Offset text presswork and binding were done by Halliday Lithograph. Color insert presswork was done by China Color Printing Co. Text paper is Glatfelter Old Forge Opaque Vellum, basis 55.